MARKETING PLANNING MODELS

STUDIES IN THE
MANAGEMENT SCIENCES

Editor in Chief

ROBERT E. MACHOL

Volume 18

1982

NORTH-HOLLAND PUBLISHING COMPANY—AMSTERDAM·NEW YORK·OXFORD

MARKETING PLANNING MODELS

Edited by

A.A. ZOLTNERS

1982

NORTH-HOLLAND PUBLISHING COMPANY—AMSTERDAM·NEW YORK·OXFORD

This North-Holland/TIMS series is a continuation of the Professional Series in the Management Sciences, edited by Robert E. Machol.

ISBN: 0 444 86369 9

Published by:

NORTH-HOLLAND PUBLISHING COMPANY
AMSTERDAM · NEW YORK · OXFORD

Sole distributors for the U.S.A. and Canada:

ELSEVIER SCIENCE PUBLISHING COMPANY, INC.
52 VANDERBILT AVENUE
NEW YORK, NY 10017

Printed in The Netherlands

CONTENTS

TIMS Studies in the Management Sciences 18 (1982) vii–ix

PREFACE

During the last fifteen years diverse marketing planning issues have been investigated using a variety of modeling approaches. Model-builders, both academic and industrial, have developed substantial literatures on such topics as pricing, advertising, personal selling, distribution, consumer and trade promotions, marketing mix, market segmentation, new product planning, product policy, strategic market planning and consumer/organizational buyer behavior. A wide range of quantitative approaches have been devised and employed in an attempt to successfully model these and other marketing planning issues. The list of approaches is extensive and spans measurement methods (e.g. econometrics, multivariate statistics), economics (e.g. Dorfman and Steiner conditions, Lancaster models), classical optimization theory and operations research (e.g. mathematical programming, stochastic models, decision theory, optimal control theory).

This model-building activity has underscored the difficulty in accurately modeling marketing phenomena. Marketing phenomena tend to be complex, ill-structured and difficult to formulate. The characterization of a market's reaction to an organization's marketing strategy has required the modeling of threshold, saturation, carry-over and decay effects as well as the complex interactions which exist between various marketing mix variables. Additionally, such factors as competitive activity, environmental influences, regional differences, economic change, public policy and technology have been incorporated into marketing models to reflect reality. Existing optimization theory has not been able to accommodate the complexity of the descriptive and predictive models of marketing phenomena which have been developed. Consequently, model-builders have had to develop heuristics or new optimization procedures to arrive at good marketing strategies using their models.

The papers in this issue represent the state-of-the-art in marketing model-building. They reflect the diversity of marketing model applications and modeling approaches mentioned above. The difficulty in modeling market behavior is demonstrated by several papers which employ alternative approaches to address related marketing planning problems.

The first two papers address the issue of product pricing. Jeuland and Dolan present a dynamic optimal-control model for new product pricing. According to their view, trial demand evolves according to a diffusion process, repeat purchasing is possible, and production costs fall with accumulated experience. The authors describe how the optimal pricing strategy is a function of the demand and cost parameters that are employed in the model. Simon develops a strategic pricing model for nondurables. The author employs a dynamic market response model and incorporates a competitive reaction function that is estimated using managerial judgment. The model is tested using data from thirty-seven brands.

New product models are developed in the next three papers. Blackburn and Clancy describe a stochastic microflow model for forecasting new product marketing performance. The model utilizes laboratory test market data to establish pre-test market estimates of brand awareness, trial, product usage, sales and market share. The model also can be used to make similar estimates after product launch. Tests for twenty-five new products are described. Zufryden presents a stochastic new product model which integrates both brand choice and product class purchase incidence behavior. The model utilizes test market data, or data for a short introductory sales period, to predict the performance of new, frequently purchased consumer brands. The model can accommodate relevant purchase-explanatory variables such as pricing, promotions, advertising media, product characteristics and segmentation characteristics. Empirical considerations are mentioned. Pessimier's ADOPTEST model is designed to develop introductory marketing strategies for a new product. ADOPTEST employs a more aggregate predictive model than the two preceding models. Pessemier's model involves a determination of optimal prices, marketing expenditures and marketing mix allocation. Competition, cost behavior and several financial variables are incorporated into the model. The sensitivity analysis component allows the model-user to test the sensitivity of model parameters.

The next two papers describe optimization procedures for marketing models that are predicated on market response relationships. Sinha and Zoltners document the evolution of a model for allocating sales force effort. The authors describe an actual model implementation where a normative model increased in complexity as management incorporated additional detail. They illustrate the type of algorithmic modifications that might be required if model-builders are to determine optimal solutions to marketing models as they evolve over time. In contrast, Morton, Mitchell and Zemel employ the discrete maximum principle to develop an optimal procedure for a general dynamic market response model. They describe how their model generalizes other models found in the literature, develop an algorithm for their model, and provide a computational comparison of their algorithm with existing approaches.

The next two papers address the topic of strategic market planning. Corstjens and Weinstein suggest a quadratic programming model for product portfolio decisions that integrates results from financial portfolio theory and strategic planning. The authors discuss the data requirements for their model, outline estimation procedures and provide an illustrative example. Mahajan,

Wind and Bradford demonstrate how the stochastic dominance rules, which have been applied in the financial portfolio literature, can be applied to product or business portfolio decisions. Their approach is illustrated using data from an insurance company.

One of the controversies among marketing model-builders is whether or not marketing models should be parameterized using managerial judgment. McIntyre and Currim assess the value of judgmental input for market response models. They develop measures of decision quality and present the results of several experimental tests comparing decisions made with and without models that were parameterized using judgmental inputs.

The final two papers in this issue are more context oriented. Farley and Sexton use cross-section surveys, known as knowledge–attitude–practice studies, to model the process by which couples adopt and continue to practice family planning in nations experiencing rapid population growth. Their model has been used to suggest program design and target population segmentation strategies for family planning programs. In their paper, Lilien and Ruzdic outline an approach for studying industrial markets in contexts where the effect of marketing spending can be measured and analyzed. Using natural experiments, the authors describe a procedure for characterizing the sales response to marketing activity. Several case studies using the approach are reported.

As editor of this volume, I wish to thank the authors who submitted manuscripts for this publication, the reviewers who provided candid and insightful evaluations of those manuscripts, Robert Machol who supplied support and encouragement, and the many individuals who participated in the final production of this publication.

Evanston, Illinois   Andris A. Zoltners
July 1981

TIMS Studies in the Management Sciences 18 (1982) 1–21
© North-Holland Publishing Company

AN ASPECT OF NEW PRODUCT PLANNING: DYNAMIC PRICING

Abel P. JEULAND
University of Chicago

and

Robert J. DOLAN
Harvard University

Two of the key factors in determining the optimal pricing strategy for a new product are how demand conditions and production costs change over time. Current theories of optimal price determination largely ignore these dynamic elements, despite the empirical evidence indicating that the firm can influence the timing of demand shifts and production cost changes. We present a methodology to determine the optimal pricing strategy when trial demand evolves according to a diffusion process, but repeat purchasing is possible, and production costs change as a function of accumulated volume. We show that the relationship among the demand and cost parameters determine which of several fundamentally different pricing strategies is optimal.

1. Introduction

Mathematical models have advanced the practice of marketing in many areas. For example, the development, testing, and application of procedures such as the ASSESSOR [38] and TRACKER [4] models for new product evaluation, conjoint measurement [14] for concept testing, and CALLPLAN [22] for sales force planning are "success stories". The distribution of "success stories" across the various areas of marketing policy is not uniform, however. The pricing area, in particular, has proven to be a difficult area for development of useful models. Although useful special purpose models exist, e.g. competitive bidding models, Oxenfeldt [29] writes: "...almost all pricing decisions have either been highly intuitive, as in the case of new product introductions, or based on routine procedures, as in cost-plus or imitative pricing". More recently, Monroe and Della Bitta [25] summarize their review of the status of models for pricing decisions with: "No models are available for the new product pricing decision.... As a product matures and price changes become necessary no relevant models are available."

To determine the factors responsible for the minimal contribution of models to the pricing area, we first examine the environment in which a firm typically operates. We then briefly discuss the literature devoted to each of the problem areas. Our review shows that an important element of the environment which most models fail to capture is the dynamic nature of the demand and supply conditions. To overcome this problem, this paper proposes a model incorporating the necessary dynamic elements. Section 2 describes the dynamic elements required in a new product pricing model. We reference the empirical evidence for the particular demand and supply dynamics considered. Section 3 presents the model and section 4 describes the optimization procedure (optimal control) used. The mathematical details are in the appendix. Section 5 interprets the results of the optimization. Section 6 assesses the utility of the model and describes possible extensions to accommodate more of the features commonly characterizing the firm's pricing problem. Our fundamental result is the identification of the critical interplay among parameters of the demand and cost models in determining the optimal pricing strategy.

2. The pricing environment

How do firms determine prices? Oxenfeldt [28] contends: "Studies of business pricing methods uniformly show cost-plus prices to be by far the most usual type." Supporters of the cost-plus position usually cite the interviews of Hall and Hitch [15] and the Brookings study [19] as evidence of the dominance of cost in pricing decisions. However, close reading of these pieces reveals little support for the cost-plus view. In Hall and Hitch, 55% of the supposed cost-plus firms stated they would cut price if business were depressed. However, in this event, a true cost-plus firm would increase price due to higher unit costs than anticipated. Similarly, the Brookings interviews reveal firms' consideration of demand and competitive conditions, e.g. while U.S. Steel "holds the philosophy of cost-plus pricing", they "meet the lowered delivered price of competition when necessary to get the business". Weston's [39] interviews with corporate executives led to formalization of the pricing process as part of a dynamic general equilibrium model based on the capital asset pricing model. A key issue is uncertainty leading the firm to use adaptive policies.

A second source of evidence for the impact of demand conditions on price is Silbertson's review [34] of econometric investigations. This review shows that demand fluctuations as well as costs do affect prices. In short, the failure of mathematical models to make a contribution to pricing practice is not due to complacency among firms deriving from the belief that the simple cost-plus procedure is correct. Rather, the lack of contribution is due to the fact that the pricing problem is a complex mixing of cost, demand, and competitive considerations which no models deal with adequately.

To be more specific about the "complex mixing", the major characteristics of the pricing environment are as follows.

(i) A firm typically markets products interrelated on the demand and cost side. Therefore, it is suboptimal to determine the price of each product offering independently.

(ii) Demand conditions are uncertain and not stable over time. The demand may grow or contract with some factor exogenous to the firm, e.g. general economic conditions, or an endogenous factor such as the number of people who have tried the product.

(iii) Production and marketing costs change over time, e.g. because of learning or experience by the firm or because of price inflation.

(iv) Since price is an easily monitored marketing variable, price changes are likely to induce reaction by the firm's competition or even affect the entry of new firms to the industry.

(v) In some situations price means more to consumers than the dollar outlay on the product. In case of uncertainty about quality, price may be used as a quality indicator. Thus, the price positions the item in the marketplace by influencing consumers' perception of the product.

(vi) Rarely does a single price suffice as a statement of the firm's pricing policy. Volume discounts, credit terms and delivery policy must be stated. Given these characteristics, it is difficult to simultaneously satisfy two major prerequisites to model implementation, i.e.

(a) the model does not omit important elements of the problem; and

(b) the necessary data for the model are easily available.

However, researchers have not conceded that "pricing is an art". Instead, research has resulted in significant progress in dealing with a number of these issues. In order to position our work on the development of dynamic pricing models, we now review some of this pricing research.

Problem 1: Demand interrelations

The existence of a product line complicates matters because the optimal strategy for a given product generally depends on the price set for other items in the line. An economic theory exists which describes optimal pricing strategies in view of these interdependencies, e.g. Bowman [5] on tie-in sales and Stigler [36] on blockbooking. In the marketing literature, Urban [37] presents a mathematical model for product line marketing mix decisions. Monroe and Zoltners [26] offer a new conceptualization of the product line pricing problem especially applicable during times of scarcity. They develop a new decision criterion called the contribution-per-resource unit. While the ideas presented have evidently yet to be applied, the approach is promising.

Problem 2: Demand dynamics

The second issue relates to the uncertainty of the demand the firm faces and how that demand may shift over time. The problem of demand curve estimation is being attacked in many ways. While the traditional econometric and field experimentation approaches have not been abandoned, much of the new work on demand curve estimation comes from laboratory experimentation. Methodologies such as those described by Sawyer, Worthing and Sendak [32] and Johnson [17] are gaining wide acceptance. The bulk of the marketing research on demand curve shifts over time concerns the development and testing of models of new product diffusion. The model first suggested by Bass [2] as a description of the diffusion of a durable good has been extended in numerous ways, e.g. Mahajan and Peterson [23] and Dodson and Muller [10]. The level of analysis here is the industry. A separate literature, e.g. Brock [6] and De Bondt [9], treats the competitive problem and the evolution of the firm's demand curve.

Problem 3: Cost dynamics

The dynamics of the supply side have been most thoroughly studied by several management consulting groups. Models of the evolution of per unit costs have been developed, tested, and applied in the determination of business strategy. The most well-known of these cost models is the experience curve productivity concept of the Boston Consulting Group (see [1] for a discussion). This particular model relating per unit cost to accumulated production volume has been employed in several optimal pricing models, first by Robinson and Lakhani [31] and subsequently by Bass [3] and Dolan and Jeuland [12].

Problem 4: Competitive reaction

Price is an easily monitored marketing variable. Hence, it is difficult to ignore the issue of competitive reaction, unless the firm is a monopolist. Unfortunately, oligopoly theory provides little hint about how competitive behavior should be modeled. The economics literature presents a variety of "limit pricing" models of potential entrants, e.g. Kamien and Schwartz [18] and Pashigian [30], but the empirical evidence supporting these models is weak. Lambin, Naert and Bultez [20] present an empirically based procedure for the derivation of competitive moves in an established industry. If entry considerations could be introduced, the model is a reasonable way to accommodate competitive reaction for new product pricing.

Problem 5: Price/quality relations

On the behavioral side, we now have improved understanding of the significance of price to consumers. Some of the evidence is at first disquieting in that consumers are found not to be the rational economic agents models suppose them to be. For example, the results of Doob et al. [13] show that factors other than current price and previous experience with the good affect current demand. The price at which those previous purchases were made positions the product in the consumer's mind. In a similar vein, many researchers, e.g. Shapiro [33] and Monroe [24], document the use of price as an indicator of quality in certain situations.

Problem 6: Discount structures

Lastly, there is the issue of price structure. Economic theory provides a rationale for quantity discounts in monopolistic situations. Buchanen [7] and Oi [27] show quantity discounts or two-part tariffs may be useful in appropriating consumer surplus. In a competitive environment, Dolan [11] provides a method for the determination of the optimal discount structure based on inventory management considerations.

This sketchy review is intended only to indicate that the problems in developing normative pricing models are recognized and are the subject of current research. It is not yet possible to propose a workable model dealing with all the factors given. Our contribution in this paper is to develop a methodology to help overcome problems 2 and 3, namely to provide a methodology for the determination of optimal prices when the demand and supply conditions change over time.

To describe demand, we use a generalization of the deterministic epidemiological model of diffusion. Demand evolves in accord with an endogenous variable, penetration of the new product. The model incorporates three characteristics of new product buying behavior:

(i) innovative trial,

(ii) imitative trial, and

(iii) repeat buying.

Innovative and imitative buying are modeled as in Bass's original use of the deterministic epidemiological diffusion model. This model postulates that the rate of trial purchases at time t is proportional to: (i) the size of the market yet to be penetrated and (ii) a linear function of previous penetration. Specifically, letting

m = market potential,

$X_1(t)$ = cumulative number of triers at time t,

$\dot{X}_1(t)$ = rate of trial purchases at t,

α = parameter of innovative trial, and

β = parameter of imitative trial,

then

$$\dot{X}_1(t) = \left[m - X_1(t)\right]\left[\alpha + \beta X_1(t)\right]. \tag{1}$$

Robinson and Lakhani [31] and later Bass [3] introduced price effects into the diffusion model of (1) by multiplying (1) by a function of price, $f(p)$. Robinson and Lakhani [31] set $f(p) = e^{-kp(t)}$, i.e. elasticity proportional to price, while Bass sets $f(p) = p(t)^{-\eta}$, i.e. constant elasticity. The demand model in section 3 follows Bass in introducing price via multiplication by $p(t)^{-\eta}$ but generalizes the "no repeat buying" diffusion model of (1) by incorporating a parameter of repeat buying. A case may be made for incorporating price differently than as a multiplicative factor (see Jeuland [16]). Future research has yet to identify tractable alternatives.

The cost dynamics considered are in the spirit of the Boston Consulting Group experience curve model, in that cost is modeled as a function of the firm's accumulated volume. However, rather than *a priori* specifying a log-linear relation between cost and volume as BCG does, we use a general function, $h(*)$, and assume only that it is decreasing in accumulated volume.

3. Optimal price model

The notation required is:

$X_1(t)$ = cumulative number of triers at time t,
$X_2(t)$ = cumulative sales at time t (includes both trial and repeat),
$X_3(t)$ = net present value of accumulated profits at t,
$\dot{X}_i(t)$ = rate of change in variable $X_i(t)$ at time t,
m = market potential,
α = parameter of innovative trial,
β = parameter of imitative trial,
b = repeat purchase parameter,
$p(t)$ = price at time t,
η = elasticity of demand curve, assumed constant over time, $\eta > 1$,
$h(X_2(t))$ = per unit production cost at time t, given accumulated production volume of $X_2(t)$, we assume $\delta h/\delta X_2 < 0$,
λ = discount rate.

The variables in the system are related via the following set of differential equations:

$$\dot{X}_1(t) = [m - X_1(t)][\alpha + \beta X_1(t)] p(t)^{-\eta}, \tag{2}$$

$$\dot{X}_2(t) = \dot{X}_1(t) + bX_1(t)p(t)^{-\eta}, \tag{3}$$

$$X_3(T) = \int_0^T [p(t) - h(X_2(t))] \dot{X}_2(t) e^{-\lambda t} dt. \tag{4}$$

Eq. (2) is identical to the Bass model and implies that the short-term elasticity of trial at time t is

$$\frac{\delta \dot{X}_1(t)}{\delta p(t)} \Big/ \frac{p(t)}{\dot{X}_1(t)} = -\eta \quad \forall t.$$

The magnitude of trial demand, $\dot{X}_1(t)$, is proportional to the unpenetrated market size, $m - X_1(t)$, and the adoptive pressure which is the linear function, $\alpha + \beta X_1(t)$, of penetration. The $\beta X_1(t)$ term measures the impetus to try due to imitative factors.

Eq. (3) specifies that the changes in total sales come from two sources: trial, $\dot{X}_1(t)$, and repeat sales, $bX_1(t)p(t)^{-\eta}$. Thus, the b parameter signifies the extent of repeat purchase activity. The magnitude of b depends on the inherent nature of the product, e.g. for durable goods $b \doteq 0$, as well as the purchase event feedback. Note that since

$$\dot{X}_2(t) = \left[(m - X_1(t))(\alpha + \beta X_1(t)) + bX_1(t)\right] p(t)^{-\eta},$$

the short-term elasticity of total demand is also $-\eta$.

Finally, eq. (4) specifies how profit accumulates since $p(t) - h(X_2(t))$ is the profit rate at t and $\dot{X}_2(t)$ is the sales rate. Thus, the optimization problem facing a single firm wishing to maximize discounted profits over the time interval $[0, T]$ is

$$\max_{p(t)} X_3(T) = \int_0^T \dot{X}_3(t)\, dt$$

$$\text{s.t. } \dot{X}_1(t) = f_1(X_1(t), p(t)),$$

$$\dot{X}_2(t) = f_2(X_1(t), p(t)),$$

$$\dot{X}_3(t) = f_3(X_1(t), X_2(t), t, p(t)),$$

$$X_1(0) = X_2(0) = 0,$$

$$p(t) \geqslant 0,$$

where $f_1(*)$, $f_2(*)$, and $f_3(*)$ are as given in eqs. (2), (3), and (4), respectively.

The initial conditions $X_1(0) = X_2(0) = 0$ specify that commercialization takes place at $t = 0$. The constraints specify the rate of change in each state variable as a function of the state variables, time, and the control variable, $p(t)$. Thus, the maximization problem is a fixed-time problem with free right-hand end conditions. The solution procedure via optimal control methods is presented in section 4.

4. Derivation of optimal price

A necessary condition for $p(t)$ to solve the maximization problem can be derived through the construction of a system of auxiliary variables. These auxiliary variables are then combined with the state variables ($X_1(t)$, $X_2(t)$, $X_3(t)$) and the control variable ($p(t)$) to form the Hamiltonian function.

In our case the auxiliary system has three variables, one corresponding to each state variable. These auxiliary variables ψ_i (which may be thought of as time varying Lagrangian multipliers), satisfy two sets of conditions.

(i) differential equation system:

$$\dot{\psi}_i(t) = -\sum_{j=1}^{3} \psi_j \frac{\delta f_j(\cdot)}{\delta X_i}, \qquad i = 1, 2, 3;$$

(ii) terminal condition:

$$\psi_i(T) = -C_i, \qquad i = 1, 2, 3$$

where C_i is the coefficient of state variable $X_i(t)$ in the objective function. The Hamiltonian function is defined as

$$H(\bar{\psi}(t), \bar{X}(t), p(t), t) = \sum_{i=1}^{3} \psi_i(t) \dot{X}_i(t)$$

$$= \sum_{i=1}^{3} \psi_i(t) f_i(\bar{X}(t), p(t), t),$$

where $\bar{\psi}(t)$ and $\bar{X}(t)$ are the vectors $(\psi_1(t), \psi_2(t), \psi_3(t))$ and $(X_1(t), X_2(t), X_3(t))$, respectively.

Pontryagin's maximum principle states that the Hamiltonian achieves an absolute minimum with respect to admissible controls at the optimal price, $p^*(t)$, for any given values of $\bar{\psi}$ and $\bar{X}$. (See Connors and Teichroew [8] for several applications.)

Because of the special structure of this pricing problem, the Hamiltonian is a simple function. Specifically, since $f_3(*)$ is not a function of X_3, the behavior of auxiliary variable ψ_3 is $\dot{\psi}_3 = 0$ and $\psi_3(T) = -1$. Therefore (dropping subscripts):

$$H(\cdot) = \psi_1 \dot{X}_1 + \psi_2 \dot{X}_2 - \dot{X}_3 = p^{-\eta} \{ (m - X_1)(\alpha + \beta X_1) \psi_1$$

$$+ [(m - X_1)(\alpha + \beta X_1) + b X_1] (\psi_2 + h e^{-\lambda t})$$

$$- p[(m - X_1)(\alpha + \beta X_1) + b X_1] e^{-\lambda t} \}.$$

$H(\cdot)$ is of the general form $p^{-\eta}(A - Cp)$, where $C > 0$. The behavior of $p^{-\eta}(A - Cp)$ is shown in fig. 1 for $p > 0$ and $C > 0$. Fig. 1 shows two cases. For

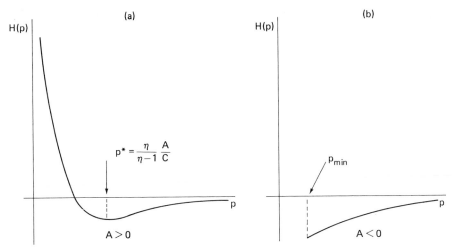

Fig. 1. Behavior of Hamiltonian.

$A > 0$, the Hamiltonian achieves an absolute minimum at some strictly positive p^*. This p^* is the optimal price if it is admissible. If some external condition $p > p_{min}$ is imposed, then the optimal price is p_{min} if $p^* < p_{min}$. For the second case, $A < 0$, in panel (b) of fig. 1, the Hamiltonian is an increasing function of price and hence the optimal strategy at time t is to charge the minimum admissible price, p_{min}.

In general, we cannot specify the sign of A. However, due to the terminal conditions on ψ_1 and ψ_2, i.e. $\psi_1(T) = \psi_2(T) = 0$, we can show $A > 0$ at T and for some time before T (due to continuity conditions). Thus, for some time interval $[t, T]$, the optimal price is $[\eta/(\eta - 1)](A/C)$. To determine the form of the expression for the optimal price over this time interval, we first define two functions:

$$g_1(X_1) = (m - X_1)(\alpha + \beta X_1),$$

$$g_2(X_1) = g_1(X_1) + bX_1.$$

These g functions correspond to the part of f functions describing trial and sales rate when the multiplicative price effect is omitted. The appendix shows that the time path of prices maximizing discounted profits for the firm is (omitting function arguments when possible):

$$p^*(t) = \frac{\eta}{\eta - 1} \left[h(X_2(T)) e^{-\lambda(T-t)} \left[\frac{g_2}{g_2(X_1(T))} \right]^{1/(\eta-1)} \right.$$

$$\left. + \lambda g_2^{1/(\eta-1)} \int_t^T h e^{-\lambda(u-t)} g_2^{-1/(\eta-1)} \, du \right], \qquad (5)$$

or equivalently,

$$p^*(t) = \frac{\eta}{\eta - 1}\left[h + g_2^{1/(\eta-1)} \int_t^T e^{-\lambda(u-t)} \frac{d}{du}\left(hg_2^{-1/(\eta-1)} \right) du \right].$$ (6)

These formulae apply only if there is no lower finite limit to admissible prices. If there is a limit, p_{min}, p_{min} may prevail for an initial period.

Eq. (6) is a generalization of the usual mark-up rule on marginal cost. From economic theory, the optimal price at time t is

$$p^*(t) = \frac{\eta}{\eta - 1} h(X_2(t))$$

under the assumption that neither supply nor demand conditions evolve in accord with a variable endogenous to the firm. This is the myopic strategy of maximizing short-term profits. The generalization in (6) specifies the adjustment necessary in the optimal price due to the endogenous dynamics. The magnitude of the adjustment is

$$\frac{\eta}{\eta - 1} g_2^{1/(\eta-1)} \int_t^T e^{-\lambda(u-t)} \frac{d}{du}\left[hg_2^{-1/(\eta-1)} \right] du.$$

Note that if production cost is constant, $h(x_2(t)) = C_1$, and there are no demand dynamics, $g_2(X_1(t)) = C_2$ (no demand side dynamics would require that the imitation coefficient β be equal to zero and the repeat rate b be equal to the innovative trial rate α), the adjustment factor is zero. With dynamic elements in the system, the adjustment factor may be positive or negative since the sign of

$$\frac{d}{du} g_2^{-1/(\eta-1)}$$

is indeterminate.

The following section investigates the implications of (6) for various demand situations.

5. Interpretation of results

The best exposition of the implications of the general pricing rule (6) is through sequential consideration of the three cases:
    (i) nondiscounted cash flow: $\lambda = 0$;
    (ii) myopic behavior: $\lambda = \infty$;
    (iii) finite positive discount rate: $0 < \lambda < \infty$.

While (iii) is the most realistic, analytical difficulties make initial consideration of the two end-point cases useful. In the case of nondiscounted profits, the optimality condition on price is obtained by simplifying (6):

$$p^*(t) = \frac{\eta}{\eta - 1} h(X_2(T)) \left[\frac{(m - X_1)(\alpha + \beta X_1) + bX_1}{(m - X_1(T))(\alpha + \beta X_1(T)) + bX_1(T)} \right]^{1/(\eta - 1)} \quad (7)$$

Eq. (7) shows that the optimal price at time t depends on the cumulative number of triers at t and several parameters which are time invariant, namely the elasticity of demand, the production cost of the final unit of output, and the cumulative number of triers at final time T. Because cash flows are not discounted, the cost of production at t does not directly affect the optimal price at t. Conceptually, not discounting collapses the behavior over $[0, T]$ into a single time period, static model where $h(X_2(t))$ is the firm's marginal cost curve. In the single period model, optimality requires output at a level equating marginal revenue and marginal cost and the optimal price is a mark-up on the cost of the final unit. The behavior of the cost curve up to final output level affects the profitability of the firm, but not the optimal price.

Eq. (7) can be written as a constant times a time varying factor,

$$\left[(m - X_1)(\alpha + \beta X_1) + bX_1 \right]^{1/(\eta - 1)}.$$

The behavior of this time varying factor governs the behavior of the optimal price over time. If the "buying potential" as a function of the number of tries, $g_2(X_1) = (m - X_1)(\alpha + \beta X_1) + bX_1$, is increasing at t, the optimal price also is increasing at t. If decreasing, the optimal price is decreasing. Hence, we now examine the behavior of g_2, the buying potential function.

The derivative of $g_2(X_1)$ with respect to X_1 is

$$\frac{dg_2(X_1)}{dX_1} = \beta m - \alpha + b - 2\beta X_1.$$

Consequently, the time path of prices is increasing at t if and only if

$$X_1 < \frac{\beta m - \alpha + b}{2\beta}.$$

Since X_1 is initially zero and becomes positive the condition for the price path to be monotonically decreasing is $\beta m - \alpha + b < 0$ or $b < \alpha - \beta m$. This would hold for example for a durable good ($b \doteq 0$), where imitative effects are unimportant. In this situation a new purchaser has an essentially negative effect on future demand since he is "out of the market" and his adoption is unlikely to positively influence others. Price is therefore initially high and allowed to fall as the initially favorable demand conditions erode over time due to market saturation.

Price will be initially low and increasing if $\beta m - \alpha + b > 0$ or $b > \alpha - \beta m$. Since $b \geq 0$, this holds if $\beta m > \alpha$ which is precisely what Bass [2] shows for a number of durable goods. The price path increases until penetration is

$$X_1(t) > \frac{m}{2} + \left[\frac{b - \alpha}{2\beta} \right].$$

From this time on, prices monotonically decline. Examination of this expression yields a sufficient condition for prices to not reach a peak and begin a decline. If $b > \alpha + \beta m$, then $m/2 + [(b - \alpha)/2\beta] \geq m$. But $X_1(t)$ cannot exceed m. Hence, if the repeat rate b is so large that it exceeds the adoption probability for a nonadopter, even when it reaches its limit $(\alpha + \beta m)$, prices are montonically increasing over time since demand conditions are continually improving. The $b > \alpha + \beta m$ case is most plausible for a new inexpensive nondurable, e.g. a grocery item, since imitation effects are small and $b > \alpha$ if the product proves satisfactory upon use.

We collect our results for the nondiscounted case in fig. 2. Each case is labeled with the typical situation leading to it.

The second end-point case is $\lambda = \infty$. Applying an infinite discount rate to future cash flows is equivalent to maximizing the current profit rate at all times. This myopic behavior entails prices given by

$$p(t) = \frac{\eta}{\eta - 1} h(X_2(t)).$$

The firm ignores the future sales promotional effects of price and if $\delta h / \delta X_2(t)$

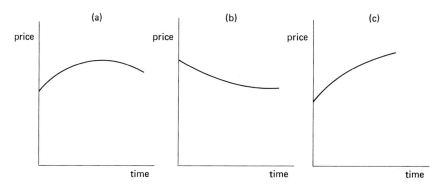

Fig. 2. (a) $\alpha - \beta m < b < \beta m + \alpha$. Durable good; imitation effects important; low introductory prices; prices peak. (b) $b < \alpha - \beta m$. (b) Durable good; imitation effects unimportant; skimming strategy: declining prices. (c) $b > \alpha + \beta m$. Nondurable good; frequent repeat; low introductory prices; prices increase.

<0, prices are monotonically decreasing, following the trend in costs.

The optimality condition for the case (iii), $0<\lambda<\infty$, is given in eq. (6). However, the properties of (6) are difficult to determine analytically. Numerical investigations employing dynamic programming yield some insight into the shape of the time path. A positive discount rate dampens the impetus to price for future market development and cost declines. We show in fig. 2(a) an "inverted U" shape for the optimal time path of prices under certain demand conditions when $\lambda=0$. As λ increases, the initial increasing portion of the curve flattens out and the optimal time path of prices becomes monotonically decreasing above some finite discount rate if production costs are falling with accumulated volume. If production costs are constant, the optimal strategy approaches the constant myopic price as $\lambda \to \infty$. The case of constant production costs is shown in fig. 3 for Bass's diffusion model (no repeat buying). The demand conditions are

$$q_t = 100 \, e^{-0.1 p_t} [0.05 + 0.9 X_t][1 - X_t],$$

where

q_t = quantity demanded in period t,
p_t = price in period t, and
X_t = percent of market penetrated at beginning of period t.

As shown in fig. 3, the myopic price (optimal if $\lambda = \infty$) is $11 assuming constant cost of $1. With an objective of maximization of nondiscounted profits over ten time periods, the optimal time path is of the "inverted U" form

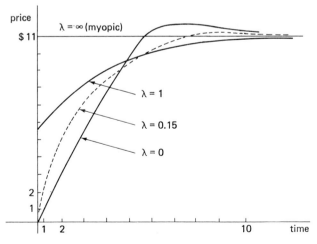

Fig. 3. Effect of discounting on optimal time path of prices.

described previously. If $\lambda = 0.15$, prices increase more rapidly at first than for $\lambda = 0$ but prices still reach a peak and then decline to the myopic price in period 10. Increasing the discount rate to $\lambda = 1$ increases the initial period price as the impetus to move from the profit-maximizing price of $11 in favor of market development is decreased due to the application of a significant discount factor to future cash flows.

In summary, the model shows that the parameters of the three aspects of purchasing behavior:

    (i) innovative trial, α,

   (ii) imitative trial, β, and

  (iii) repeat buying, b,

interact with one another and the behavior of costs in special ways which lead to fundamentally different optimal pricing strategies. Depending upon the relationship among these buying parameters, the optimal time path of prices may take one of the three shapes shown in fig. 2 for $\lambda = 0$. Numerical results show that for $\lambda > 0$, the same basic shapes are encountered generally. However, as λ becomes large the optimal strategy becomes like the myopic strategy in which price follows cost.

The model has succeeded in identifying some key factors in planning the pricing of a new product over the life cycle. The factors have been incorporated into the model to permit assessment of the key interactions. The model gives insight into the question of what market conditions warrant the adoption of various pricing strategy alternatives. The introductory remarks in section 2 set out the major limitations of our model. The conclusions section now discusses possible advancement of the methodology given here to overcome the limitations.

6. Conclusions: Toward a comprehensive characterization of new product pricing strategy

The classical economic model of price determination assumes that demand and supply conditions are stable or evolve due to exogenous factors. There is, however, empirical evidence that the firm can influence the timing of these demand and supply condition changes. In demand situations characterized by diffusion of innovations, demand shifts in accord with the number of previous adopters. The firm's price controls the adoption rate and thus the timing of demand shifts. Similarly, experience curve productivity maintains that the firm's previous output levels determine current cost. Thus, the shifts in production costs are again controllable. The model proposed here accommodates these timing effects into the determination of the optimal pricing strategy. As such, it is a step toward realism and implementation.

These two timing factors are the whole story in only very special situations, e.g. a natural monopoly. Typically, the pricing activities of the firm also impact the rate of entry into the industry. Consequently, inclusion of this third factor would significantly expand the applicability of the model.

There are two main difficulties. First, one must specify the behavior of potential entrants. The "limit pricing" literature, e.g. Pashigian [30], Kamien and Schwartz [18], contains many models but the empirical support for any particular one is weak. Secondly, once entry does occur, we must specify how prices evolve (e.g. does the entrant follow leader's price?) and how market shares are determined. Market share equations have been proposed and tested in the marketing literature (e.g. Little [21]) and Smiley and Ravid [35] consider the entry problem in the context of experience curve productivity. This work may be useful in extending the monopolistic model here to competitive situations. Competitive entry may be modeled as a third "timing effect" of price and thus the optimal control framework may work. Successful addition of this factor will result in a methodology incorporating the major influences on a firm's profitability.

The analysis in the paper shows that a key advantage of the optimal control solution (see eq. (6)) is that this general solution allows one to more readily identify the nature of the interaction effects among several factors. In addition, derivation of optimality conditions such as (6) may suggest more appropriate functional forms for econometric models designed to measure price behavior. For example, an econometric model following from the continuous time optimality condition in (6) is derived as follows. Recalling that h is the per unit cost function and g_2 is the "buying potential", the optimality condition on price, p, can be rewritten as

$$\frac{d}{dt}\left\{\left(\frac{\eta-1}{\eta}p-h\right)g_2^{-1/(\eta-1)}e^{-\lambda t}\right\} = -e^{\lambda t}\frac{d}{dt}\left\{hg_2^{-1/(\eta-1)}\right\}.$$

Denoting the functions $g_2^{-1/(\eta-1)}$ by g and $e^{-\lambda t}$ by k, the equation is

$$\frac{\eta-1}{\eta}(pgk)' = (hgk)' - k(hg)',$$

which implies

$$\frac{\eta-1}{\eta}(p'g+p(g'-\lambda g)) = -\lambda hg,$$

where a prime denotes the derivative. This expression suggests the nonlinear econometric model specification:

$$\frac{\eta-1}{\eta}\left[(p_t-p_{t-1})g_t + p_t((1-\lambda)g_t - g_{t-1})\right] = -\lambda h_t g_t$$

or

$$p_t((2-\lambda)g_t - g_{t-1}) - p_{t-1}g_t = \frac{-\lambda\eta}{\eta-1}h_t g_t$$

or

$$p_t\left((2-\lambda) - \frac{g_{t-1}}{g_t}\right) = p_{t-1} - \frac{\lambda\eta}{\eta-1}h_t,$$

where the subscripts on functions denote the values at that particular time.

In summary, we have demonstrated the utility of optimal control methods in analyzing new product pricing strategies. The methodology provides insights into the key factors and interactions of supply and demand. Secondly, it may suggest appropriate models of price behavior. Generalization to incorporate more factors, in particular competition, is possible. As such, the methods presented here should prove useful in conjunction with other measurement and optimization tools, in the development of a comprehensive characteriziation of optimal new product pricing strategies.

Appendix: Derivation of necessary conditions for optimal price

The problem:

$$\max_{p(t)} \quad X_3(T)$$

s.t.
$$\dot{X}_1(t) = [m - X_1(t)][\alpha + \beta X_1(t)]p(t)^{-\eta},$$
$$\dot{X}_2(t) = \dot{X}_1(t) + bX_1(t)p(t)^{-\eta},$$
$$\dot{X}_3(t) = [p(t) - h(X_2(t))]\dot{X}_2(t)e^{-\lambda t},$$
$$X_1(0) = X_2(0) = 0.$$

Now define:

$$g_1(X_1(t)) = (m - X_1(t))(\alpha + \beta X_1(t)),$$

$$g_2(X_1(t)) = g_1(X_1(t)) + bX_2(t).$$

Dropping time subscripts, the auxiliary system ψ is

$$\dot{\psi}_1 = -\psi_1 \dot{g}_1 p^{-\eta} - \psi_2 \dot{g}_2 p^{-\eta} + [p - h(X_2)]\dot{g}_2 p^{-\eta}e^{-\lambda t}, \tag{A1}$$

$$\dot{\psi}_2 = h\dot{g}_2 p^{-\eta}e^{-\lambda t}, \tag{A2}$$

where

$$\dot{g}_1 = \frac{dg_1}{dX_1}; \qquad \dot{g}_2 = \frac{dg_2}{dX_1}; \qquad \dot{h} = \frac{dh}{dX_2}.$$

We have made use of the fact that $\dot{\psi}_3 = 0$, $\psi_3(T) = -1$. The Hamiltonian is

$$H(\cdot) = \psi_1 \dot{X}_1 + \psi_2 \dot{X}_2 - \dot{X}_3 = p^{-\eta}\left[\psi_1 g_1 + \left(\psi_2 + h\,e^{-\lambda t}\right) g_2 - p g_2\,e^{-\lambda t}\right]. \quad (A3)$$

Letting

$$A = \psi_1 g_1 + \left(\psi_2 + h\,e^{-\lambda t}\right) g_2,$$

$$C = g_2\,e^{-\lambda t}.$$

Differentiation of (A3) with respect to p implies the optimal price satisfies

$$p^* = \frac{\eta}{\eta - 1}\frac{A}{C}. \qquad (A4)$$

This expression involves auxiliary variables and thus is not directly usable. We seek to obtain an expression involving only characteristics of the original system. Rearranging terms in (A4):

$$(p - h)\,e^{-\lambda t} = \frac{\eta}{\eta - 1}\left(\frac{\psi_1 g_1 + \psi_2 g_2}{g_2}\right) + h\,e^{-\lambda t}\left(\frac{1}{\eta - 1}\right).$$

Substituting into (A1), we obtain:

$$\dot{\psi}_1 = -\psi_1\left(\dot{g}_1 - \frac{\eta}{\eta - 1}\frac{\dot{g}_1}{g_2}\dot{g}_2\right)p^{-\eta} - \psi_2\left(\dot{g}_2 - \frac{\eta}{\eta - 1}\dot{g}_2\right)p^{-\eta}$$

$$+ \frac{h\,e^{-\lambda t}}{\eta - 1}\dot{g}_2\,p^{-\eta}.$$

Eliminating $p^{-\eta}$ via the substitution $p^{-\eta} = \dot{X}_1/g_1$:

$$\dot{\psi}_1 = -\psi_1\left(\frac{\dot{g}_1}{g_1} - \frac{\eta}{\eta - 1}\frac{\dot{g}_2}{g_2}\right)\dot{X}_1 + \frac{1}{\eta - 1}\frac{\dot{g}_2}{g_1}\dot{X}_1\left(\psi_2 + h\,e^{-\lambda t}\right),$$

$$\dot{\psi}_1 + \psi_1 \cdot \frac{d}{dt}\left[\ln g_1 g_2^{-\eta/(\eta - 1)}\right] = \frac{1}{\eta - 1}\left(\psi_2 + h\,e^{-\lambda t}\right)\frac{\dot{g}_2 \dot{X}_1}{g_1}. \qquad (A5)$$

After multiplying both sides of (A5) by $F(t) = g_1 g_2^{-\eta/(\eta-1)}$, the left-hand side is $d[\psi_1 \cdot F(t)]/dt$. This, together with the terminal condition $\psi_1(T) = 0$, allows us to write

$$\psi_1 = \frac{-g_2^{\eta/(\eta-1)}}{(\eta-1)g_1} \int_t^T \left(\psi_2 + h\, e^{-\lambda u}\right) \dot{X}_1 \dot{g}_2 g_2^{-\eta/(\eta-1)}\, du$$

$$= \frac{g_2^{\eta/(\eta-1)}}{g_1} \left[h(X_2(T))\, e^{-\lambda T} g_2(X_1(T))^{-1/(\eta-1)} - \left(\psi_2 + h\, e^{-\lambda t}\right) g_2^{-1/(\eta-1)} \right.$$

$$\left. - \int_t^T \left(\dot{\psi}_2 + h\dot{X}_2\, e^{-\lambda u} - \lambda h\, e^{-\lambda u}\right) g^{-1/(\eta-1)}\, du \right]. \tag{A6}$$

ψ_2 has a relatively simple form. From (A2),

$$\dot{\psi}_2 = -h\dot{X}_2\, e^{-\lambda t},$$

and the terminal condition is $\psi_2(T) = 0$. Thus,

$$-\psi_2 = -h(X_2(T))\, e^{-\lambda T} + h\, e^{-\lambda t} - \lambda \int_t^T h\, e^{-\lambda u}\, du.$$

Substituting this into (A6):

$$\psi_1 = \frac{g_2^{\eta/(\eta-1)}}{g_1} \left\{ h(X_2(T))\, e^{-\lambda T} g_2(X_1(T))^{-1/(\eta-1)} \right.$$

$$\left. - \left(\psi_2 + h\, e^{-\lambda t}\right) g_2^{-1/(\eta-1)} + \int_t^T \lambda g_2^{-1/(\eta-1)} h\, e^{-\lambda u}\, du \right\}$$

$$= \frac{g_2^{\eta/(\eta-1)}}{g_1} \left\{ h(X_2(T))\, e^{-\lambda T} g_2(X_1(T))^{-1/(\eta-1)} - g_2^{-1/(\eta-1)} \right.$$

$$\times \left(h(X_2(T))\, e^{-\lambda T} + \lambda \int_t^T h\, e^{-\lambda u}\, du \right)$$

$$\left. + \lambda \int_t^T g_2^{-1/(\eta-1)} h\, e^{-\lambda u}\, du \right\}.$$

Both auxiliary variables have now been written in terms of state and control variables and time. Substitution into the expression for p yields

$$p^* = \frac{\eta \, e^{\lambda t}}{\eta - 1} \left\{ g_2^{1/(\eta-1)} \left[h(X_2(T)) \, e^{-\lambda T} g_2(X_1(T))^{-1/(\eta-1)} \right. \right.$$

$$\left. - \left(h(X_2(T)) \, e^{-\lambda T} + \lambda \int_t^T h \, e^{-\lambda u} \, du \right) g_2^{-1/(\eta-1)} \right.$$

$$\left. + \lambda \int_t^T g_2^{-1/(\eta-1)} h \, e^{-\lambda u} \, du \right] + h(X_2(T)) \, e^{-\lambda T} + \lambda \int_t^T h \, e^{-\lambda u} \, du \right\}$$

$$= \frac{\eta}{\eta - 1} \left(h(X_2(T)) \, e^{-\lambda(T-t)} \left(\frac{g_2}{g_2(X_1(T))} \right)^{1/(\eta-1)} \right.$$

$$\left. + \lambda g_2^{1/(\eta-1)} \int_t^T h \, e^{-\lambda(u-t)} \frac{d}{du} \left(h g_2^{-1/(\eta-1)} \right) du \right)$$

$$= \frac{\eta}{\eta - 1} \left(h + g_2^{1/(\eta-1)} \int_t^T e^{-\lambda(u-t)} \frac{d}{du} \left(h g_2^{-1/(\eta-1)} \right) du \right).$$

This is eq. (6) in section 4.

References

[1] D.F. Abell and J.S. Hammond, Strategic Market Planning (Prentice-Hall, Englewood Cliffs, N.J., 1979).

[2] F. Bass, A new product growth model for consumer durables, Management Science 15 (1969) 215–227.

[3] F. Bass, The relationship between diffusion rates, experience curves, and demand elasticities for consumer durable technical innovations, Presented at Conference on Interfaces between Marketing and Economics, University of Rochester, April 1978.

[4] R. Blattberg and J. Golanty, Tracker: An early test market forecasting and diagnostic model for new product planning, Journal of Marketing Research 15 (1978) 192–202.

[5] W.S. Bowman, Tying arrangements and the leverage problem, The Yale Law Journal 67 (1957) 19–36.

[6] G.W. Brock, The U.S. Computer Industry: A Study of Market Power (Ballinger, Cambridge, Mass., 1975).

[7] J.M. Buchanen, The theory of monopolistic quantity discounts, Review of Economic Studies XX (1953) 199–208.

[8] M. Connors and D. Teichroew, Optimal Control of Dynamic Operations Research Models (International Textbook Co., Scranton, Pa., 1967).

[9] R.R. De Bondt, On the effects of retard entry, European Economic Review 9 (1977) 361–371.

[10] J.A. Dodson and E. Muller, Models of new product diffusion through advertising and word-of-mouth, Management Science (1978) 1568–1578.

[11] R.J. Dolan, Determination of optimal quantity discount schedules, working paper, University of Chicago, February 1980.

[12] R.J. Dolan and A.P. Jeuland, The experience curve concept: Implications for optimal pricing strategies, Journal of Marketing 45 (1981) 52–62.

[13] A. Doob et al., Effects of initial selling price on subsequent sales, Journal of Personality and Social Psychology 11 (1969) 345–350.

[14] P.E. Green and V. Srinivasan, Conjoint analysis in consumer research: Issues and outlook, Journal of Consumer Research 5 (1978) 103–123.

[15] R.L. Hall and C.J. Hitch, Pricing theory and business behavior, Oxford Economic Papers No. 2 (1939).

[16] A.P. Jeuland, Epidemiological modeling of diffusion of innovation: Evaluation and future direction of research, Proceedings, 1979 Marketing Educators' Conference, American Marketing Association.

[17] R. Johnson, A new procedure for studying price–demand relationships, unpublished memo, Market Facts, Inc., December 1972.

[18] M.J. Kamien and N.L. Schwartz, Limit pricing and uncertain entry, Econometrica (1971) 441–454.

[19] A.D.H. Kaplan, J.B. Dirlam and R.F. Lanzillotti, Pricing in Big Business (Brookings Institute, Washington, D.C., 1958).

[20] J.J. Lambin, P.A. Naert, and A. Bultez, Optimal marketing behavior in oligopoly, European Economic Review (1975) 105–128.

[21] J.D.C. Little, BRANDAID: A marketing-mix model, parts 1 and 2, Operations Research (1975) 628–673.

[22] L.M. Lodish, CALLPLAN: An interactive salesman's call planning system, Management Science (1971) 25–40.

[23] V. Mahajan and R.A. Peterson, Innovation diffusion in a dynamic potential adopter population, Management Science (1978) 1589–1597.

[24] K.B. Monroe, Buyers' subjective perceptions of price, Journal of Marketing Research (1973) 70–80.

[25] K.B. Monroe and A.J. Della Bitta, Models for pricing decisions, Journal of Marketing Research (1978) 413–428.

[26] K.B. Monroe and A.A. Zoltners, Pricing the product line during periods of scarcity, Journal of Marketing (1979) 49–59.

[27] W. Oi, A Disneyland dilemma: Two-part tariffs for a Mickey Mouse monopoly, Quarterly Journal of Economics (1971) 77–96.

[28] A.R. Oxenfeldt, Industrial Pricing and Market Practices (Prentice-Hall, New York, 1951).

[29] A.R. Oxenfeldt, A decision making structure for price decisions, Journal of Marketing (1973) 48–53.

[30] B.P. Pashigian, Limit price and the market share of leading firm, Journal of Industrial Economics (1968) 165–177.

[31] B. Robinson and C. Lakhani, Dynamic price models for new product planning, Management Science (1975) 1113–1122.

[32] A.G. Sawyer, P.M. Worthing and P.E. Sendak, The role of laboratory experiments to test marketing strategies, Journal of Marketing (1979) 60–67.

[33] B. Shapiro, The psychology of pricing, Harvard Business Review (1968) 14–16ff.

[34] A. Silbertson, Surveys of applied economics: Price behavior of firms, Economic Journal (1970) 511–582.

[35] R. Smiley and A. Ravid, The importance of being first: Learning price and strategy, working paper, Cornell University, July 1979.

[36] G. Stigler, A note on block-booking, in: The Organization of Industry (Irwin, Homewood, Ill., 1968).

[37] G. Urban, A mathematical modeling approach to product line decisions, Journal of Marketing Research (1969) 40–47.
[38] G. Urban and A.J. Silk, Pre-test-market evaluation of new packaged goods: A model and measurement methodology, Journal of Marketing Research (1978) 171–191.
[39] J.F. Weston, Pricing behavior of large firms, Western Economic Journal (1972) 1–18.

TIMS/Studies in the Management Sciences 18 (1982) 23–41
North-Holland Publishing Company

PRICESTRAT—AN APPLIED STRATEGIC PRICING MODEL FOR NONDURABLES

Hermann SIMON
University of Bielefeld

The implications of strategic versus myopic pricing are clarified by means of an empirically applied model. Both qualitative and quantitative recommendations for strategic pricing are derived. The difficulties in incorporating empirical competitive reaction patterns are demonstrated and a procedure based on managerial experience is proposed to cope with this problem. Various applications and experiences for both established and new products are reported.

1. Introduction

There are few areas in marketing where the gap between theory and application is larger than in pricing. In Monroe and Bitta's [15] survey on price decision models the average age of references at the time of publication was 12.3 years, documenting the poor state of the art in this field.

As a matter of fact, price theory and pricing research have won little recognition in business practice.

Besides the reasons given in the survey [15], namely

(1) the dominance of economics' price theory (versus business price theory), and

(2) the seller's problem having been demand stimulation rather than pricing; two further reasons seem important:

(3) the prevalence of a static orientation which implies the neglect of phenomena like carryover effects, product life cycle, obsolescence, experience curve, etc. and

(4) the lack of empirical foundations and verification of price response functions.

In spite of prices, costs and sales being quantitative phenomena by their very nature, a great part of the management-oriented pricing literature is nonquantitative [17, 20, 21 and the numerous references therein].

More recently, the area has attracted increasing attention. Robinson and Lakhani [18] were the first US researchers to introduce price and experience curve effects into the well-known Bass model [2]. Bass [3], Bass and Bultez [4], and Dolan and Jeuland [5] have further advanced these models. With the exception of one model in [5] these models are confined to durable goods.

It is interesting to compare this development with the research activities in Germany where price has traditionally played a more important role in business, partially due to the rather rigorous restrictions on TV advertising.

Spremann [26] was probably the first (in 1975) to derive general control theoretic optimality conditions for various diffusion models (including the Bass model). In a later paper [27] he provided also a numerical solution procedure. Simon [22] developed a price-dependent product life cycle model for nondurables and also investigated the impact of experience curve effects on the optimal pricing strategy. His analysis was confined to numerical simulations, as was Schmalen's [19] work. Schmalen conceived a marketing mix model based on Bass's diffusion model and clarified the strategic implications. The empirical foundation of these contributions was rather weak or missing. But more recently, empirical and measurement issues have been clearly on the rise. Kaas [9] developed a psychology-based methodology to measure price response and Eckhardt [6] took advantage of scanning data in a cash-and-carry market in order to evaluate deal effectiveness. Albach [1] and Simon [23,24] calibrated dynamic price models for different product categories.

The inclusion of dynamic interrelations increases the complexity of the models, in particular with respect to the optimization issue. This raises the question of managerial applicability, the importance of which is increasingly being emphasized [13,16].

The main focus of the present paper is on this issue. In section 2 a strategic pricing model for nondurables (abbreviated PRICESTRAT) is developed. In sections 3 and 4 the strategic implications are clarified in a way which has proved to make them communicable to managers. Finally, various applications and experiences with the model are reported and discussed.

2. The PRICESTRAT response function

PRICESTRAT is a brand life cycle model for nondurables. Its core is the dynamic response function whose structure is clarified in fig. 1. The dependent variable is explained by nonprice factors and price factors, which are linked *additively*. The nonprice factors are the initial demand potential which can be either constant or time-decreasing and the carryover effect which is assumed to be subject to an "obsolescence". The underlying rationale is that in a dynamic market due to the introduction of new competitive brands the percentage of repeat purchases is likely to decrease over time.

The price influence is split into two parts. The absolute price is hypothesized to affect sales or market share linearly.

For the competitive price effect two alternative hypotheses seem feasible. The first goes back to Gutenberg [7] and states that the competitive price effect increases more than proportionally with the magnitude of the price differential

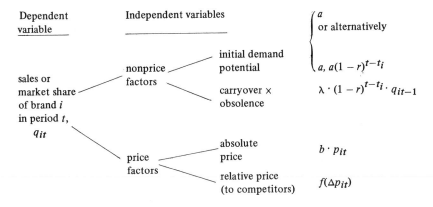

a, λ, r, b = parameters,
t_i = period of introduction of brand i,
p_{it} = price of brand i in period t,
Δp_{it} = price differential to competitive prices.

Fig. 1. The structure of PRICESTRAT.

$\Delta p_{it} = (\bar{p}_{it} - p_{it})/\bar{p}_{it}$ between brand i's price, p_{it}, and the market share weighted average price of competing brands, $\bar{p}_{it}$. This relation can be represented by a sinh function:

$$f(\Delta p_{it}) = c_1 \cdot \sinh(c_2 \, \Delta p_{it}). \tag{1}$$

Alternatively, a linear function can be considered:

$$f(\Delta p_{it}) = c \cdot \Delta p_{it}. \tag{2}$$

Linking the various terms, the following modular dynamic response function is obtained:

$$q_{it} = \begin{Bmatrix} a \\ a(1-r)^{t-t_i} \end{Bmatrix} + \lambda(1-r)^{t-t_i} q_{it-1} + bp_{it} + \begin{Bmatrix} c_1 \sinh(c_2 \, \Delta p_{it}) \\ c \, \Delta p_{it} \end{Bmatrix} + u_{it}, \tag{3}$$

where u_{it} is the error term. The terms in curly brackets are alternatives so that (3) implies four alternative versions of the function, which have been tested for a great number of brands. The function is nonlinear in the parameters r and c_2 which, therefore, had to be determined by an iterative search procedure so that no significance measures for these parameters are available. A detailed description of the estimation procedures and results (as well as a more extensive substantiation) are provided in [23,24] and need not be repeated here. For

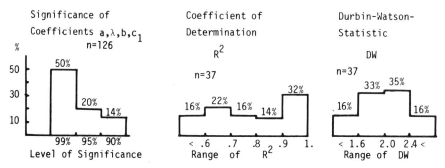

Fig. 2. Statistical criteria for 37 price response tests.

different brands different versions of model (3) fitted best. The statistical criteria of the regressions for 37 brands (detergents, household cleaners, food, pharmaceuticals) are summarized in fig. 2.

These global criteria may suffice here to demonstrate that the PRICESTRAT hypotheses are strongly supported by the empirical evidence and seem to be an adequate representation of reality.

3. Implications for strategic pricing

The strategic objective is to maximize the present value (the product index is omitted)

$$\Pi_t = \sum_{\tau=0}^{T} \left[p_{t+\tau} q_{t+\tau} - C_{t+\tau}(q_{t+\tau}) \right](1+i)^{-\tau}, \tag{4}$$

where T is the planning horizon, C denotes a cost function, and i is the discount rate. Since competitive markets are considered, the issue of competitive reaction arises. For the present we accept the no-reaction (Cournot) hypothesis [10]. However, we shall return to this issue below.

Under the no-reaction assumption the derivative of (4) with respect to p_t is

$$\frac{\partial \Pi_t}{\partial p_t} = q_t + (p_t - C_t')\frac{\partial q_t}{\partial p_t} + \sum_{\tau=1}^{T} (p_{t+\tau} - C_{t+\tau}')\frac{\partial q_{t+\tau}}{\partial p_t}(1+i)^{-\tau}, \tag{5}$$

where C' denotes marginal cost.

The partial derivative $\partial q_{t+\tau}/\partial p_t$ can be rewritten as

$$\frac{\partial q_{t+\tau}}{\partial p_t} = \frac{\partial q_t}{\partial p_t} \cdot \frac{\partial q_{t+\tau}}{\partial q_t}. \tag{6}$$

From the carryover term in (3) it follows that

$$\frac{\partial q_{t+\tau}}{\partial q_t} = \lambda^\tau (1-r)^{\tau t + \tau(\tau-1)/2}, \tag{7}$$

where the introduction period t_i is assumed to correspond to zero, so that $t = t - t_i$.

Taking advantage of (7) and (6) we can rewrite the sum term in (5) as

$$m_t \cdot \partial q_t / \partial p_t, \tag{8}$$

where

$$m_t = \sum_{\tau=1}^{T} (p_{t+\tau} - C'_{t+\tau})\lambda^\tau (1-r)^{\tau t + \tau(\tau-1)/2}(1+i)^{-\tau}. \tag{9}$$

From (8) and (9) it is easily verified that m_t measures the cumulative future effects (expressed in present value terms) of the current price as a *multiple* of the short-run price response $\partial q_t / \partial p_t$, therefore m_t is labeled "marketing multiplier". Note that m_t is a function of future prices which are to be determined.

The present value Π_t is maximized if (5) equals zero. Inserting (8) into (5) yields

$$(p_t - C'_t)\frac{\partial q_t}{\partial p_t} = -m_t\frac{\partial q_t}{\partial p_t} - q_t. \tag{10}$$

We multiply by p_t/q_t and insert the price elasticity term

$$e_t = \frac{\partial q_t}{\partial p_t} \cdot \frac{p_t}{q_t}. \tag{11}$$

Solving for p_t leads to

$$p_t^* = \frac{e_t}{1+e_t}(C'_t - m_t). \tag{12}$$

This formulation is very suitable for economic interpretation but it is not a solution for p_t^* since e_t and m_t on the right-hand side still depend on p_t (eq. (12) is a so-called fixed point equation). Note that $e_t < -1$ is required if the term in parentheses is positive.

According to (12) the myopic or short-run profit-maximizing price is simply obtained by setting $m_t = 0$; i.e. neglecting all future effects of the current price.

This is the well-known Amoroso–Robinson relation [10] from static price theory according to which an elasticity-dependent mark-up on marginal costs leads to the optimal (myopic) price.

Under dynamic conditions, this relationship remains fundamentally the same. Marginal cost C_t' is, however, reduced by the marketing multiplier, i.e. the present value of future sales changes attributable to a change in p_t^* or, more precisely, to the resulting change in the state variable q_t. To those familiar with control theory it is evident that m_t is equivalent to the adjoint variable of the control-theoretic model. Spremann [26] derived a control-theoretic optimality condition for a continuous time model which is completely analogous to (12). Note that if $(C_t' - m_t) = 0$, condition (12) cannot be applied and p_t^* (which is then equal to the sales value maximizing price where $e_t = -1$) must be calculated from (10).

If $(C_t' - m_t) < 0$, i.e. the value of the long-term effects is greater than the marginal cost, p_t^* must be less than the sales value-maximizing price because then $0 > e_t > -1$. An extreme "pricing" of this type is free sampling.

Compared to the control-theoretic model, our model and condition (12) have two advantages: (1) owing to their simplicity (both in derivation and structure) they are rather easily explainable to managers and (2) are based on a discrete time model, the *discrete* maximum principle does not allow for an equally simple derivation.

In short, the optimal strategic price depends on three factors:

  (i) the short-run price elasticity, e_t;
  (ii) the marginal cost, C_t'; and
  (iii) the marketing multiplier, m_t.

The short-run price elasticity, e_t, determines the optimal mark-up on marginal cost, be it myopic marginal cost, C_t', or "strategic" marginal cost $(C_t' - m_t)$. The marketing multiplier thus determines the *difference* between myopic and strategic price.

According to (9) the multiplier is positive if the future contribution margins and the carryover-coefficient λ are positive. The magnitude of m_t depends on these factors, on the rate of obsolescence, r, the discount rate, i, and the planning horizon, T. If m_t is positive, then the strategic price is *lower* than the myopic price.

From (9) and (12) we can readily verify that the difference between strategic price and myopic price is, *ceteris paribus*, the greater:

  (i) the greater the future contribution margins are;
  (ii) the greater the carryover-coefficient λ is;
  (iii) the smaller the rate of obsolescence r is;
  (iv) the smaller the discount rate i is; and
  (v) the more extended the planning horizon T is.

Note that if $m_t < 0$, the reverse relations apply. Compared with mainly intuitively based pricing rules these simple considerations clearly reveal the causality and the structure of the strategic price and are understandable for managers.

4. Linking pricing strategy and the life cycle

In order to be able to make inferences on the relative magnitude of the strategic prices at different stages of the life cycle, knowledge of the magnitudes of the price determinants, e_t, m_t and C'_t, at these stages is required. This is an empirical question.

The evidence on the development of the short-run price elasticity, e_t, over the life cycle is still uncertain. According to the author's empirical findings for 37 brands (reported in [23,24]) the *magnitude* of e_t decreases over the introduction and growth stage, reaches its minimum at the maturity stage, and increases during the decline stage.

This pattern, which holds true for all product groups under investigation, is —exemplarily for detergents—depicted in fig. 3. The elasticity values were calculated by inserting the actual price and sales data into the elasticity term $e_t = \partial q_t / \partial p_t \cdot p_t / q_t$. From these values the resulting mark-up factors, $e_t / (1 + e_t)$, were computed in order to demonstrate the mark-up *theoretically* implied by the actual price elasticity. These mark-ups are also given in fig. 3.

We can infer that the mark-up on "relevant" marginal cost (myopic or strategic) is relatively smaller in the early LC-stages, increases up to the maturity stage, and then again decreases. Note that this statement does not refer to the absolute level of prices since we have not yet made any assumption on the development of marginal cost.

The second price determinant derived from the PRICESTRAT response function is the marketing multiplier, m_t. From (9) we can readily infer that if the future contribution margins ($p_{t+\tau} - C'_{t+\tau}$) are nonincreasing, and the rate

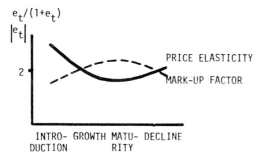

Fig. 3. Price elasticities and mark-up factors at different stages of the product life cycle (values for detergents).

of obsolescence r is positive, then the multiplier m_t decreases over time. Under these conditions the difference between myopic and strategic price *shrinks* over the life cycle.

Economically this means that a higher short-run profit should be sacrificed in the *early* stages of the life cycle in order to build goodwill (to improve the product's market position measured by the state variable, q_{t-1}). The difference between myopic and strategic profit in a certain period can be considered as an "investment" into goodwill, market position or market share (cf. also [5]). In the later stages of the life cycle the pay-off of this "investment" deteriorates due to the obsolescence, i.e. myopic and strategic prices come closer and closer.

In all 37 cases investigated the rates of obsolescence, r, turned out to be positive so that (for nonincreasing future contribution margins) the described pattern holds. In fig. 4 three empirical examples of the developments of m_t are given. The values of m_t were calculated according to (9) and based on an assumed future contribution margin of 30% of marginal cost and a discount rate of 10%, so the future prices were not optimized in this computation. The multiplier, m_t, is expressed as a percentage of C_t'.

The example of brand (1) in the figure shows that m_t may temporarily be greater than C_t'. Although the empirical evidence on this issue is highly shaky, this author contends that a decrease of m_t is a likely development. The examples provided below support this contention.

Marginal cost, the third price determinant, can develop in different ways over the life cycle. Three basic types of cost hypotheses are economically reasonable: (1) constant marginal cost, (2) marginal cost decreasing with sales volume per period (economies of scale), and (3) marginal cost decreasing with accumulated sales volume (experience curve effect; see [8]). In fig. 5 these basic

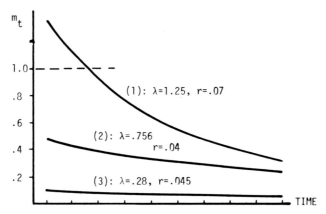

Fig. 4. The development of the marketing multiplier, m_t, over time (examples from different product classes).

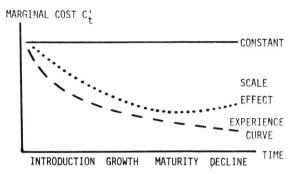

Fig. 5. Basic patterns of development of marginal cost over time.

patterns are—in a merely schematic way—related to the life cycle.

We do not expand here on the functional representation of these curves (see [3,5]). The schematic representation suffices to make inferences on the development of myopic and strategic prices for the empirically most relevant cases (the development of e_t according to fig. 3, and m_t decreasing over time). For these conditions possible price trajectories for the different marginal cost patterns are given in fig. 6.

Thus, general statements on the *absolute* levels of optimal prices at different life cycle stages are *not feasible* because these levels depend on marginal cost, which can develop in different ways.

The optimal price is always a *compound* of the influences of both demand

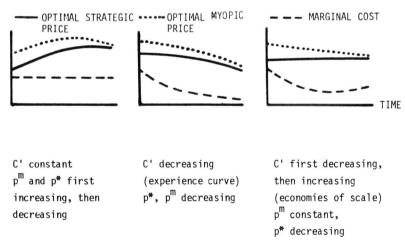

Fig. 6. Possible trajectories of optimal prices (schematically).

Table 1

Stage of product life cycle		Introduction	Growth	Maturity	Decline
Price elasticity, e_t		high	medium	low	medium
Mark-up factor, $e_t/(1+e_t)$		low	medium	high	medium
Marketing multiplier, m_t		high	medium–high	low	very low
Optimal strategic price, p_t^*:	in relation to optimal myopic price p_t^s	low	increasing	high	very high
	in relation to marginal cost	low	increasing	high	decreasing

and cost factors and, consequently, depends in any single case on the relative importance of these factors. Simple generalizations, as are occasionally expressed in recommendations of the "skimming" and "penetration" type, are not feasible.

We can, however, make general statements on the level of the strategic price in relation to the myopic price and to marginal cost. These qualitative recommendations (again under the assumption that m_t *decreases* over time) are summarized in table 1.

5. The competitive reaction issue

Since most of the applications of PRICESTRAT have been related to oligopolistic markets the competitive reaction issue is of crucial importance for the maximization of the objective function (4). In the theoretical price literature (both in the classical literature and in the more recent game-theoretic approaches) this issue has attracted wide attention (for a comprehensive survey see [10]); empirical studies are, however, extremely rare and not at all conclusive [11,27]. It should be emphasized that under the application aspect the competitive reaction is much less a mathematical than an empirical problem. It is extremely difficult to explain the actually observed reactive behavior by means of mathematically simple and econometrically measurable reaction functions.

A few examples may support this contention. In fig. 7 the price developments of four products and the respective market share weighted average prices of competing products are depicted. The variety of patterns is amazing.

Each reduction of product A's price is matched by a larger reduction of the competitive price (or is the causality reverse?). For product B, the competitors seem to raise their prices when B's price is reduced. For products C and D no reasonable or consistent reaction pattern seems identifiable.

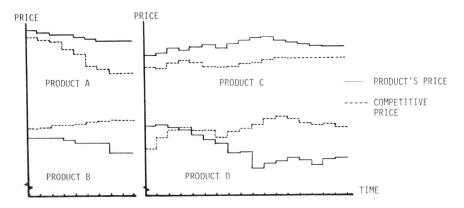

Fig. 7. Actual price developments on four markets.

None of the classical (static) hypotheses (like Cournot, Hotelling, Chamberlin, von Stackelberg, etc.; see [10]) is capable of adequately explaining such a variety of patterns. If we consider, however, the specific situations of the products (e.g. stage in the life cycle, relative competitive strength, market share shifts) many of the observed reaction moves appear conclusive.

Product A has a dominant position and is in the growth stage of its life cycle. Most of the competitors have only recently entered the market and attempt to take market shares from A by means of aggressive pricing. Rather moderate reductions of A's price were sufficient to compensate the effects and to retain the old market share.

Product B has a minor market share. In spite of cumulative price reductions of 27% its share did not increase. Obviously, competitors can behave without paying much attention to this weak product.

Product C has maintained a relatively high market share throughout the period under investigation. Slight losses occurred in the high-price phase but could be compensated by the subsequent price reductions. Those affected the competitors only slightly so that no reaction occurred. Product C, and most of its competing products, are in the maturity stage of their life cycles and the observed market share shifts were not dramatic, nor were the reactions.

Product D has entered its decline stage; in spite of considerable price cuts, its market share decreased to 60% of the initial value. Evidently competitive products were perceived as superior by consumers, and in spite of price increases their accumulated share increased. It seems unlikely that competitors react to any action of product D.

In spite of a certain logical consistency these considerations are not easily incorporated into an estimable reaction function. The hypothesis of a constant reaction elasticity adopted by Lambin et al. [12] is completely inadequate in our cases.

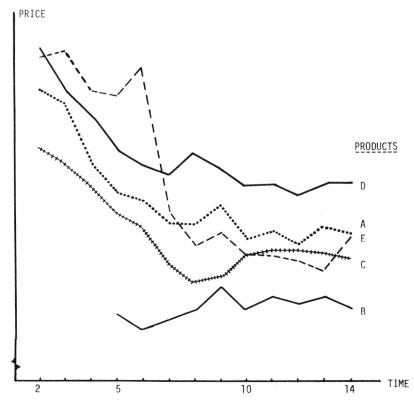

Fig. 8. Actual price developments on a market with five products.

The issue becomes even more complex if, instead of the aggregate price, individual prices of competing products are considered. The disaggregation might be important since the competitors are likely to be affected in different ways by a certain action and thus should be supposed to react differently.

Fig. 8 provides an illustrative example for a market with five products. In periods 2–5 price relations remained relatively stable, in period 7 product E's price was cut by more than 20% and E's market share increased considerably; A and D lost market shares. Nevertheless, no discernible reaction occurred. In the subsequent periods the price changes are again relatively proportional. Obviously, the reaction behavior is not stable over time.

So far no satisfactory mathematical representation of the empirical reaction patterns has been attained. The explanation is complicated by the fact that no certain information on the cost situation of competitors is available. *For the time being*, and in particular under the aspect of managerial application, a simplified two-step procedure for the inclusion of the competitive reaction has been adopted.

First step. The management predicts expected competitive prices for the periods under consideration. The optimization is run with these prices considered as given (Cournot hypothesis or Nash solution in a game-theoretic context [10]).

Second step. The managers reconsider their original estimate of competitive prices under the assumption that the "optimal" prices (obtained in the first step) will be realized. If the original estimates prove still realistic under this assumption, then the final optimal strategy is obtained. If not, the estimates are revised and a new optimization is run. In four out of five applications a "sufficient convergence" was achieved after one or two re-estimations. It is, however, not unusual that the oligopolistic situation corresponds to the "prisoner's dilemma" known from game theory [10] and the managers are necessarily very uncertain about the competitive reaction. This simplified procedure is certainly not fully satisfactory and must be improved. It should, however, be observed that it is appealing to managers and the input of their subjective judgments on possible competitive reaction increases their confidence in the model's results. Since our main concern is to improve the practice of strategic pricing, the applicability aspect is, for the time being, more highly evaluated than a theoretically more elegant inclusion of a competitive reaction function.

A thorough investigation of this issue is under way. So far *ex post* forecasts of competitive prices within a system of equations are good, but *ex ante* forecasts are not yet satisfactory.

6. Applications and experiences

In order to find the optimal pricing strategy over all planning periods a dynamic programming problem with (4) as objective function and one of the alternative versions of (3) as equation of motion has to be solved.

In most of the present applications a heuristic algorithm which optimizes over a finite number of price alternatives by means of a limited enumeration has been used. Note that this algorithm does not take direct advantage of condition (12), which is preferable since the nonlinear price response function (3) may imply several local profit maxima and, thus, the problem may not be convex. The considerations in connection with (12) served to clarify the economic structure of the strategic price.

Application type 1. In the first type of applications past pricing strategies were analyzed in order to gain insights into the strategic price impact and its dynamics.

An example is given in fig. 9. The actual price of this brand (which was not superior to its competitors) has been held constant over 12 periods after the

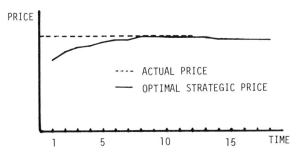

Fig. 9. Example of a strategically nonoptimal price policy,

introduction. In this case the price effect was best represented by a response function of the sinh-type ($R^2 = 0.89$). Marginal cost remained approximately constant (no experience curve!). The model indicates the optimality of a penetration type strategy with a move to a higher price level in the later periods. The profit associated with the penetration strategy would have exceeded the actual one by 33%. A competitive reaction would have been unlikely since the predicted market share gain is only three share points.

Obviously, strategic considerations had not played an important role in the actual price decision for this product. The same diagnosis applied to various other products. The majority of managers agreed with these conclusions.

Actually, penetration strategies of the proposed type are not at all unusual. Often a low initial price is provided in the form of a special introduction deal or, in the case of pharmaceuticals, by excessive free sampling (price = 0).The strategy is also usual with durables.

In 1977, RWE AG, the largest electricity supplier in Germany, offered a substantial discount for the first 1,000 purchasers of heat-pumps. In the aircraft business the "launching carrier" (i.e. the first airline which adopts a new aircraft) normally gets very attractive price conditions. Dolan and Jeuland [5] quote an example of a pocket book which was initially sold at $2.95, later the price was raised to $3.50. Last, but not least, the Japanese entry successes provide strong evidence in support of this strategy. Though still unusual, this strategy may be more rewarding then the popular "down the ladder" approach to pricing.

Application type 2. This application type refers to the determination of optimal current and future prices for established brands. An example is depicted in fig. 10. The brand under consideration is in its maturity stage, a linear version of the competitive price effect gave a satisfactory representation of reality ($R^2 = 0.66$). The figure provides both the strategic and the myopic prices as of the current period. Both optimal prices are higher than the actual price of the last period, in the early periods the myopic price again exceeds the strategic one. The curve of the accumulated profit differences clearly shows

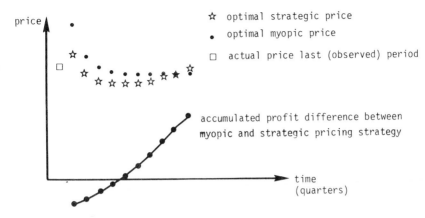

Fig. 10. Myopic and strategic prices for a mature product.

that with the strategic price some profit is sacrificed in the beginning, but with a payoff period of about $4\frac{1}{2}$ quarters, or 14 months, this "investment" is highly profitable. At the end of the 10-period planning horizon the "strategic" present value exceeds its myopic counterpart by 8.6%.

Application type 3. A very recent application was related to a new pharmaceutical product. This product was expected to be without equivalent competitors for about one year after its introduction. Entries of competitors were only expected after this time.

A worldwide simultaneous introduction was planned, and due to superior, compelling reasons a uniform "world" price had to be determined for the first year. The responsible managers in three key countries were asked to provide estimates of the lowest and the highest feasible price of the first year sales associated with these two prices, and also the middle price. The results are depicted in the upper part of fig. 11 (meanwhile the managers provide even their estimates graphically on prepared diagram sheets).

From these data the price range DM 1.10–1.50 was considered feasible. If necessary the managerial estimates were extrapolated to cover this range (dashed). The aggregation of the three countries yields the (static) price response curve (solid line) in the lower part of fig. 11. On the basis of this curve and the cost figures the total contributions obtained with each price are readily calculated (dashed line), showing that the optimal myopic price is somewhere in the region of DM 1.20–1.30.

The price response function can also be formalized. A subjectively determined (decision calculus!) form is

$$q_1 = 189 - 90p_1. \tag{13}$$

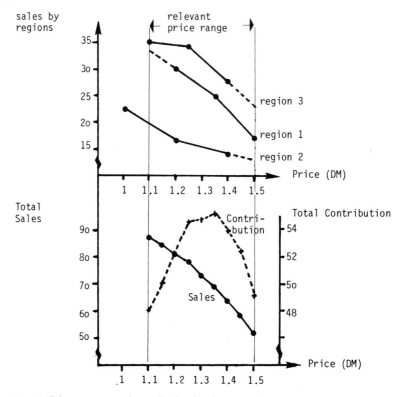

Fig. 11. Price response and contribution for three countries.

Note that this is the first year's response function (no carryover) and that a competitive price effect does not exist owing to the absence of competing products.

The marginal costs are $C_t' = 0.55$. The *myopic* price p_1^m (note that $m_1 = 0$) is easily calculated from (10) as

$$p_1^m = \tfrac{1}{2}\left(\tfrac{189}{90} + 0.55\right) = 1.325. \tag{14}$$

In order to find out about the strategic price the managers were asked to provide sales forecasts for the years 2, 3 and 4 under the assumption that their respective middle prices became effective. Additionally, the year and the magnitude of the sales maximum in the brand's life cycle were sought. By means of these data an aggregate life cycle forecast was made and used to determine subjectively the magnitude of the carryover coefficient, λ, and the obsolescence rate, r. The dynamic sales function with $\lambda = 0.60$ and $r = 0.05$, i.e.

$$q_t = 189 + 0.6 \times 0.95^t q_{t-1} - 90 p_t, \tag{15}$$

reproduced the managerial forecasts quite satisfactorily. These carryover values were also substantiated by the econometric results for the predecessor brand. A long-run mechanical optimization (e.g. for 5 years) on the basis of (15) was not considered reasonable since this function does not adequately represent the price effect after the entry of competitors. Owing to the uncertainty associated with this entry the price decision should be confined to the first period but, nevertheless, observe the long-term effects of the initial price which are measured by the marketing multiplier, m_t. According to (9) an estimate of the future contribution margins is required to calculate m_t. These margins were estimated to be about DM0.50, so that a value of $m_1 = $ DM0.47 is obtained from (9) ($i = 0.10$).

The strategic price, p_1^*, is readily calculated by replacing $C_1' = 0.55$ in (14) by $(C_1' - m_1) = 0.55 - 0.47 = 0.08$ so that

$$p_1^* = \tfrac{1}{2}\left(\tfrac{189}{90} + 0.08\right) = 1.09. \tag{16}$$

This price is—owing to the initially high carryover—considerably lower than the myopic price of DM 1.32. The profit sacrifice or "market investment" amounts to about 10% of the first year's maximal profit.

Owing to the extreme uncertainty as to the competitive entry and to the market conditions thereafter, it may be impossible to recover this (absolutely) high "investment". Moreover, experience curve effects did not exist. Therefore the actual price was set closer to the myopic than to the strategic price. This amounts to applying a high discount rate to the future profits, e.g. 40% instead of the 10% used in (16).

The conclusions were substantiated by a simulation study which included both the monopoly and the presumed oligopoly stage. This study, which cannot be reported here, indicated that in this special case it is probably optimal to set the initial price rather close to the myopic price but to cut it early enough before the competitive entry in order to build up "goodwill". More details on this strategy are reported in [25].

In all of the present applications the model's relative simplicity has proved to be its most valuable asset. Actually, in the applications the model has continuously been "desophisticated". The managerial willingness to use the model and to adopt the results was clearly related to the difficulties in understanding the model and the measurement procedures. The reduction of the response dynamics to two easily understandable measures, the short-run price elasticity and the marketing multiplier, and the revelation of the "investment" character of the strategic price proved highly relevant in this regard. Perhaps the hitherto most satisfactory application was that of type 3 (real novelty), and it has to be admitted that the static response curve in fig. 11 had a relatively greater impact on the decision than the dynamic considerations. The availability of graphically displayed price response and contribution curves made the price decision process more efficient and objective. The influence of subjective factors was considerably reduced. The quantitative, market oriented substantiation of the price recommendation strengthened the pricing group's position in front of the top executives who have to approve all price decisions.

The PRICESTRAT model is in an exploratory stage and is being continuously improved. One improvement in the data collection stage is that the managers are now asked to provide their estimates (like the ones in fig. 11) graphically on a prepared diagram. This seems to yield more consistent estimations. Many issues are not yet solved, e.g. the competitive reaction problem. Others remain completely outside the model, e.g. the psychological effects of prices, and the political and antitrust aspects.

The focus of future improvements is, however, less on making the model more complex than rather on better substantiating the entering parameters.

References

[1] H. Albach, Market organization and pricing behavior of oligopolistic firms in the ethical drugs industry—An essay in the measurement of effective competition, Kyklos 32 (1979) 523–540.

[2] F.M. Bass, A new product growth model for consumer durables, Management Science 15 (1969) 215–227.

[3] F.M. Bass, The relationship between diffusion rates, experience curves, and demand elasticities for consumer durable innovations, Journal of Business 53 (July 1980) 551–567.

[4] F.M. Bass and A.V. Bultez, Generating of optimal strategic pricing policies with learning, Paper presented at the ORSA/TIMS Joint National Meeting, Milwaukee, 15–17 October 1979.

[5] R.J. Dolan and A.P. Jeuland, Experience curves and dynamic demand models: Implications for optimal pricing strategies, Journal of Marketing 45 (Winter 1981) 52—62.

[6] K. Eckhardt, Sonderangebotspolitik in Warenhandelsbetrieben Eine empirische Studie (Dealing Policy in Stores, An Empirical Study) (Gabler, Wiesbaden, 1977).

[7] E. Gutenberg, Grundlagen der Betriebswirtschaftslehre, Band II, Der Absatz (Fundamentals of Business Administration), 15th edn. (Springer, Berlin–Heidelberg–New York, 1976).

[8] B.D. Henderson, Perspectives on Experience, 4th edition (Boston Consulting Group, 1972).

[9] K.P. Kaas, Empirische Preisabsatzfunktionen bei Konsumgütern (The Empirical Measurement of Price Response Functions) (Springer, Berlin–Heidelberg–New York, 1977).

[10] W. Krelle, Preistheorie, 2nd edn. (Mohr-Siebeck, Tübingen, 1976).

[11] J.J. Lambin, Advertising, Competition and Market Conduct in Oligopoly over Time (North-Holland–Elsevier, Amsterdam, 1976).

[12] J.J. Lambin, Ph. Naert and A. Bultez, Optimal marketing behavior in oligopoly, European Economic Review 6 (1975) 105–128.

[13] J.D.C. Little, Decision support for marketing management, Journal of Marketing 43 (July 1979) 9–26.

[14] K.B. Monroe, Pricing (Prentice-Hall, Englewood Cliffs, 1979).

[15] K.B. Monroe and A.J.D. Bitta, Models for pricing decisions, Journal of Marketing Research 15 (August 1978) 413–428.

[16] J.G. Myers, St.A. Greyser and W.F. Massy, The effectiveness of marketing's "R&D" for marketing management: An assessment, Journal of Marketing 43 (January 1979) 17–27.

[17] A.R. Oxenfeldt, Pricing Strategies (Amacom, New York, 1975).

[18] B. Robinson and CH. Lakhani, Dynamic price models for new product planning, Management Science 21 (June 1975) 1113–1122.

[19] H. Schmalen, Ein Diffusionsmodell zur Planung des Marketing-Mix bei der Einführung langlebiger Konsumgüter auf einem Konkurrenzmarkt (A diffusion model for the introduction of consumer durables onto a competitive market), Zeitschrift für Betriebswirtschaft 47 (November 1977) 697–714.

[20] B.P. Shapiro, The Pricing of Consumer Goods: Theory and Practice (Marketing Science Institute, Cambridge, 1972).

[21] B.P. Shapiro and B.B. Jackson, Industrial pricing to meet customer needs, Harvard Business Review 56 (Nov.–Dec. 1978) 119–127.

[22] H. Simon, Preisstrategien für neue Produkte (Pricing Strategies for New Products) (Gabler, Wiesbaden, 1976).

[23] H. Simon, Produktlebenszyklus und Preisstrategie (PLC and pricing strategy), Wirtschaftswissenschaftliches Studium 7 (March 1978) 116–123.

[24] H. Simon, Dynamics of price elasticity and brand life cycles: An empirical study, Journal of Marketing Research 16 (November 1979) 439–452.

[25] H. Simon, Preismanagement, (Gabler, Wiesbaden, 1982).

[26] K. Spremann, Optimale Preispolitik bei dynamischen deterministischen Absatzmodellen (Optimal pricing for dynamic deterministic sales models), Zeitschrift für Nationalökonomie 35 (1975) 63–73.

[27] K. Spremann, The Nerlove–Arrow theorem and dynamic marginal costs, Working Paper No. 74 (University of Karlsruhe, 1976).

TIMS/Studies in the Management Sciences 18 (1982) 43–61
North-Holland Publishing Company

LITMUS: A NEW PRODUCT PLANNING MODEL *

Joseph D. BLACKBURN
Vanderbilt University

and

Kevin J. CLANCY
Boston University

The LITMUS model is an interactive stochastic model which serves as a decision aid to the marketing manager in the development of a marketing strategy for a new product introduction. In addition to early forecasts of market performance for a new product, the model also provides diagnostics for refinement of the marketing plan. LITMUS is designed to work with a limited amount of consumer data, such as would be provided by a Laboratory Test Market (LTM). In this paper we describe the theoretical development and empirical tests of the LITMUS model.

1. Introduction

The introduction of new products and services continues to be a risky, but essential, marketing function. Contemporary marketing managers expend a disproportionate amount of effort and expense developing new products and yet few of these products achieve success on a national level. It is estimated that less than one in one hundred new product concepts are taken into test markets. This reluctance to enter a test market is due, in part, to the fact that intense competition has caused dramatic increases in the cost (often more than one million dollars), accompanied by a high rate of failure. Recent data reported by the A.C. Nielsen Company indicate that the risk of new product failure continues to increase with a current failure rate of more than 60% for new grocery products introduced into test markets, compared to about 50% a decade ago [2]. (The failure rate is even higher if one counts all products dropped prior to test marketing.)

Nevertheless, although the risk is high, new product introductions are necessary for survival in certain product categories. Watching the market share of established brands be eroded by competitive entries, the intelligent marketer

* This research was funded, in part, by Yankelovich, Skelly and White, Inc., who also provided data for the model tests reported here.

must continue to seek out new product opportunities, if only for defensive reasons.

Recent developments in marketing research have provided some new methods of reducing the risk of new product introductions. Some firms have turned to a combination of sophisticated test market research integrated with mathematical models of the new product introduction process. The objective is to provide more accurate forecasts of new product market performance and to discern how the product concept or marketing plan should be shaped to maximize the likelihood of success. Several mathematical models, which are designed to use test market data as input, have been developed in recent years. These include NEWS [3,4], TRACKER [1], and SPRINTER [6].

Many firms have taken a different approach to this problem, choosing the alternative of relatively inexpensive simulated test markets, such as Yankelovich, Skelly and White's Laboratory Test Market (or LTM). Such simulations attempt to compress in time and dollars a test market experience. Some marketing managers use them as a low risk step prior to a full-scale test market, while others have replaced traditional test markets with their simulated counterparts. Still other firms have adopted systems which combine the simulated test market with a mathematical model. Management Decision System's ASSESSOR [5] is a pioneering example of this approach. LITMUS, a new mathematical model developed in conjunction with Yankelovich's LTM, is another.

LITMUS is an interactive stochastic model designed to forecast, diagnose and improve the performance of alternative marketing strategies for new packaged goods either before *or* after test marketing. Using inputs derived from the new product's marketing plan, other empirical relationships, and laboratory test market research, LITMUS forecasts brand awareness, trial, current usage, sales and market share. The model's built-in sensitivity analysis then provides the planner with insights into the likely effects of changes in each strategic and tactical input on key measures of campaign effectiveness, notably sales and market share. In this manner the reasons underlying the predicted success or failure of the new product launch can be quickly diagnosed and recommendations made which will improve the expected performance of the new product entry.

On the surface, LITMUS appears similar to its predecessors, especially NEWS, TRACKER and ASSESSOR, in terms of its objectives, easy-to-use conversational mode, input parameters, and published evidence of successful forecasting. However, surface similarities can be deceiving, for although LITMUS shares some of the strengths and weaknesses of other models, it has some distinctive features. Two such features are the large number of marketing mix variables and the extensive number of states of nature used to capture the richness and complexity of the new product introduction process.

In this paper we describe the development, structure and empirical tests of the LITMUS model. The empirical tests were carried out on 25 new products originally tested in LTM and later evaluated in the real world (either a test market or a regional/national introduction). Using a marketing plan and LTM data as input, the model's forecasts were compared to actual in-market performance. Though these tests indicate that the model can, in most cases, provide accurate predictions, the failures are more instructive from a research perspective in that they indicate where future research is needed to refine the empirical relationships used in the model.

1.1. Model development

The genesis of LITMUS was a need for a model which could be used with laboratory test market results to evaluate the individual and simultaneous effects of a variety of marketing mix variables on new product performance. Since its introduction in 1968, Yankelovich, Skelly and White's LTM, a service designed to compress the traditional marketing of new products into a shorter time span at a fraction of the cost, has enjoyed a considerable degree of success as a forecasting and diagnostic tool. Given one or several marketing plans, including product concept and advertising, LTM provides clients with estimates of market share and recommendations for improvements in the marketing plan. A comparison of these LTM estimates with real world performance suggests a high level of construct and predictive validity.

The heart of LTM is the laboratory test. A cross section of 300–500 potential buyers are invited to a theater (in groups of 30–35); the theaters are located in three different markets in the U.S. Following the completion of a brief, self-administered questionnaire (mostly demographic information), consumers are exposed to a television program in which a commercial for the new brand and competitive products are embedded. Afterwards, consumers are led in small groups to the "store", a store which stocks the brands advertised in the commercial and others which enjoy a significant market share in the testing area. Upon entering the "store" consumers are provided with a fixed amount of money to stimulate purchase. A fraction of the people go on to buy the "test" brand, others do not. This fraction, adjusted by LTM norms, experience, and marketing plan data, leads to an estimate of the probability of brand trial, given awareness.

Some time later (the lag dependent on the product category), consumers are reinterviewed by telephone to gauge their reactions to the product. These data, again adjusted by norms and experience, generate an estimate of first repeat purchase probability. Often, however, a sales wave or extended use test is incorporated into the research design and these data are used to estimate multiple repeat purchase probabilities. All of this information is then used to forecast brand sales and/or market share.

What LTM cannot easily do, however, is to evaluate many plans or assess the individual contribution of many variables in the marketing mix to market share. As the more creative use of media flourishes, for example, there is a growing need by LTM management to forecast the effects of media variables, such as GRPs and advertising impact, on new product performance. Hence, the interest in coupling the LTM output with a contextual model.

In its early stages of development, the archetype for the LTM model was the highly successful NEWS model. In fact, both models assume the same basic structure for the new product introduction process (as shown in fig. 1). However, as the number of the modifications increased, a new and more complex model emerged. Given its purpose and LTM parentage, we call it LITMUS.

1.2. Model structure and input

An outline of the new product introduction process, as modeled by LITMUS, is shown in fig. 1. A target group of consumers (i.e. the market) is exposed to

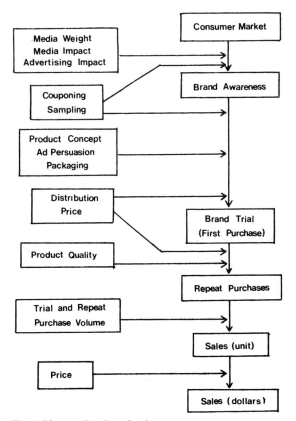

Fig. 1. New product introduction process.

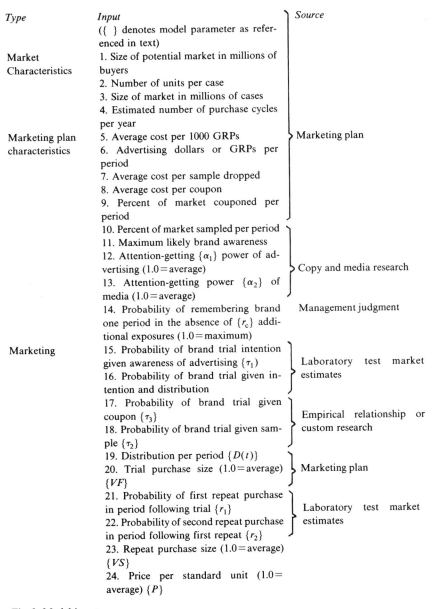

Type	Input ({ } denotes model parameter as referenced in text)	Source
Market Characteristics	1. Size of potential market in millions of buyers 2. Number of units per case 3. Size of market in millions of cases 4. Estimated number of purchase cycles per year	
Marketing plan characteristics	5. Average cost per 1000 GRPs 6. Advertising dollars or GRPs per period 7. Average cost per sample dropped 8. Average cost per coupon 9. Percent of market couponed per period	Marketing plan
	10. Percent of market sampled per period 11. Maximum likely brand awareness 12. Attention-getting $\{\alpha_1\}$ power of advertising (1.0=average) 13. Attention-getting power $\{\alpha_2\}$ of media (1.0=average)	Copy and media research
	14. Probability of remembering brand one period in the absence of $\{r_c\}$ additional exposures (1.0=maximum)	Management judgment
Marketing	15. Probability of brand trial intention given awareness of advertising $\{\tau_1\}$ 16. Probability of brand trial given intention and distribution	Laboratory test market estimates
	17. Probability of brand trial given coupon $\{\tau_3\}$ 18. Probability of brand trial given sample $\{\tau_2\}$	Empirical relationship or custom research
	19. Distribution per period $\{D(t)\}$ 20. Trial purchase size (1.0=average) $\{VF\}$	Marketing plan
	21. Probability of first repeat purchase in period following trial $\{r_1\}$ 22. Probability of second repeat purchase in period following first repeat $\{r_2\}$	Laboratory test market estimates
	23. Repeat purchase size (1.0=average) $\{VS\}$ 24. Price per standard unit (1.0=average) $\{P\}$	

Fig. 2. Model inputs.

advertising and/or promotion for the new product. Depending upon the intensity (e.g. media weight) and effectiveness (e.g. media impact) of this exposure, brand awareness (expressed as a percent of the target group) is generated.

The output process continues from awareness through purchase, converted to sales dollars. Note that different factors affect the transitions between stages. For example, product concept, but not media weight or impact, is hypothesized to affect the conversion from awareness to trial (i.e. first purchase).

More specific information on the inputs required to run the model and the sources for each are displayed in fig. 2. These inputs are sequenced to correspond to the process shown in fig. 1. Experience has shown that when the model is run in conjunction with the laboratory test market, these inputs are readily assembled. They are derived from a combination of the marketing plan, laboratory test market estimates, empirical relationships and management judgment. These inputs are then entered into the model in a conversational mode.

In its current state of development, LITMUS bases its projections on a given marketing plan (variables 1–10 and 19 in fig. 2). However, as an interactive aid to the marketing manager, sensitivity analysis of the relationship between projected sales and specific components of the marketing plan can be carried out to indicate how to improve the plan. The program could be imbedded in an optimization model in which the marketing plan is characterized perhaps by a budget constraint. Then nonlinear search techniques could be employed to determine optimal (or near-optimal) levels for each component in the marketing plan by purchase period. Future research will be directed toward this end.

2. Model description

In ths LITMUS model the new product introduction is characterized by a Markov process with transition probabilities that are nonstationary in time. The basic structure of the model through the first trial state is shown in fig. 3. All consumers begin in the unaware pool. The general state categories that can be achieved over the product introduction period are shown as rectangles; circles denote points in the process at which consumer behavior is subject to chance, or probabilistic, effects which can alter the consumer's awareness of the product.

The time periods (or purchase periods) in this model correspond to the normal purchase cycle for the product category. In each purchase period, all members of the unaware pool have the potential to become aware of the new product due to some combination of advertising, promotions (samples) or coupons. As a result, a certain fraction of the consumers move into the *awareness state*, which denotes brand awareness prior to trial.

Seven separate categories are used to characterize specific forms of consumer awareness:

(1) advertising awareness;

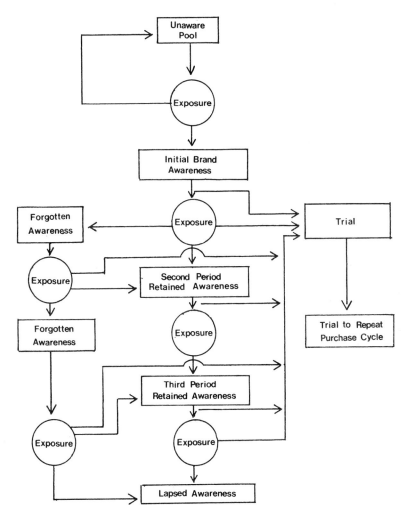

Fig. 3. Awareness-to-trial process.

    (2) promotion awareness;
    (3) coupon awareness;
    (4) combined advertising and promotion awareness;
    (5) advertising and coupon awareness;
    (6) promotion and coupon awareness; and
    (7) advertising, promotion and coupon awareness.
  In what follows, the awareness states will be identified by the number given above. For completeness, two more states are used:

(8) unexposed to product in current period; and
(9) forgotten awareness.

2.1. Awareness probabilities

The probability that a consumer is in a particular awareness category in a time period is determined from the unconditional probabilities of awareness due to advertising, promotions and coupons. Exposure to advertising and exposure via promotion and/or coupons are assumed to be *independent* effects:

$P_A(t)=$ unconditional probability of awareness due to advertising in time period t,
$P_p(t)=$ unconditional probability of awareness due to sample promotion in time period t,
$P_c(t)=$ unconditional probability of awareness due to coupon offer in time period t.

The advertising awareness probability ($P_A(t)$) is computed by weighing the current period's advertising exposure in Gross Rating Points or GRPs (G_t) by advertising impact (a), the attention power of advertising with respect to the industry (α_1) and attention power of the media (α_2). This can be represented using the following expression for the probability of advertising awareness:

$$P_A(t) = 1 - \exp\left[-(\alpha_1\alpha_2 \cdot a \cdot G_t)\right],$$

where $P_p(t)$ is taken to be the fraction of the population made aware due to coupon promotion in time period t, and $P_c(t)$ is taken to be the fraction of the population made aware due to coupon promotion in time period t.

The expression for $P_A(t)$ is similar to that used in [1] and [3]. It assumes diminishing returns to advertising so that if awareness is already high, a very high level of advertising would be required to raise it even further. Parameters are estimated using historical data or actual in-market experience.

Using these unconditional probabilities and assuming independence, the joint probability of advertising, promotion and coupon awareness in period t is

$$P_7(t) = P_A(t) \cdot P_p(t) \cdot P_c(t);$$

promotion and coupon awareness:

$$P_6(t) = P_p(t) \cdot P_c(t) \cdot (1 - P_A(t));$$

advertising and coupon:

$$P_5(t) = P_A(t) \cdot P_c(t) \cdot (1 - P_p(t));$$

advertising and promotion:

$$P_4(t) = P_A(t) \cdot P_p(t) \cdot (1 - P_c(t));$$

coupon awareness only:

$$P_3(t) = P_c(t) - P_5(t) - P_6(t) - P_7(t);$$

promotion awareness only:

$$P_2(t) = P_p(t) - P_4(t) - P_6(t) - P_7(t);$$

advertising awareness only:

$$P_1(t) = P_A(t) - P_4(t) - P_5(t) - P_7(t).$$

2.1.1. New awareness

For each of the seven awareness categories, the fraction of new awares in the current purchase period, $A_i(1)$, $i = 1, \ldots, 7$, is the product of the unaware fraction in time period $t(U(t))$ and the probability of new awareness in category $i(P_i(t))$:

$$A_i(1) = P_i(t) \cdot U(t).$$

2.1.2. Updating the unaware pool

To update the unaware fraction at the beginning of the next purchase period:

$$U(t+1) = U(t)\left[1 - \sum_{i=1}^{7} P_i(t)\right].$$

That is, the unaware pool of consumers is reduced by the fraction who become aware of the product in period t.

2.1.3. Awareness-to-trial probability

Once awareness has been achieved, a consumer is assumed to have up to three periods to try the product, i.e. make a transition from an awareness state to a new trier state. The probability of purchase diminishes over this time interval, but also depends on the number and type of exposures. For example, a consumer can be exposed to advertising in period 1, experience no exposure in period 2, and exposure via coupon and promotion in period 3. The probability of trial in period 3 would then be based on the entire history of exposures by the consumer.

Therefore, the probability of trial in time period t depends on the consumer's states of awareness in the three most recent periods—t; $t-1$ and $t-2$. The trial probabilities for new awares are described first, followed by the two-period aware consumers, and finally consumers who first achieved awareness in period $t-2$. It should be noted that, in LITMUS, a much larger number of states of nature are used to capture the richness and complexity of the awareness to trial process than its precursors, NEWS and TRACKER.

2.1.4. New awares

Newly aware consumers have a trial probability τ_i, where i denotes the consumer's particular awareness state:

$\tau_1 =$ advertising awareness to buying intention coefficient (probability of trial given awareness due to advertising alone),

$\tau_2 =$ promotion (sample to trial coefficient),

$\tau_3 =$ coupon to trial coefficient,

$\tau_4 = \tau_1 + \tau_2 - (\tau_1)(\tau_2)$,

$\quad =$ probability of trial given advertising and promotion awareness,

$\tau_5 = \tau_1 + \tau_3 - (\tau_1)(\tau_3)$,

$\tau_6 = \tau_2 + \tau_3 - (\tau_2)(\tau_3)$,

$\tau_7 = \tau_1 + \tau_2 + \tau_3 - (\tau_1)(\tau_2) - (\tau_1)(\tau_3) - (\tau_2)(\tau_3) + (\tau_1)(\tau_2)(\tau_3)$.

These estimates of trial probability are based on an assumption of independence with respect to the joint effect of different forms of awareness. For example, in the expression for τ_4, if a consumer is aware of the product due both to advertising and receipt of a sample, then trial is assumed to occur as a result of one of these two effects. Let event A denote trial due to advertising awareness and event S denote trial due to sample awareness; then

$$\tau_4 = P(A \cup S) = P(A) + P(S) - P(A \cap S)$$
$$= \tau_1 + \tau_2 - \tau_1 \cdot \tau_2 \qquad\qquad (1)$$

under the independence assumption. The expressions for τ_5, τ_6 and τ_7 are similarly derived.

Our model essentially assumes no interaction between the different forms of awareness and, as such, satisfies the following inequalities:

$$\max\{\tau_1, \tau_2\} \leqslant \tau_4 \leqslant \tau_1 + \tau_2.$$

Although some might hypothesize a positive interaction exceeding that suggested by (1), there is a dearth of empirical evidence in support of this hypothesis. Experience with LTM products suggests that the interactive effect is negligible.

2.1.5. Two-period awares

The computation of trial probabilities for consumers who have maintained awareness for two purchase periods is complicated by two additional factors. Since these consumers have failed to try the product during one purchase period, their probability of trial should be diminished from that of newly aware consumers. In addition, these consumers have been exposed to new advertising or a promotion in the current period and this will alter the degree of awareness and, as a result, trial probability. To account for the latter factor, the state of awareness is denoted by two indices (i,j) where

$i =$ awareness state in time period t (one of the eight possible awareness states), and
$j =$ awareness state in time period $t - 1$.

For example, $(1,4)$ is the additional awareness due to advertising (state 1) in period t, initial awareness due to advertising and promotion (state 4) in period $t - 1$.

State 8 indicates no new awareness in the current time period. So $(8,1)$ would indicate a consumer who was initially aware due solely to advertising and then simply retained the awareness in period t (no new exposure). State 9 indicates forgotten awareness and so the state $(2,9)$ denotes a consumer who became aware in period $t - 1$, forgot the product, and then had renewed awareness achieved due to exposure to a promotion in period t.

The trial probability is given by $(\tau_{ij})^2$. The probability is squared to show the diminishing effect of a failure to try in period $t - 1$, the period of initial awareness (the relationship used here is an extension of the relationship used in [3]):

$$\tau_{ij} = \tau_i + \tau_j - (\tau_i)(\tau_j),$$

where $\tau_1,\ldots,\tau_7$ are defined as for new awares, and thus τ_{ij} depends on the mix of exposures over the previous two time periods. Also, $\tau_8 = \tau_9 = 0$.

2.1.6. Three-period awares

These consumers first achieved awareness in period $t - 2$ and have failed to try the product in the two time periods prior to t. Developing the consumer states analogously to the two-period awares, the state is denoted by a triplet (i,j,k), where

$i =$ awareness state in time period t,
$j =$ awareness state in time period $t - 1$, and
$k =$ awareness state in time period $t - 2$; $i, j, k = 1,\ldots,9$.

The trial probability is given by $(\tau_{ijk})^3$ and

$$\tau_{ijk} = \tau_1 + \tau_j + \tau_k - (\tau_i)(\tau_j) - (\tau_j)(\tau_k) - (\tau_i)(\tau_k) + (\tau_i)(\tau_j)(\tau_k).$$

As before, $\tau_1,\ldots,\tau_7$ are the awareness-to-trial probabilities for new awares and $\tau_8 = \tau_9 = 0$.

2.2. Updating awareness and new trier fractions

Consumers who first achieve awareness in period $t(A_i(1), i = 1,\ldots,7)$, can be in one of three states in period $t + 1$:
 (1) new trier,
 (2) retained awareness (but did not try in preceding period), or
 (3) forgotten awareness.

In calculating the fraction of new triers, the effect of imperfect distribution in period t is to diminish the probability of trial by a factor, $D(t)$, which denotes the probability that the product is available to a prospective purchaser. The trial fraction from new awares in period t is

$$T_1(t) = \sum_{i=1}^{8} A_i(1) \cdot \tau_i \cdot D(t).$$

$A_i(1)(1 - \tau_i D(t))$ is the fraction of the new awares who did not try the product in period t. Of the nontriers, a fraction will retain awareness and the remainder will fail to retain awareness. The *retention coefficient*, $r_c(i)$, denotes the probability that a consumer in awareness state i will retain awareness in the succeeding purchase period. Then the fraction of consumers in two-period awareness state (j, i) in period $t + 1$ is given by

$$A_{ji}(2) = P_j(t + 1)r_c(i)A_i(1)(1 - \tau_i D(t)), \qquad i = 1,\ldots,7; \quad j = 1,\ldots,8.$$

A consumer who fails to retain awareness of the product can still become a trier, given that renewed exposure regenerates awareness within two time periods of initial exposure. Otherwise, it is assumed that the consumer will not become a trier of the product. In the event of regenerated awareness, the probability of trial will, of course, be lower than that of a newly aware consumer.

The fraction of consumers who fail to retain awareness is

$$\sum_{i=1}^{7} (1 - r_c(i)) \cdot A_i(1) \cdot (1 - \tau_i D(t)).$$

These consumers can achieve new awareness states in period $t + 1$:

$$A_{j9}(2) = P_j(t + 1)\left[\sum_{i=1}^{7} (1 - r_c(i))A_i(1)(1 - \tau_i D(t)) \right], \qquad j = 1,\ldots,8.$$

An analogous process is used to update two-period awareness in period t. The trial fraction $T_2(t)$ is given by

$$T_2(t) = \sum_{j=1}^{9} \sum_{i=1}^{9} A_{ji}(2) \cdot \tau_{ji}^2 \cdot D(t).$$

Awareness in $t + 1$:

$$A_{kji}(3) = P_k(t+1) \cdot r_c(j, i) \cdot A_{ji}(2) \cdot \left(1 - \tau_{ji}^2 D(t)\right),$$

$$i = 1,\ldots,9; \quad j = 1,\ldots,8; \quad k = 1,\ldots,8.$$

New awareness created from the pool of consumers who had failed to retain earlier awareness:

$$A_{k99}(3) = P_k(t+1) \sum_{j=1}^{7} \sum_{i=1}^{7} \left[\left(1 - r_c(j, i)\right) \cdot A_{ji}(2) \cdot \left(1 - \tau_{ji}^2 D(t)\right)\right].$$

Consumers who have been aware of the product for three periods either become triers in the period or have a negligible probability of trial thereafter. This group of consumers, called *lapsed awares*, remains in this (absorbing) state for the duration of the study.

The trial fraction ($T_3(t)$) is

$$T_3(t) = \sum_{k=1}^{9} \sum_{j=1}^{9} \sum_{i=1}^{9} A_{kji}(3) \tau_{kji}^3 D(t)$$

The lapsed awareness fraction ($L(t)$) is computed as follows:

$$L(t) = \sum_{k=1}^{9} \sum_{j=1}^{9} \sum_{i=1}^{9} A_{kji}(3)\left(1 - \tau_{kji}^3 D(t)\right).$$

2.3. The trial–repeat purchase process

The fraction of consumers who are new triers in period t is

$$NT(t) = T_1(t) + T_2(t) + T_3(t).$$

Once a consumer has tried the product, then in each succeeding purchase period there is an opportunity to make a repeat purchase. The probability of a repeat purchase increases with the number of prior purchases and is di-

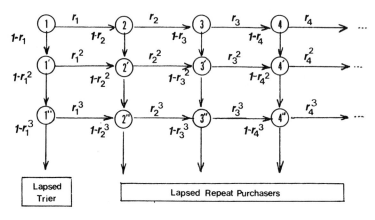

Fig. 4. Repeat purchase process.

minished whenever a consumer fails to purchase in a period.

The repeat purchase process is shown schematically in fig. 4. The nodes represent states of the repeat purchase process and the arrows denote the probability of moving from one state to another between purchase cycles. Primes indicate the number of purchase periods in which a consumer has failed to make a purchase since trying the product. For example,

① denotes a new trier, one who first tried the product in the preceding time period;

② denotes a consumer who made his second purchase in the preceding purchase cycle;

①' denotes a new trier who failed to purchase last period;

①'' denotes a new trier who has failed to purchase in the preceding two periods;

②' denotes a consumer who has made two purchases, but has failed to purchase in one purchase cycle;

r_1 is the trial-to-repeat purchase probability; and

r_2 is the loyalty factor ($r_2 \geqslant r_1$).

For $k = 1, 2, \ldots$, the kth repeat purchase probability is

$$r_k = r_{max} - \frac{(r_{max} - r_2)^{k-1}}{(r_{max} - r_1)^{k-2}}.$$

Therefore, $r_1 \leqslant r_2 \leqslant r_k \leqslant r_{max}$. The repeat purchase probabilities increase with k and approach maximum awareness, r_{max}, asymptotically (this relationship is adapted from one used in [3]).

A failure to purchase in a period leads to a reduced probability of purchase in the next time period. The first failure reduces the probability of purchase from p to p^2 and the second missed purchase reduces it by another factor of p. After three purchase periods without a purchase, a consumer's purchase probability drops to zero; these consumers move into the lapsed purchaser state.

The total fraction of repeat buyers in a period is composed of those who repeat for the first, second, third time, etc.

$$R(t) = R_1(t) + R_2(t) + \ldots + R_n(t).$$

2.3.1. Unit sales

Consumers who buy the product for the first time (i.e. trial) purchase it in a given package size of volume (VF). The most common package size in the product category is indexed at 1.0. For example, if the average package size is 16 ounces, then a 16-ounce purchase is associated with a VF of 1.0 while for an 8-ounce package VF is 0.5. Therefore the (standardized) fraction of units purchased by triers in a period is $NT(t) \cdot VF$.

Similarly, repeat purchasers may buy the product in the same size or a different size. The size or volume of this repeat purchase is indicated by VS. Thus, the (standardized) fraction of units purchased by repeat purchasers in a period is $R(t) \cdot VS$. The total fraction of buyers in the period, then, is $NT(t) + R(t)$ and the total fraction of units sold (i.e. market share in units), or U, equals $NT(t) \cdot VF + R(t) \cdot VS$. Here it is assumed that the size of the total market in units is essentially unaffected by the purchase volumes for the new product.

2.3.2. Dollar sales

The proportion of units sold in a period (U) is then adjusted by an indexed price (P), where $P = 1$ for the average price per unit of volume in the category. The total fraction of dollar sales (i.e. market share in dollars) in a period is therefore

$$\frac{U \cdot P}{(U \cdot P) + (1 - U) \cdot 1}.$$

3. Model output

3.1. Forecasts

After the input data (see fig. 2) have been entered, LITMUS forecasts Brand Awareness, Cumulative Trial, Repeat Buyers, Total Buyers, Sales (in cases)

Table 1

Predicted values
            Client: ABC Foods
        Product: frozen food product
    No. of periods: 12
No. of periods/yr: 12

No.	Awareness	Cumul. trial	Repeat buyers	Total buyers	Sales—000 cases	Share ($)
1	0.2276	0.0252	0.0000	0.0252	100.9	0.0143
2	0.3833	0.0532	0.0101	0.0381	172.6	0.0245
3	0.4899	0.0794	0.0189	0.0450	217.9	0.0309
4	0.5547	0.1001	0.0250	0.0457	232.7	0.0330
5	0.5999	0.1168	0.0275	0.0442	231.8	0.0328
6	0.6315	0.1304	0.0279	0.0415	221.8	0.0314
7	0.6505	0.1415	0.0272	0.0382	207.2	0.0294
8	0.6640	0.1506	0.0258	0.0349	191.2	0.0271
9	0.6734	0.1581	0.0242	0.0317	175.3	0.0248
10	0.6774	0.1642	0.0226	0.0287	160.1	0.0227
11	0.6801	0.1693	0.0210	0.0261	146.2	0.0207
12	0.6821	0.1736	0.0194	0.0237	133.6	0.0189
Total				0.4231	2191.4	0.0259 (avg.)

and Market Share (in dollars) for each purchase period. Sample output is presented in table 1. For a more careful analysis, the model also can provide period-by-period profiles of the predicted fractions of the consumer pool in each of the awareness and repeat purchase states.

3.2. Sensitivity analysis

Included in LITMUS output is an analysis of brand sales to each of the key input values. Importantly, among these are all those variables over which the product manager exercises some control, such as:
  (1) media weight,
  (2) advertising impact (i.e. attention-getting power),
  (3) distribution,
  (4) awareness-to-trial probability,
  (5) promotion,
  (6) couponing,
  (7) trial-to-repeat purchase probability,
  (8) loyalty factor, and
  (9) maximum awareness.
Sensitivity analysis enables us to detect which variables have strong effects on

sales, given the marketing plan under which a particular new product will be introduced.

In the case which we are using for the model output illustration (table 1), the LITMUS projection of case sales did not meet the sales objective for this brand. Sensitivity analysis is, therefore, used to see which variables are influential in determining sales. In this case, we discovered that trial-to-repeat purchase probability and distribution are critical variables and represent the key to any change in sales. An increase in either trial-to-repeat or distribution could result in a large increase in sales. On the other hand, we noted that sales were not particularly sensitive to changes in media weight or promotion. An increase or decrease in these factors may have little effect on sales. This suggests to the marketing manager that the planned heavy advertising and promotion budget might be reduced and the dollars reallocated to improving more sensitive factors (e.g. product improvements and distribution).

4. Applications

Following model development, LITMUS was applied to 20 additional cases with promising results. For each product, LTM managers provided the authors with marketing plan data and LTM estimates of trial and repeat purchase probabilities. Only after we ran the forecasts were we shown data on the actual, real world performance of the 20 brands. Tables 2–4 show comparisons between model predictions and brand performance in the marketplace for each of these cases. Eight of these cases (table 2) are regarded as "bulls-eyes", i.e. the forecast was right on target. Eight were close to target (table 3), while only four were disappointing (table 4). However, even the disappointments were instructive. For some of the products we discovered that there was some uncertainty on the part of the client as to the appropriate value for certain

Table 2

Bull's eye

Case	Product	LITMUS forecast	Actual
2	Food product A	2.0 share	2–4 share
6	Food product B	3.2 share	2–3 share
9	Beauty aid A	3.5 million units	3.8 million units
11	Health product A	3.1 share	3–4 share
13	Health product B	2.2 share	2.0 share
17	Beauty aid B	3.1 share	3–4 share
19	Beauty aid C	3.2 share	2–3 share
20	Beauty aid D	1.2 share	1–2 share

Table 3

Near miss

Case	Product	LITMUS forecast	Actual
3	Food product	14–18 million units	7–10 million units
5	Food product D	1.2 share	0.75–1.0 share
7	Food product E	0.6–2.2 share	0.5–1.0 share
8	Food product H	4.0 share	5.0 share
10	Beauty aid E	8.6 share	6–7 share
12	Health product C	5.8–7.6 share	4–6 share
14	Laundry product A	11.0 share	9.0 share
16	Laundry product B	6.3 share	4.5 share

input parameters, such as media impact or repeat purchase probability. In some cases we found that the sales target could be "bounded" by using the high and low estimates for inputs. Although an average of the high and low input might have yielded reasonable predictions, we were not given these values initially and, consequently, they are not reported as part of the results. This tends to support our belief, and the experience of LTM managers, that team planning and accurate inputs are essential to the new product planning process. If an input parameter such as awareness-to-trial probability can only be estimated by a confidence interval, then it is important to investigate the sensitivity of the sales projection to the uncertainty in the input value.

We have also discovered some factors which could contribute to potential model failure and call for closer examination as we plan ahead. LITMUS, as we have seen, assumes that paid advertising drives brand trial. Yet, observing recent test market results, we have noted situations in which advertising plays a minor role in product success. In one case involving a product category with low advertising budgets (a favored potato chip) high trial rates were achieved from shelf visibility alone. In another case, a combination of new product technology, word-of-mouth advertising and distribution propelled a new candy

Table 4

Off target

Case	Product	LITMUS forecast	Actual
1	Food product F	20–50 million units	37.7 million units
4	Food product G	41–62 million units	20–22 million units
15	Laundry product C	25.4 share	10–12 share
18	Laundry product D	17–40 million units	28 million units

product to significant trial levels. This has led us to consider ways to model the effects of shelf visibility (or distribution) and word-of-mouth advertising on product awareness. In its current form, LITMUS can introduce alternative sources of awareness and trial through judicious choices of the values of initial awareness and the initial trial fraction. However, this method is not entirely satisfactory because it loads the awareness and trial into the initial purchase period instead of distributing it over the introduction period. Additional model refinements in this area are needed and will be the subject of future research.

In summary, LITMUS is a new product planning model, used in conjunction with LTM, designed to forecast, diagnose and improve the performance of alternative marketing strategies and tactics for new packaged goods before or after test marketing. Though still in an exploratory stage of development, the model has shown evidence of the kind of construct and predictive validity that might be expected given its "genetic structure" through its "parents" LTM and NEWS.

References

[1] R. Blattberg and J. Golanty, Tracker: An early test market forecasting and diagnostic model for new product planning, Journal of Marketing Research 15 (1978) 192–202.

[2] L. Ingrassia, There's no way to tell if a new food product will please the public, The Wall Street Journal 195, no. 89 (February 26, 1980) 1.

[3] NEWS, The Theoretical Basis of NEWS, Technical Report BBDO, Inc. (1971).

[4] NEWS, The NEWS Model: A Technical Description, Technical Report BBDO, Inc. (no date).

[5] A.J. Silk and G. Urban, Pre-test market evaluation of new packaged goods: A model and measurement technology, Journal of Marketing Research 15 (1978) 171–191.

[6] G.L. Urban, Sprinter Mod III: A model for the analysis of new frequently purchased consumer products, Operations Research 18 (1970) 805–853.

TIMS/Studies in the Management Sciences 18 (1982) 63–83
North-Holland Publishing Company

A GENERAL MODEL FOR ASSESSING NEW PRODUCT MARKETING DECISIONS AND MARKET PERFORMANCE

Fred S. ZUFRYDEN

University of Southern California

A model is developed to predict the market performance of new, frequently purchased, consumer brands. The model is designed to be implemented on the basis of data from either a pre-introduction test market or a short introductory sales period. The generalized structure of the model permits marketing managers to evaluate the market performance of a new brand as a function of any relevant purchase-explanatory variables. These variables may include alternative marketing mix aspects, such as pricing, promotions, advertising media decisions, and product characteristics, as well as segmentation characteristics of potential consumer target markets.

1. Introduction

The introduction of successful new products is a key determinant of the viability of business organizations. Unfortunately, the introduction of new products is not without serious risks. Typically, a sequence of stages takes place prior to a product's commercialization which include (1) generation of product ideas, (2) screening of ideas, (3) business analysis, (4) development of product prototypes, and (5) test marketing. [1] However, most ideas generated are doomed to failure during the pre-commercialization stages. Moreover, most products encounter market failures during commercialization as well. This is a particularly serious problem in the case of consumer packaged goods where the rate of market failure can be staggering. [2]

The first four steps of new product development exhibit failures due to aspects such as the incompatibility of new ideas with company objectives or resources, low expectations of demand or profitability, and engineering difficulties with prototype development. In contrast, failures during the latter stages are often directly attributable to a lack of consumer or trade acceptance in response to ineffective marketing plans. Given the overwhelming risks during the latter stages, this paper proposes a model that is designed to be used on the basis of test market or early introductory period data; at which time,

---

[1] See Booz, Allen and Hamilton [2] and Spitz [20].

[2] O'Meara [16] has reported an 80% rate of failure based on a survey of 200 packaged foods companies. More recently, Booz, Allen and Hamilton [2] and Silk and Urban [19] have also reported substantial failure rates for consumer products.

the evaluation and development of the final components of the marketing plan become key considerations in relation to the new brand's likely market success.

The proposed model provides a general structure that is to be used to predict the market performance of a new brand as a function of purchase-explanatory variables. The purchase-explanatory variables may reflect any aspect that a marketing manager deems potentially relevant to a market situation of interest. For example, the variables may include consumer segmentation characteristics (e.g. demographic or geographic descriptions of consumers). Marketing decision aspects such as product characteristics (e.g. package size, quality, color), price, advertising, distribution, and promotional incentives (e.g. cents off, coupons and point of purchase displays) may also be considered. Moreover, the model is general enough to permit the inclusion of other exogenous variables, including economic factors or other descriptors of the market environment. Hence, the aim of the study is to provide a general model formulation that may be custom-designed to suit a particular marketing situation and that can thereby help a marketing manager to evaluate alternative marketing plans. Moreover, model tractability is given prime consideration to promote model use in practice.

Many other new product forecasting models have previously been proposed. These include those of Fourt and Woodlock [8], Parfitt and Collins [17], Eskin [6], Massy [15], Silk and Urban [19], Urban [21], Greene [11], and Blattberg and Golanty [1]. Of these, the Blattberg and Golanty TRACKER model comes closest to the purpose and scope of the model to be developed herein. These authors show how their model can be used to forecast year-end market performance of a new frequently purchased brand on the basis of planned media effort, price, and promotional activities. On the basis of survey data, TRACKER is shown capable of providing useful diagnostic information from which alternative marketing plans may be evaluated.

There are several structural differences between the proposed model and its predecessors, including TRACKER. First, the proposed model is based on stochastic model components that integrate *both* brand choice and product class purchase incidence behavior.[3] Most previous models do not explicitly consider brand choice behavior, while others ignore purchase incidence behavior. Moreover, a particularly important feature of the brand choice model component is that it offers a completely general structure through which any type and number of relevant purchase-explanatory variables can readily be considered. In contrast, most past models provide conditional forecasts without specifically considering *any* exogenous variables. On the other hand, the few models that consider explanatory variables might require a substantial reformulation to accommodate additional variables within their present structures.

The following discusses the foundations of the model, the development of

---

[3] For a review of related stochastic models, the reader is referred to Jones and Zufryden [13].

market performance measures as a function of explanatory variables, as well as empirical considerations for the implementation of the model for managerial use.

2. Model components

The model consists of three basic components that will be developed in turn: (1) a conditional brand choice model which examines brand choice probability as a function of an arbitrary set of explanatory variables; (2) a purchase incidence model that reflects the frequency of product class purchase outcomes over time; and (3) an advertising awareness model that is designed to specifically incorporate the characteristics of the advertising phenomenon and the effect of alternative media plans. It is noted that advertising is singled out within a separate model component. A reason for this is that its complex characteristics, including carryover effects, make it difficult to consider directly as an explanatory variable within the brand choice model component.

2.1. The conditional brand choice model

An individual-based brand choice model is now proposed that is conditional upon product class purchase occurrences *and* exogenous variables. Thus, consider a particular consumer at a given purchase occasion. We define p as the consumer's probability of choosing a new brand (brand A) *given* that a product class purchase occurs at this purchase occasion. Moreover, it is assumed that p is functionally related to an arbitrary vector of purchase-explanatory variables x as $p(x)$ with

$$x = (x_1, x_2, ..., x_V).$$

The explanatory variables may be expressed in either categorical (0/1) or continuous form. The arbitrary elements x_i can include consumer segmentation characteristics or particular marketing mix aspects which may influence brand choice at the time of purchase. For example, Jones and Zufryden [13] have related purchase probability to variables including consumer income level, presence of children, and relative net price through a model structure that is basically similar to that which will be proposed here. Typically, managerial judgment, data availability, and the nature of the market situation of interest should guide in the specification of the vector x. Moreover, Jones and Zufryden [13] have shown how an adaptive modeling technique can also be used for this purpose.

It is assumed that a Logit model relates the mean purchase probability

$E[p(x)]$ and x as

$$\phi(x) = \ln\left[\frac{E[p(x)]}{1 - E[p(x)]}\right] = \beta_0 + \sum_{i=1}^{V} \beta_i x_i + \varepsilon, \tag{1}$$

with $\beta_0, \beta_1, \ldots, \beta_V$ constant parameters and ε an error term.

The Logit model has been suggested in previous marketing applications. For example, Green et al. [10] emphasize the useful statistical properties of the Logit model in the context of predicting the probability of a durable product's adoption, while Jones and Zufryden [13] have recently applied this model to the prediction of the market performance of a frequently purchased consumer good.

The present study extends the Logit model form of the previous studies in important ways. First, whereas past research considers static, or zero-order, type formulations, the present formulation casts the Logit model in the form of a first-order Markov structure [26,27]. This enables the consideration of purchase-event feedback from past purchase outcomes. In this manner the model becomes better suited to consider a transient new product introduction situation in which the probability of brand choice may readily evolve over time on the basis of a consumer's recent experience with the product.

In addition, the present model version permits the specific consideration of advertising media impact by defining an "advertising awareness state" variable. This variable is subsequently linked to an advertising awareness probability model component which is allowed to change over time as a function of a company's cumulative advertising media efforts.

In order to incorporate the latter extensions, we draw upon the inherent flexibility of the Logit model to consider categorical variable specifications through appropriate coding of explanatory variables. Thus, the following variable components of x are defined:

$$x_{V-1} \begin{cases} 1, & \text{if a consumer is aware of any company advertising for brand A,} \\ 0, & \text{otherwise,} \end{cases}$$

and

$$x_V = \begin{cases} 1, & \text{if brand A was purchased at the last purchase occasion,} \\ 0, & \text{if any one of the competing brands} \\ & \text{(O) was purchased at the last purchase occasion.} \end{cases} \tag{2}$$

It is noted that the basic model assumes a two-brand market in the sense that all brands that compete with A are aggregated. The model may, however, be extended to consider a multibrand market situation, as will be described below.

Given the above definitions, the following conditional probabilities may be derived from (1):

$$P_x(A|A) = \frac{1}{1 + e - \phi(x_A)},$$

$$P_x(A|O) = \frac{1}{1 + e - \phi(x_O)},$$

(3)

where $P_x(A|A)$ and $P_x(A|O)$ are the probabilities of purchasing brand A *given* that A or O, respectively, were purchased at the previous occasion. In this instance, the conditional Logit variables $\phi(x_A)$ and $\phi(x_O)$ are obtained by appropriately setting the last purchase indicator variable x_V as in (2) above. More specifically, we define:

$$\phi(x_A) = (\beta_0 + \beta_V) + \sum_{i=1}^{V-1} \beta_i x_i,$$

$$\phi(x_O) = \beta_0 + \sum_{i=1}^{V-1} \beta_i x_i,$$

(4)

with x_A and x_O being the original vector x given the specification of the last brand choice indicator variable x_V.

Given the additional specification of the advertising awareness state variable, x_{V-1}, two-state first-order Markov transition matrices may be structured using (3) as a function of the remaining purchase-explanatory variables. Thus, we define the matrix $T_{x|x_{V-1}}$, conditional on the alternative awareness states, as

$$
\begin{array}{c}
\text{Purchase at} \\
\text{current occasion}
\end{array}
$$

		A	O	
Purchase at previous occasion	A	$P_{x|x_{V-1}}(A|A)$	$1 - P_{x|x_{V-1}}(A|A)$	
	O	$P_{x|x_{V-1}}(A|O)$	$1 - P_{x|x_{V-1}}(A|O)$	

(5)

with $x_{V-1} = 0$ or 1.

In (5), it is assumed, as in Herniter [12], that the matrices $T_{x|x_{V-1}}$ are homogeneous over the consumer population and are stationary over time. However, in this case they are *conditional* on a particular setting of the explanatory variables vector x, such that the transition matrices are assumed to change with changes in x.

Results to date have supported the empirical viability of this model component. For example, the author has applied the Logit–Markov brand choice model form to a frequently purchased consumer brand for which data was available from the purchase panel diaries of NPD Research, Inc. [26]. In this particular application, Logit regression with independent variables including family income level, presence of children in the family, price of the brand relative to competing brands and the last brand purchase, were shown to provide a good explanation of brand choice probability at successive purchase occasions. Moreover, empirical analysis confirmed the compatibility of model predictions with the observed data. [4]

2.2. The purchase incidence model

The previous model describes brand choice behavior *given* exogenous variables *and* the occurrence of product class purchases. In order to provide useful dynamic market results, it is necessary to specify a model to characterize the occurrence of product class purchases.

A model that may be used for this purpose is the Negative Binomial Distribution (NBD). It has been shown that if an individual's purchases are Poisson distributed with a mean purchase rate that is Gamma distributed over the population of consumers, then the proportion of consumers making $k = 0$, 1,..., etc. purchases in the aggregate market will follow an NBD (e.g. Ehrenberg [4]). This model has been used routinely in practice and has been shown to provide a remarkably good empirical fit to brand purchase data. [5] More recently, Zufryden [24,25] has empirically studied the viability of this model in the context of *product class* purchase distributions and has found similarly good empirical results.

Given the relative tractability of the NBD, it is also used in this study. [6] However, it is slightly modified to better suit the situation of a new product.

It is noted first that the standard NBD, if applied directly to product class purchases, assumes that as $T \to \infty$, eventually all consumers of the population will make a product class purchase and hence may eventually have some chance of choosing the new brand. However, often a substantial fraction of a consumer population will never buy products within a particular product class. By taking this fraction of the population into consideration, a ceiling can be defined on the market potential of the new brand. Thus, we define ω_0 as the population proportion who will never make a purchase of the product class

---

[4] See Zufryden [26] for a detailed discussion of these and related empirical results.

[5] See Ehrenberg [4,5] and Chattfield and Goodhardt [3].

[6] Zufryden [22,23] has also studied the Condensed Negative Binomial Distribution (CNBD) first proposed by Chattfield and Goodhardt [3] as a product class incidence distribution. This theoretically attractive distribution, founded on different assumptions than the NBD, was also found empirically viable. Such an alternative might also be used in the present model structure without altering the basic nature of the mathematical developments discussed herein.

(including the new brand). Given a time interval $(0, T)$ from the introduction of brand A, then the aggregate population distribution of product class purchases is defined in a form similar to that described by Greene [11]:

$$P(k|T) = \begin{cases} \omega_0 + (1 - \omega_0)P_{\text{NBD}}(0|T), & \text{for } k = 0, \\ (1 - \omega_0)P_{\text{NBD}}(k|T), & \text{for } k = 1, 2, \text{ etc. product} \\ & \text{class purchases,} \end{cases} \quad (6)$$

where

$$P_{\text{NBD}}(k|T) = \frac{\Gamma(k+a)}{\Gamma(a)k!} \left(\frac{T}{T+b} \right)^k \left(\frac{b}{T+b} \right)^a, \quad \text{for } k = 0, 1, 2, \dots, \text{ etc.,}$$

is the NBD, with mean aT/b, representing product class purchases within the "buyer" segment of the population and a, $b > 0$ are constant model parameters.

For reasons of model tractability, it is assumed that product class purchase incidence is not affected by the explanatory variables x, including advertising. However, at the risk of some complication, different product class purchase distributions could be assumed under alternative x values. Although this refinement would not alter the nature of the subsequent theoretical developments, it would impose a potential burden in terms of model implementation is practice.

2.3. The advertising awareness model

Given the properties of the advertising phenomenon, a separate model component is developed. This model draws upon a recent study by Blattberg and Golanty [1]. These authors have proposed and empirically evaluated a useful model of brand awareness in response to advertising media efforts. In this model, advertising media efforts are defined in terms of gross rating points (GRPs) corresponding to a particular media plan. Besides its tractability, this model offers several advantages with respect to its ability to realistically reflect the advertising phenomenon. For example, the formulation considers advertising carryover effects as well as diminishing returns and saturation as advertising weight increases to high levels. An essentially similar basic model structure is used in the present study. However, in contrast to the consideration of brand awareness, this study examines advertising awareness as the dependent variable. Also, the model is cast into a form that considers *cumulative* time rather than time period effects. Moreover, it assumes an arbitrary saturation level of advertising awareness.

The basic advertising awareness model is stated as:

$$\ln \left[\frac{A_\infty - A_T}{A_\infty - A_{T-1}} \right] = \alpha_0 + \alpha_1 G_t, \quad (7)$$

where

A_T = proportion of consumers who are aware of any brand A advertising over $(0, T)$,

G_t = gross rating points corresponding to the media plan during *period t* defined over interval $(T - 1, T)$,

α_0, α_1 = constant model parameters, and

A_∞ = maximum saturation level (proportion) of advertising awareness.

In order to state A_T in terms of cumulative period advertising efforts, it is useful to first restate (7) as

$$A_T = A_\infty - (A_\infty - A_{T-1})\exp(\alpha_0 + \alpha_1 G_t). \tag{8}$$

Then, consider N advertising periods over $(0, T)$ during which the GRPs $G_t (t = 1, 2, \ldots, N)$ are achieved. By recursive substitution of (8) back to the initial time of product introduction, (8) becomes

$$A_T = A_\infty - (A_\infty - A_0)\exp\left(N\alpha_0 + \alpha_1 \sum_{t=1}^{N} G_t\right) \tag{9}$$

or, alternatively,

$$\ln\left(\frac{A_\infty - A_T}{A_\infty - A_0}\right) = N\alpha_0 + \alpha_1 G_T, \tag{10}$$

where A_0, the awareness level at the initial time $t = 0$, may be assumed equal to 0 and $G_T = \sum_{t=1}^{N} G_t$ is the cumulative sum total of GRPs over interval $(0, T)$.

It should be noted that the basic form of the above model provides a flexible structure that easily lends itself to other possible refinements. For example, the model can be extended to consider multiple media influences and even competitive effects. Thus, a recent proprietary study by the author has shown empirical support for a model formulation of the general form

$$\ln\left(\frac{A_\infty - A_T}{A_\infty - A_{T-1}}\right) = \alpha_0 + \sum_i \alpha_i E_{it}, \tag{11}$$

where E_{it} is the ratio of company expenditures to that of competition during time period t in medium i (with $i = $ TV, radio, and newspaper), and the remaining variables and parameters are defined as before.

The above models, being of inherently linear form (by logarithmic transformation), lend themselves to standard parameter estimation techniques that are discussed in a later section.

3. Development of market performance model

Now that the basic model components have been described, the following develops several useful measures of market performance by integrating these components within an overall composite model. In the development of these results, it is assumed that a given vector x remains in effect over successive purchases through time.

3.1. Cumulative brand penetration

A central model result is the cumulative penetration of the new brand, within the consumer population, over time interval $(0, T)$.

Consider a consumer who is initially a brand O purchaser (i.e. who starts in brand state (0) at time $t = 0$. After K purchases, the probability that none of the K purchases is of brand A, conditional on a vector x of explanatory variables, is given by

$$P_x(j = 0 | K, O) = P_x(O|O)^K, \tag{12}$$

where j denotes the index for the number of brand purchase occurrences. In contrast, for a consumer starting in brand state A,

$$P_x(j = 0 | K, A) = P_x(O|A)P_x(O|O)^{K-1}. \tag{13}$$

By conditioning on the initial brand state and taking expected values,

$$P_x(j = 0 | K) = [(1 - m_0)P_x(O|O) + m_0 P_x(O|A)] P_x(O|O)^{K-1}, \tag{14}$$

where m_0 is the mean brand A purchase probability at time $t = 0$.

If m_0 is assumed to be equal to zero at $t = 0$, (14) becomes identical to (12). In this case, the population proportion of consumers who make $j = 0$ brand purchases over $(0, T)$ can be obtained by conditioning on the occurrence of product class purchases. Thus,

$$P_x(j = 0 | T) = \sum_{K=0}^{\infty} P_x(O|O)^K P(K|T), \tag{15}$$

or

$$(\quad) = \omega_0 + (1 - \omega_0) \left[\frac{b}{b + T[1 - P_x(O|O)]} \right]^a$$

after summation and some manipulations. (See appendix A.)

From (15), the cumulative brand penetration (or in this case, the proportion of triers) is obtained as: [7]

$$\text{PEN}_x(T) = 1 - P_x(j = 0 | T).\tag{16}$$

3.2. Mean number of brand purchases

The mean number of brand purchases per consumer in the population over $(0, T)$ provides another useful measure of brand performance.

Again, consider a particular vector x of explanatory variables over $(0, T)$. It can be shown that the probability of purchasing brand A at a consumer's kth purchase occasion is given by the recursive equation:

$$P_x(k) = \alpha_x + \beta_x P_x(k - 1),\tag{17}$$

where $\alpha_x = P_x(A|O)$ and $\beta_x = P_x(A|A) - P_x(A|O)$. By recursive substitution (17) becomes

$$P_x(k) = \alpha_x \sum_{i=0}^{k-1} \beta_x^i + \beta_x^k P_0,\tag{18}$$

where P_0 is the consumer's brand A purchase probability at time $t = 0$. Using a well-known result of geometric series, (18) becomes

$$P_x(k) = \alpha_x \left(\frac{1 - \beta_x^k}{1 - \beta_x} \right) + \beta_x^k P_0.\tag{19}$$

Taking expectations, (19) becomes

$$\text{E}[P_x(k)] = \alpha_x \left(\frac{1 - \beta_x^k}{1 - \beta_x} \right) + \beta_x^k \text{E}[P_0].\tag{20}$$

---

[7] Note that in the general case, where $m_0 \neq 0$ at $t = 0$, $\text{PEN}_x(T)$ is obtained using (14). This yields:

$$\text{PEN}_x(T) = 1 - \left[\omega_0 + (1 - \omega_0) \left(\frac{(1 - m_0) P_x(O|O) + m_0 P_x(O|A)}{P_x(O|O)} \right) \right.$$

$$\left. \times \left(\frac{b}{b + T[1 - P_x(O|O)]} \right)^a \right].$$

Alternatively, (20) may be re-stated in the form

$$m_x(k) = m_x(\infty) + [m_0 - m_x(\infty)]\beta_x^k, \tag{21}$$

where $m_x(\infty) = \alpha_x/(1 - \beta_x)$ is the steady state equilibrium share of brand A and, for notational convenience, we define $m_0 = E[P_0]$ and $m_x(k) = E[P_x(k)]$, respectively.

Now, under the assumption that $m_0 = 0$ at $t = 0$, (21) becomes

$$m_x(k) = m_x(\infty)(1 - \beta_x^k). \tag{22}$$

Hence, the mean number of brand purchases can be computed by summing up the expected number of brand purchases corresponding to each possible number of product class purchases $(k = 1, 2, \ldots, \text{etc.})$ and weighting these values by the product class purchase distribution:

$$M_x(T) = \sum_{K=1}^{\infty} P(K|T) \sum_{k=1}^{K} m_x(k). \tag{23}$$

Appendix B provides a derivation of $M_x(T)$ leading to the following result: [8]

$$M_x(T) = (1 - \omega_0) m_x(\infty) \left\{ \frac{aT}{b} - \left[\frac{\beta_x}{1 - \beta_x} \right] \times \left[1 - \left(\frac{b}{b + T(1 - \beta_x)} \right)^a \right] \right\}. \tag{24}$$

3.3. Integrated model results

The model developments thus far are conditioned upon the vector x of purchase explanatory variables over $(0, T)$. It is recalled that the $V - 1$st component of x denotes the advertising awareness state of consumers. Consequently, by appropriately setting x_{V-1}, the results of (16) and (24) can be stated contingently on the advertising awareness state. Using our customary notation, we define $\text{PEN}_{x|x_{V-1}}(T)$ and $M_{x|x_{V-1}}(T)$ as the penetration and mean

---

[8] In the general case, where $m_0 \neq 0$ at $t = 0$, (21) is used in the derivation of $M_x(T)$. In this instance

$$M_x(T) \doteq (1 - \omega_0) \left\{ m_x(\infty) \frac{aT}{b} + [m_0 - m_x(\infty)] \left[\frac{\beta_x}{1 - \beta_x} \right] \right.$$

$$\left. \times \left[1 - \left(\frac{b}{b + T(1 - \beta_x)} \right)^a \right] \right\}.$$

number of brand purchases over $(0, T)$ respectively, *given* awareness state x_{V-1} (with $x_{V-1} = 0$ or 1 as in (2)).

The above market performance measures can be stated directly as a function of the cumulative advertising effort G_T by conditioning on the awareness state alternatives using (9). That is,

$$\text{PEN}_x(T, G_T) = \text{PEN}_{x|1}(T)A_T + \text{PEN}_{x|0}(T)(1 - A_T) \qquad (25)$$

and

$$M_x(T, G_T) = M_{x|1}(T)A_T + M_{x|0}(T)(1 - A_T). \qquad (26)$$

Dividing (26) by the mean of the product class purchase distribution (6) the brand market share over $(0, T)$ can likewise be stated as a function of explanatory variables:

$$S_x(T, G_T) = bM_x(T, G_T)/aT(1 - \omega_0). \qquad (27)$$

Another useful result is the complete repeat purchase distribution. Although the latter can be developed analytically, a considerably simpler and more practical approach is to assume that this distribution can be approximated by an NBD. Consequently, given the values $1 - \text{PEN}_x(T, G_T)$ and $M_x(T, G_T)$, corresponding NBD parameters $a_x(T, G_T)$ and $b_x(T, G_T)$, which are dependent upon x and G_T over $(0, T)$, can be determined according to the root search procedure that is described in the estimation section. Once determined, the corresponding repeat brand purchase distribution can be developed from an NBD (i.e. as that used in (6)). This distribution becomes $P_{\text{NBD}}(j|T)$, for $j = 0$, $1, 2, \ldots$, etc. brand purchases, with parameters $a = a_x(T, G_T)$ and $b = b_x(T, G_T)$. Consequently, this distribution becomes a function of x and G_T as well.

4. Model uses

The integrated model results above provide a useful framework for evaluating alternative marketing plans. Thus, a manager can evaluate alternative marketing decisions as reflected by specified levels of the vector x and media plans and forecast such performance criteria for the new brand as penetration, mean number of purchases per consumer, market share, and repeat purchase patterns. Based on cost considerations for implementing the proposed plans, comparisons with market performance criteria goals, and profitability analysis, the model may guide in the selection of a preferred alternative. For example, a recommended pricing policy could be suggested through model use (e.g. see [13] and [26]). Moreover, appropriate GRP levels (and a corresponding media plan) may be established for an introductory advertising campaign.

An interesting aspect of the model approach is that the general brand choice structure can easily incorporate demographic or other variables designed to describe consumer segments. This is an important feature of the model because it enables a marketing manager to pinpoint the variables, including consumer characteristics, that are the most statistically significant predictors of brand choice probability (e.g. see [13] and [26]). This may provide useful guidance both in defining and effectively reaching a new brand's best target market opportunity.

To the extent that the model aids in identifying and relating marketing aspects to brand purchase behavior and various criteria of market performance, it may provide a useful tool for diagnostic analysis leading to refinements of preliminary marketing plans. For example, the merits of eliminating (or emphasizing) particular promotional incentives, changes in product features, increases in advertising budget, and other refinements, could be assessed through model usage.

Because the model is dynamic, it can help a manager assess the impact of particular marketing decisions upon the market performance criteria over time. Moreover, the Markovian structure permits a marketing planner to estimate the magnitudes of brand loyalty and switching as a function of alternative plans. This capability should become even more advantageous if the model is cast into a multi-brand market form. In the latter form, it becomes possible to assess the particular brands from which the new brand's franchise will be gained (or lost) under different marketing settings. This model extension is discussed in the following section.

5. Model extension to the multi-brand market case

The Logit model that has been proposed is of the binomial (i.e. two-brand state) form. However, the multivariate brand choice model can be extended to consider a multi-brand market. This can be handled using the general multinomial version of the Logit model that has been described by McFadden [14]. Such a model formulation has received attention in a number of previous studies (e.g. McFadden [14], Punj and Staelin [18], Gensch and Recker [9], and Silk and Urban [19]).

In this case, let $T_x = [P_x(j|i)]$ be the matrix of size $B \times B$ (where B represents the total number of brands including brand A in the market). Then, the generalization of (3) becomes the multinomial Logit model:

$$P_x(j|i) = v_x(j,i) \Big/ \sum_k v_x(k,i), \tag{28}$$

with

$$v_x(j, i) = \exp(\beta_j x + \alpha_{ji} + \varepsilon_j),$$

for brands $i, j = 1, 2, \ldots, B$, where

β_j = $(\beta_{j0}, \beta_{j1}, \ldots, \beta_{jV})$ are parameters where β_{jv} ($v = 1, 2, \ldots, V$), correspond to the explanatory variables, excluding the last brand choice, and β_{j0} is a constant;

α_j = $(\alpha_{j1}, \alpha_{j2}, \ldots, \alpha_{jB})$ are the parameters corresponding to last purchase indicator variables;

x = $(1, x_1, x_2, \ldots, x_V)$ are the purchase explanatory variables, including the advertising awareness state, with the unit element corresponding to the β_{j0} parameter;

y = $(y_1, y_2, \ldots, y_B)$ are $0/1$ last purchase state indicator variables such that

y_b = $\begin{cases} 1, & \text{if brand b was bought at the last purchase occasion}, \\ 0, & \text{if another brand was bought at the last purchase occasion}, \end{cases}$

and

ε = $(\varepsilon_1, \varepsilon_2, \ldots, \varepsilon_B)$ is a vector of random error terms.

The multinomial Logit model is based on the assumption that if $v_x(j, i) > v_x(j', i)$, for $j \neq j'$, then brand j would be chosen over j' by an individual. If V_x is defined as a utility function, this implies that an individual will choose the brand alternative perceived to have the greatest utility. However, given the random error components, ε_j, of the utility functions, there is some uncertainty about the actual choice outcome. In order to consider this uncertainty, it has been assumed (e.g. [14]) that the vector of random errors, ε, has elements that are independently and identically distributed, across individuals and choice alternatives, as a double exponential (Gnedenko extreme value) distribution. Given this error term distribution, McFadden [14] has shown that a probabilistic choice model of the form of (28) results. This formulation further assumes that the choice of any brand is independent of the presence (or absence) of a third brand alternative.

Market performance measures, such as those given for the two-brand state case, can be obtained for the multi-brand state version by following steps similar to those that have been described. However, these developments are beyond the scope of this paper. [9]

---

[9] The reader is referred to Herniter [12] who has provided the derivation of a model that includes a multi-brand, homogeneous Markov brand choice model (without exogenous variable influences) and a purchase incidence model which is based on different assumptions from those of the present model.

6. Parameter estimation and empirical considerations

In order to implement the model in practice, it is necessary to estimate the parameters of its three basic component parts.

6.1. Estimation of purchase incidence model

The NBD-based purchase incidence model parameters can easily be estimated on the basis of a root search method similar to that which has commonly been used by Ehrenberg [4] and others (e.g. [3] and [23]).

First, assume that an estimate of ω_0, the proportion of nonbuyers of the product class, has been obtained (e.g. directly from survey data). Next, consider an observation period $(0, T_1)$ over which both the mean number of product class purchases, $\bar{x}$, and the proportion of the population making *no* product class purchases, $P(0)$, have been obtained. These data may be obtained from survey data or consumer purchase diary panels. Then, the following equations can be used to set the observed values to the corresponding theoretical values from (6):

$$\bar{x} = (1 - \omega_0) a T_1 / b, \tag{29}$$

$$P(0) = \omega_0 + (1 - \omega_0) \left(\frac{b}{b + T_1} \right)^a. \tag{30}$$

By substituting b from (29) into (30) and solving the resulting equation by a root search algorithm (e.g. Newton method), an estimate of $\hat{a}$ is obtained. Then, substituting $\hat{a}$ in (29) and solving for b provides the parameter estimate $\hat{b}$.

6.2. Estimation of brand choice model

The binomial Logit model can be estimated by the method of weighted least squares (WLS). This method can be applied in the case of all categorical variables and even with mixtures of categorical and continuous variable specifications. [10]

Another alternative that has been held as a superior method is maximum likelihood (e.g. see Flath and Leonard [7]). This method has been widely used in previous studies. [11] Thus, consider an individual n within a consumer

---

[10] See Jones and Zufryden [13] for a detailed discussion of WLS estimation in this context.

[11] For example, see Flath and Leonard [7], Gensch and Recker [9], Punj and Staelin [18], and Silk and Urban [19].

sample. For each n, (28) can be used to define:

$$P_n(j) = \left[1 + \sum_{k \neq j} \exp\left[(\beta_k - \beta_j)x_n + (\alpha_k - \alpha_j)y_n + (\varepsilon_k' - \varepsilon_j) \right] \right]^{-1}. \qquad (31)$$

Furthermore, let z_{jn} be an index denoting the occurrence of state j for individual n corresponding to the vector of explanatory variable setting (x_n, y_n). Thus,

$$z_{jn} = \begin{cases} 1, & \text{if individual } n \text{ purchased brand } j \text{ at the current occasion,} \\ 0, & \text{otherwise.} \end{cases}$$

The following likelihood function can then be formulated:

$$L(z; \beta, \alpha) = \prod_n \prod_j P_n(j)^{z_{jn}}. \qquad (32)$$

The parameters of the multinomial Logit can be obtained by maximizing the log of L by choice of the parameters β and α. Several computer programs are available that perform maximum likelihood parameter estimation. [12] The basic data requirements for Logit estimation consist of at least two consecutive individual purchase observations from a sample of consumers, including the corresponding settings of the purchase-explanatory variables at the time of purchase and the previous brand choice. Such data could be obtained from surveys or consumer purchase diary panels. Thus, for similar Logit models, which did not include advertising effects, Jones and Zufryden [13] and Zufryden [26] describe the data reduction and model estimation procedures based on consumer panel data for a frequently purchased consumer good.

Recent technical advances promise to render the proposed brand choice model framework even more useful in the future. For example, the use of UPC scanning data, which is currently growing at the retail level, permits the instantaneous measurement of many potential purchase-explanatory variables (e.g. prices, promotional deals, product characteristics) at the specific time of purchase. Such data, ideally, could be coupled with advertising awareness tracking data. For example, a survey could be administered as consumers check out of the supermarket, at which time an appropriate unaided recall question might be used to establish if any brand ads are recalled by the consumer.

---

[12] For example, see Gensche and Recker [9], Silk and Urban [19], and McFadden [14] for descriptions of relevant computer programs.

(23) becomes

$$M_x(T) = \sum_{K=1}^{\infty} P(K|T) S_x(K)$$

$$= m_x(\infty) \sum_{K=1}^{\infty} P(K|T) \left[K - \frac{\beta_x (1 - \beta_x^K)}{1 - \beta_x} \right];$$

or, substituting for $P(K|T)$ using (6),

$$M_x(T) = m_x(\infty)(1 - \omega_0) \sum_{K=1}^{\infty} P_{\mathrm{NBD}}(K|T) \left[K - \frac{\beta_x}{1 - \beta_x} (1 - \beta_x^K) \right]. \qquad (B3)$$

Now,

$$\sum_{K=1}^{\infty} P_{\mathrm{NBD}}(K|T) = 1 - (1 - \theta)a, \qquad (B4)$$

with θ defined as in appendix A.

Moreover, from (A2)

$$\sum_{K=1}^{\infty} \frac{\Gamma(a+K)}{\Gamma(a)K!} Y^K = (1 - Y)^{-a} - 1, \quad \text{for } 0 < Y < 1. \qquad (B5)$$

Using (6) and the result of (B4) in (B3) yields

$$M_x(T) = m_x(\infty)(1 - \omega_0) \left\{ \frac{aT}{b} - \frac{\beta_x}{1 - \beta_x} \left[1 - (1 - \theta)^a \right] \right.$$

$$\left. + \frac{\beta_x}{1 - \beta_x} (1 - \theta)^a \sum_{K=1}^{\infty} \frac{\Gamma(a+K)}{\Gamma(a)K!} \theta^K \beta_x^K \right\}. \qquad (B6)$$

Then, letting $Y = \theta \beta_x$ and applying (B5), (B6) becomes

$$M_x(T) = m_x(\infty)(1 - \omega_0) \left\{ \frac{aT}{b} - \frac{\beta_x}{1 - \beta_x} \left[1 - (1 - \theta)^a \right] \right.$$

$$\left. + \frac{\beta_x}{1 - \beta_x} (1 - \theta)^a \left[(1 - Y)^{-a} - 1 \right] \right\}. \qquad (B7)$$

Upon substitution of θ and Y in (B7) and some simplification, (B7) can be shown to be equivalent to expression (24).

References

[1] R. Blattberg and J. Golanty, Tracker: An early test market forecasting and diagnostic model for new product planning, Journal of Marketing Research 19 (May 1978) 192–202.

[2] Booz, Allen and Hamilton, Management of New Products (Booz, Allen and Hamilton, Inc., New York, 1971).

[3] C. Chattfield and G.J. Goodhardt, A consumer purchasing model with Erlang inter-purchase times, Journal of the American Statistical Association 68, no. 346 (December 1973) 828–835.

[4] A.S.C. Ehrenberg, The pattern of consumer purchases, Applied Statistics 8 (1959) 26–41.

[5] A.S.C. Ehrenberg, Repeat Buying: Theory and Applications (North-Holland Publishing Co., Amsterdam, 1972).

[6] G.J. Eskin, Dynamic forecasts of new product demand using a depth of repeat model, Journal of Marketing Research 10 (May 1973) 115–129.

[7] D. Flath and E.W. Leonard, A comparison of two Logit models in the analysis of qualitative marketing data, Journal of Marketing Research 16 (November 1979) 533–538.

[8] L.A. Fourth and J.W. Wooklock, Early prediction of market success for new grocery products, Journal of Marketing 24 (October 1960) 31–38.

[9] D.H. Gensch and W.W. Recker, The multinomial, multiattribute Logit choice model, Journal of Marketing Research 16 (February 1979) 124–132.

[10] P. Green, T. Carmone and D.P. Watchpress, On the analysis of qualitative data in market research, Journal of Marketing Research 14 (February 1977) 52–59.

[11] J.D. Greene, Projecting test market trial-repeat of a new brand in time, Proceedings of the American Marketing Association (1974) 419–422.

[12] J. Herniter, A probabilistic market model of purchase timing and brand selection, Management Science 18 (December 1971) 102–113.

[13] J.M. Jones and F.S. Zufryden, Adding explanatory variables to a consumer purchase behavior model—An exploratory study, Journal of Marketing Research (August 1980) 323–334.

[14] D. McFadden, Conditional Logit analysis of qualitative choice behavior, in: P. Zarembka, ed., Frontiers in Econometrics (Academic Press, New York, 1974) 105–142.

[15] W.F. Massy, Stochastic models for monitoring new product introduction, in: F.M. Bass, C.W. King and E.A. Pessemier, eds., Application of the Science in Marketing Management (John Wiley and Sons, Inc., New York, 1978).

[16] J.T. O'Meara, Selecting profitable products, Harvard Business Review (January–February 1961) 83.

[17] J.H. Parfitt and B.J.K. Collins, Use of consumer panels brand-share predictions, Journal of Marketing Research 5 (May 1968) 131–145.

[18] G.N. Punj and R. Staelin, A model of the college choice process, Proceedings of the American Marketing Association (1976) 324–329.

[19] A.J. Silk and G.L. Urban, Pre-test market evaluation of new packaged goods: A model and measurement methodology, Journal of Marketing Research 15 (May 1978) 171–191.

[20] A.E. Spitz, Product Planning (Auerbach Publishers, New York, 1972).

[21] G.L. Urban, Springer MOD III: A model for the analysis of new frequently purchased consumer products, Operations Research 17 (September–October 1969) 805–854.

[22] F.S. Zufryden, A composite heterogeneous model of brand choice and purchase timing behavior: Theoretical development, Management Science 24, no. 2 (October 1977) 121–136.

[23] F.S. Zufryden, An empirical evaluation of a composite heterogeneous model of brand choice and purchase timing behavior, Management Science 24, no. 7 (March 1978) 761–763.

[24] F.S. Zufryden, A dynamic model of market response to influences of explanatory variables, USC Graduate School of Business Working Paper, presented at the XXIV International TIMS Meeting, Hawaii, June 1979.

TIMS/Studies in the Management Sciences 18 (1982) 85–98
North-Holland Publishing Company

STRATEGY DEVELOPMENT FOR NEW PRODUCT INTRODUCTIONS: PREDICTING MARKET AND FINANCIAL SUCCESS

Edgar A. PESSEMIER

Purdue University

This paper describes the ADOPTEST model. It can evaluate alternative marketing strategies for a potential new product and can demonstrate the influence of important policy variables on financial success. The model is sufficiently flexible to handle the data requirements and structural properties of most applied new-product problems.

1. Introduction

The task of formulating and evaluating alternative introductory marketing strategies for a new product is strongly conditioned by the nature of the product and market. For example, the product may join many competing brands in an established, well-understood product class. In this case, communications on behalf of the new entry can concentrate on developing brand awareness and emphasizing comparative advantages. On the other hand, a novel or innovative item typically has features that will not be immediately understood or appreciated by potential buyers. During the early market life of this type of product, communications should reduce the perceived risk of purchase by emphasizing the nature and reliability of the use benefits. Furthermore, the communication content, marketing mix and cost behavior for a new product tend to change as the product moves from introduction to maturity. Some of the more important elements in the above process are as follows.

Market definition. The size and character of the market for a product improvement is much easier to accurately judge than is the size and character of the market which will emerge for a novel or innovative product.

Competitive climate. In an established product class, the number and behavior of competitors can be confidently estimated, but in a new or emerging product class, decision-makers usually face a high degree of uncertainty about the competitive climate.

Rate of trial or adoption. The rate at which a new brand can gain trial purchases can be judged from experience in a mature product class but the expected rate of adoption for an innovation is hard to estimate. Trial purchases is an established product class are a function of the firm's marketing effort but adoption purchases in a new product class are a function of the marketing efforts of all competing firms.

Cost behavior. The genuinely innovative product will usually require new production methods and be subject to important declines in unit cost as experience accumulates. Much smaller cost reductions are typically available to improved products that require little change in current production methods.

Time horizons. Adoption of an innovation by most potential buyers may be strongly dependent on the observed purchase and use behavior of others. This time-consuming process is less influential in the case of product improvements introduced into an established product line.

The above list of differences is not exhaustive but it is extensive enough to emphasize the need to recognize a new product's position along the newness continuum. Furthermore, this list is long enough to demonstrate the wide range of cost and revenue factors that must be considered when appraising the alternative marketing strategies which can be employed on behalf of a new market entry. The ADOPTEST model which is described below is designed to evaluate marketing strategies for both innovative products and product improvements, and to integrate all of the significant elements which influence the effectiveness of a strategy. The principal decision variables entering the analysis are period by period marketing expenditures, the allocation of marketing effort to each marketing mix element, the unit prices charged, and the associated annual nonmarketing investments.

2. A brief literature review

Since the body of potentially relevant literature is very large and diffuse, the following review simply highlights some important contributions to knowledge about the major topics introduced in the foregoing section.

2.1. Market potential

Estimating the number of individuals who will ultimately be willing to buy a new product is not particularly difficult in the case of a well-established product class. A variety of commercial services are available which use a simulated-shopping or a controlled in-store environment. The Yankelovich Test Marketing System [10], the ESP system offered by NPD Research [12], Management Decision Systems' ASSESSOR procedure [30], and Elrick and Lavidge's COMP system [7] illustrate models that rely on these types of early test data to forecast the market potential and brand sales for new, frequently purchased consumer products.

The problem of estimating sales for truly innovative products and infrequently purchased products is more difficult and solutions are not as well developed. The principal difficulty is the potential buyer's state of knowledge. When a new product must be evaluated, this knowledge is typically far less developed than it will be at the time a real decision will be made to adopt or not adopt the product. Recent experiments that exposed potential buyers to audio-visual discussions of an innovation's pros and cons appear to offer an efficient way to accelerate the development of suitable levels of knowledge. In the case reported by Wilton [32], predictions of market shares were comfortably close to the observed market results with the average absolute deviation across ten brands being less than 0.8%.

2.2. Competitive climate

Methods for estimating competitive responses to a new product introduction are even less well developed than methods for appraising the number, characteristics and expected behavior of potential adopters. Although the literature in game theory, microeconomics and industrial organization [9,19,23,28] addresses numerous theoretical and aggregate aspects of the problem, decision-makers usually must resort to using *ad hoc* methods to predict the likely behavior of potential competitors. Careful observation of possible competitors' past behavior and a thorough analysis of the payoffs they might realize from alternative actions appears to be the most dependable basis for forecasting competitive responses.

2.3. Rate of adoption or trial

Studies of the adoption of innovations have produced a number of models. For example, Bass [3] proposed and tested an epidemiological model, Mansfield [21] developed and tested econometric models for technological innovation, and a substitution function has been examined by Fisher and Pry [13]. In addition to the approaches employed in ASSESSOR, ESP and COMP, a number of alternative models of the trial process have been proposed [2,8,15,20,31]. Nevertheless, most applied adoption/trial processes can be satisfactorily approximated by the Weibull distribution. The wide use of this distribution in the analysis of survival data and the similarity of the survival process to the adoption process support its use in this application [14,17,26].

In a specific case, the problem is selecting a shape of the distribution which will closely approximate the rate of adoption or trial as a function of the effort expanded on the new product introduction. It seems likely that the shape of observed adoption/trial curves are a function of each product's degree of newness and the level and temporal distribution of the introductory effort. Unfortunately, only a small amount of empirical evidence has been collected about this subject. As a practical matter, company and trade association records may be the best source for practical guidance concerning entries into an established product class. The literature on adoption and diffusion offer modest help with respect to innovative products but the related evidence from substitution studies is somewhat more extensive [13,16].

2.4. Cost behavior

For more than a decade the Boston Consulting Group and some of its competitors have diffused an experience curve approach to business strategy [1,6]. This curve shows a constant percentage reduction in the cost of the last unit produced for a constant percentage increase in the number of units produced. Although most of the evidence presented in support of the experience curves is based on observed price behavior, there is little doubt about the tendency of cumulative experience to reduce unit cost, especially in the case of products that require new or novel production methods [30]. Recent studies have built analytical links between this form of cost behavior and optimal pricing policies. For example, see Bass and Bultez [4], Dolan and Jeuland [11] and Robinson and Lakhani [27].

2.5. Time horizon

The time required for an innovation to be adopted by the vast majority of potential buyers is usually long. For example, when a new industrial product replaces an inferior product, the modal time required to go from 1 to 50% substitution is 12–15 years. Periods of more than 30 years are not uncommon [22]. On the other hand, it may take just a few months for a new entry into an established class of frequently purchased consumer products to reach 90% of the maximum level of trial.

Since the time to achieve a given level of adoption or trial is a function of the product-market characteristics of the product and its introductory strategy, it is difficult to generalize about the process. Here, decision-makers must rely principally on experience and knowledge about such matters as the "normal" relationships between decision variables such as advertising expenditures and product awareness, and between the levels of awareness and adoption or trial.

A joint graphic representation of market size and market effort is instructive. Here, the effort (and time) required to reach two important market-development milestones are displayed. Although the number of buyers can be shown as a function of time given the size and distribution of marketing expenditures, the more instructive approach is to make the number of buyers a function of cumulative expenditures with time being separately accounted for. In the following discussion, cumulative expenditures always carry a time subscript.

In fig. 1, the largest or target market includes the general types of buying

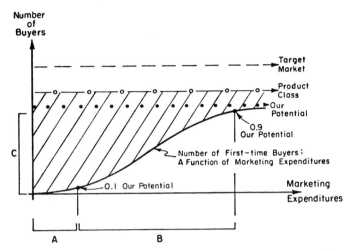

Fig. 1. Defining characteristics of the adoption/trial process. Critical elements: A = takeoff expenditures or time, B = takeover expenditures or time, C = takeover market.

units who may be prospects for the product. For a variety of reasons, such as special requirements, buyer limitations or the availability of substitutes, some of these units will never buy a product from the product class. Among the remaining product class buyers, some may never become buyers of a firm's product due to the product's performance or size limitations, its unavailability in remote geographic regions and so on. This leaves the real potential buyers of the firm's product.

The responsible decision-maker must have a good estimate of the number of potential buyers or, equivalently, the Takeover Market shown in fig. 1. It is also important for the decision-maker to have good estimates of the Takeoff Expenditures (and Time) and the Takeover Expenditures (and Time). The former defines the effort needed to convert 10% of the potential buyers into first-time buyers, and the latter defines the effort needed to convert 90% of the potential buyers into first-time buyers. Once these data are in hand, the less critical problem of defining the complete shape of the adoption/trial function can be completed.

3. Structure of the ADOPTEST model

The ADOPTEST model was developed as an interactive computer program designed for use by a marketing analyst or a manager who is comfortable working with a computer terminal. Considerable effort was devoted to emphasizing salient economic elements and to asking for data in a form that is compatible with the way these data arise in a managerial setting. Wherever possible, helpful intermediate computations and analyses are performed by the computer and presented for information and/or approval.

The system is divided into several major sections which perform the sequential tasks displayed in the following flow diagram.

Define the nature of the problem
↓
Provide the data required to *define the characteristics of the adoption/trial curve*
↓
Provide the data concerning the *firm's and competitors' marketing activities, product test results and buyer needs*
↓
Model the market and develop an "optimal" marketing mix for the firm in each period
↓
Define unit cost behavior and compute unit costs
↓
Define financial variables, compute periodic contribution profit and the discounted cash flow of each marketing strategy
↓
Perform sensitivity analysis on alternate prices and marketing expenditures
↓
Repeat analysis until a nearly globally optimal introductory strategy has appeared

Little needs to be said about problem definition except to note three principal parts: specify whether the product will enter a new product class or an established product class, specify the beginning and ending dates of the analysis, and choose the time period t (60 day, quarter or annual) which will be used.

Once the problem has been defined, the basic data about the adoption/trial process can be developed. They include the number of potential adopters/triers, a; the fraction of all buyers, x_t, who will have adopted or tried given cumulative total marketing expenditures of y_t; the frequency of purchase among buyers during the period ending at t, u_t; and the price per unit, v_t. Estimated or observed cumulative total marketing expenditures and the associated fraction (or number) of adopters or triers can be used to fit the Weibull response function using either graphical methods or by regressing linearized transformations [14]. Alternatively, the parameters of the function can be supplied directly by the user.

At this point, enough data is on hand to predict w_t, the total dollar sales in the interval ending at t for the spending pattern on behalf of the new product or product class. In slightly simplified form,

$$w_t = (v_t u_t) \quad (a x_t).$$ (1)

total	revenue	number of
dollar	per buyer	buyers during
sales	during t	period t

It is worth noting that in the case of an adoption process, adoption is influenced by the marketing efforts of all sellers and nonadopters do not buy any product in the product class. In the case of a trial process, trial is influenced solely by the sponsor's marketing effort and nontriers of a new product are buyers of other products in the product class.

To test the effects of alternative pricing and marketing expenditures on behalf of a firm, a convenient procedure is needed to adjust total demand for the effects of each strategy. Instead of re-estimating x_t in eq. (1), the parameters of eq. (2) can be easily estimated:

$$z_t = (y_t^*/y_0)^\alpha (v_t^*/v_0)^\beta,$$ (2)

where the asterisk indicates a possible new price or spending level and the subscript zero indicates the original level. The respective elasticity coefficients, α and β, can readily be computed from an estimate of the percent changes in z_t for the percent change in either total marketing or unit price. To obtain an estimate of the adjusted total dollar sales, w_t^*, under an alternative strategy, appropriate values of the various variables are used to compute

$$w_t^* = w_t z_t.$$ (3)

The division of dollar sales between the firm and its competitors is made by computing part-worths contributed by each element of the firm's marketing mix. First, estimates are made of the relative importance, s_k, of each marketing mix element to potential buyers, and of the amounts which will be spent by the firm and its competitors on each marketing element. Past or expected total spending for mix elements serve as a guide to estimating importance weights. These data should be supplemented by decision-makers' constant sum judgments about the benefits conveyed by expenditures on each mix element. Next, the firm's relative spending on each nonproduct mix element, r_k, $k = 1, ..., K - 1$, is weighted by the element's relative importance. Finally, the new product's relative appeal due to design and price, $0 < b < 1$, is determined from a blind use test or some similar method and this value is weighted by its relative importance, s_K. Since the importance weights sum to one across the mix elements and the relative spending components sum to one across all competitors, the estimated market share that a firm's strategy will yield is estimated from

$$m_t = s_1 r_1 + \ldots + s_{k-1} r_{k-1} + s_k b. \tag{4}$$

This form of the market share equation is closely related to Luce's choice theorem [18] and to the market share theorem of Bell, Keeney and Little [5]. The firm's estimated dollar sales are

$$W_t = w_t^* m_t. \tag{5}$$

In a separate report [24] the author describes how eq. (4) can be used to optimize the distribution of marketing expenditures across the nonproduct elements of the marketing mix. The optimization method sequentially chooses the least costly change in the expenditure for a mix element that achieves a desired incremental change in market share [24]. This procedure is used in the ADOPTEST algorithm to improve the efficiency of the firm's marketing expenditures during each period. The most efficient allocations are used in eq. (5) to compute the dollar revenue from each marketing strategy.

The cost of the units sold are usually computed with the aid of an experience curve. The slope coefficient, λ, and the imputed cost of the first

Table 1
Illustrative summary ADOPTEST results for the firm

Summary of alternatives

Alternative	Budget			Price			Total contribution profits ($)	Discounted cash flow ($)
	0	+	−	0	+	−		
1	*			*			946 879	827 629
2	*				*		1 242 575	1 107 926
3	*					*	569 025	470 321
4		*		*			914 661	797 032
5		*			*		1 212 735	1 079 594
6		*				*	533 928	436 993
7			*	*			978 483	857 641
8			*		*		1 271 723	1 135 602
9			*			*	603 595	503 150

Best alternative:
  market budget decrease, 4%,
  price increase, 5%.
Discounted net cash flows:
  original, 827629,
  best alternative, 1135602.

unit, c^*, are both computed from input data about marginal unit costs and rates of cost improvement. In turn, the total dollar cost of the units produced in time period t is

$$\pi_t = \left(c^*/(1-\lambda)\right)\left(c_t^{1-\lambda} - c_{t-1}^{1-\lambda}\right),$$

where c_t is the cumulative unit sales through period t for the marketing strategy being analyzed.

With total dollar revenue and total dollar product cost available for each period and introductory strategy, the discounted net cash flows can be calculated after the marketing and investment flows have been accounted for in each period. In addition to this important index of effectiveness, a wide range of other statistics are reported for each strategy being tested. For example, annual dollar and unit sales, average unit costs, market shares and contribution profit are displayed.

To improve the analyst's appreciation of the new product's economic characteristics and to help him identify a superior introductory strategy, the program automatically performs sensitivity analysis. For each user specified percentage increase and decrease in the firm's unit price and the firm's marketing expenditures, results are calculated for all combinations of these prices and levels of marketing effort. An illustrative final summary of a sensitivity sequence appears in table 1, where the best alternative is selected on the basis of the discounted cash flows. The contribution profit criterion usually but not necessarily produces the same result.

By reviewing the data in table 1, the analyst can formulate and test new alternatives. In this process, shifts may be made in other decision variables such as the time distribution of marketing effort. Finally, the analyst should examine the results obtained under alternative competitive climates. Once this iterative process is complete, the analyst or manager should be able to identify one or more excellent introductory strategies, and forecast the effect of adopting each one in the face of each of the more significant market environments in which they might become operative.

4. Some experience with the algorithm

The nature of the ADOPTEST algorithm does not lend itself to standard optimization methods or to simple sensitivity tests. Nevertheless, it is instructive to use a $3 \times 3 \times 2 \times 2 \times 2$ set of experimental data to see how the model responds to important changes in the characteristics of an introductory strategy. The nature of the experimental treatments are shown in table 2 and some of the treatment characteristics are displayed in fig. 2.

The results of analyzing the experimental data sets shown in table 2 appear

Table 2

The experimental treatments used in test no. 1: An adoption process covering 5 years

Total marketing expenditures		Level ($000)		
Timing	Year	High	Medium	Low
Up and down	1	$1,200	$600	$300
	2	1,600	800	400
	3	1,800	900	450
	4	1,400	700	350
	5	1,000	500	250
Total		$7,000	$3,500	$1,750
High and declining	1	$2,500	$1,250	$625
	2	2,000	1,000	500
	3	1,500	750	375
	4	500	250	125
	5	500	250	125
Total		$7,000	$3,500	$1,725
Constant	1	$1,400	700	350
	2	1,400	700	350
	3	1,400	700	350
	4	1,400	700	350
	5	1,400	700	350
Total		$7,000	$3,500	$1,725

Form of Weibull distribution
　Shape parameter: 1.5, 3.0.
Unit price (annual levels): $12.00 through 8.00, $9.00 constant.
Experience curve slope: -0.322, -0.152.

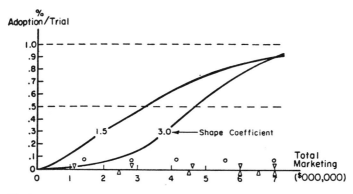

Fig. 2. Effect of different shape coefficients on the impact of spending levels over the adoption/trial process.

Table 3
Sensitivity of discounted cash flow results to select input variable and parameter levels, test no. 1.
(See table 1 for details of the experimental design)

	Number of cases	Mean discounted cash flows (000)
All cases	72	$7,400
Timing of total marketing		
Increasing and decreasing	24	7,071
Initially high and then decreasing	24	8,784
Constant	24	6,345
Level of total marketing expenditures		
High ($7,000,000)	24	5,960
Medium ($3,500,000)	24	7,855
Low ($1,750,000)	24	8,385
Form of adoption/trial function		
Weibull shape parameter = 1.5	36	8,528
Weibull shape parameter = 3.0	36	6,272
Unit Price		
High and declining ($12.00 − 8.00)	36	8,005
Low and constant ($9.00)	36	6,795
Slope of experience curve		
"Normal" ($\lambda = 0.15$)	36	8,798
Steep ($\lambda = 0.32$)	36	6,003

in table 3. The latter table summarizes the discounted cash flow results (using a 10% cost of capital).

The differences produced by each experimental treatment are substantial. Although results like those displayed in table 3 are conditional on such matters as the length of the introductory period, the cost of capital, the relative appeal of the firm's product, and a sizable number of other factors, it is fair to state that in the vast majority of practical cases, none of these treatment variables can be ignored or grossly misspecified without accepting a serious risk of choosing an inefficient introductory strategy.

The tests summarized in table 3 deal principally with aggregate changes in markets and programs. Only unit price and unit cost data apply solely to the analysis firm. To examine the sensitivity of results to changes in the relative size of the firm's marketing expenditures, a second set of analyses were run for one of the above cases (medium level of expenditures, an up and down pattern of spending through time, a Weibull adoption function shape parameter of 1.5, and an experience curve slope coefficient of 0.152). The results for five levels of company spending are shown in table 4.

Table 4
Sensitivity of results to the firm's share of total marketing expenditures, test no. 2. Total marketing, all competitors 1980–1984: $3,500,000. (No change in adoption pattern or primary demand)

Our total mktg.	Market share		Discounted cash flow
1980–1984	1980	1984	
$1,250,000	50.90%	70.37%	$6,990,747
1,600,000	56.25	71.57	6,647,952
1,950,000	61.61	72.80	7,034,581 [a]
2,300,000	66.95	74.03	7,116,568
2,650,000	72.30	75.26	7,081,750

[a] Base case.

As the data indicate, strategies that vary the relative amount spent on marketing can produce substantial shifts in the firm's market share. Nevertheless, the size of the discounted cash flows are very similar to those for the base case. In other words, market share is gained at a cost or lost at a saving in marketing expenditures which produce net results that are similar to one another. This outcome emphasizes the often overlooked fact that market share gains and losses may not be closely related to changes in financial performance.

5. Conclusion

The numerical results which have been examined do not provide evidence about the behavior of specific markets or company strategies. They do indicate, however, that when suitable data are used in the ADOPTEST system, it can provide just the type of analysis needed to make thoughtful decisions about a new-product introduction. Furthermore, sensitivity analysis performed with the aid of the model should improve managerial judgments about fruitful strategic actions by the firm and possible responses by its competitors. For example, the model can be used to help formulate various competitive actions and test their effectiveness in the hope of better assessing both the likelihood and effect of competitive moves.

Although the principal value of the ADOPTEST model is its capacity to help management formulate and test introductory strategies, other ancillary benefits are noteworthy. First, it provides the essential estimates needed to monitor market performance during the first three phases of the product's life cycle. By adding similar estimates for the less volatile last two phases of the product's life cycle, the full-life performance of a potential new product may be appraised before making a final go, no-go decision. Secondly, although the model does not provide direct measures of the risk associated with each strategy, it provides much of the basic input data required to conduct a full venture analysis of each strategy [25]. The principal new data required to complete this latter analysis are confidence estimates for unit sales, unit prices, unit costs and annual investments.

References

[1] William Abernathy and Kenneth Wayne, Limits of learning curve, Harvard Business Review (September–October 1974) 109–116.
[2] Gert Assmus, NEWPROD: The design and implementation of a new product model, Journal of Marketing (January 1975) 16–23.
[3] Frank M. Bass, A new product growth model for consumer durables, Management Science 15 (January 1969).
[4] Frank M. Bass and Alain V. Bultez, Optimal strategic pricing policies with learning, Krannert Graduate School of Management, Purdue University (August 1980).
[5] David E. Bell, Ralph E. Keeney and John D.C. Little, A market share theorem, Journal of Marketing Research (May 1975) 136–141.
[6] Boston Consulting Group, Inc., Perspectives on Experience (1968).
[7] Phillip C. Burger, COMP: A new product forecasting system, Working Paper 123–172, Northwestern University (August 1972).
[8] Henry Claycamp and Lucien Liddy, Prediction of new product performance, Journal of Marketing Research 6 (November 1969) 414–420.
[9] Kalman J. Cohen and Richard M. Cyert, Theory of the Firm: Resource Allocation in a Market Economy (Prentice-Hall, Englewood Cliffs, N.J., 1965).
[10] Linda Cyrog, Marketing simulation cuts risk of product failures, Marketing News (20 April 1979) 8.
[11] Robert J. Dolan and Abel P. Jeuland, The experience curve concept: Implications for optimal pricing strategies, Graduate School of Business, University of Chicago (December 1978).
[12] G.J. Eskin and John Malec, A model for estimating sales potential (ESP) prior to the test market, Proceedings, Fall Educators Conference, no. 39 (American Marketing Association, Chicago, 1976) pp. 230–233.
[13] John C. Fisher and Robert H. Pry, A simple substitution model of technological change, in: Marvin Citron and Christine Ralph, eds., Industrial Applications of Technological Forecasting (Wiley–Interscience, New York, 1971).
[14] Norman L. Johnson and Samuel Katz, Distributions in Statistics: Continuous Univariate Distributions, Vol. 1 (John Wiley, New York, 1970) pp. 250–271.
[15] Lawrence Light and Lewis Pringle, New product forecasting using recursive regression, in: David Kollat, Roger Blackwell and James Engle, eds., Research in Consumer Behavior (Holt, Rinehart and Winston, New York, 1970) pp. 702–709.
[16] Harold A. Linstone and Devendra Sahal, eds., Technological Substitution (Elsevier, New York, 1976).
[17] David K. Lloyd and Myron Lipow, Reliability: Management, Methods and Mathematics (Prentice-Hall, Englewood Cliffs, N.J., 1962).
[18] R. Duncan Luce, Individual Choice Behavior (John Wiley and Sons, New York, 1959).
[19] R. Duncan Luce and Howard Raiffa, Games and Decisions (Wiley, New York, 1957).
[20] William F. Massy, David B. Montgomery and Donald G. Morrison, Stochastic Models of Buyer Behavior (MIT Press, Cambridge, 1970) pp. 325–443.

[21] Edwin Mansfield, Industrial Research and Technological Innovation (W.W. Norton, New York, 1968).

[22] Joseph P. Martino, Kuei-Lin Chen and Ralph C. Lenz, Jr., Predicting the Diffusion Rate for Industrial Innovation, NTIS, PS-286 693 (March 1978).

[23] John McDonald, The Game of Business (Doubleday, Garden City, 1975).

[24] Edgar A. Pessemier, A model for product management, Institute Paper no. 683, Krannert Graduate School, Purdue University (January 1980).

[25] Edgar A. Pessemier, Product Management: Strategy and Organization, 2nd edn. (Wiley, New York, in press).

[26] Erich Pieruschka, Principles of Reliability (Prentice-Hall, Englewood CLiffs, N.J., 1963).

[27] Bruce Robinson and Chet Lakhani, Dynamic price models for new product planning, Management Science 21, no. 1 (June 1975) 1113–1122.

[28] F.M. Sherer, Industrial Market Structure and Economic Performance (Rand McNally, Chicago, 1970).

[29] Alvin Silk and Glen Urban, Pretesting market evaluation of new package goods: A model and measurement methodology, Journal of Marketing Research 15 (May 1978) 171–191.

[30] Robert Stobaugh and Phillip Townsend, Price forecasting and strategic planning: The case of petrochemicals, Journal of Marketing Research 12 (February 1975) 19–29.

[31] Glen L. Urban, SPRINTER mod. III: A model for the analysis of new frequently purchased consumer products, Operations Research 18 (September–October 1970) 805–854.

[32] Peter C. Wilton, Choice dynamics: A cross sectional analysis of maturation in perceptual and preferential structures as a function of information, Doctoral Dissertation, Purdue University, 1979.

TIMS/Studies in the Management Sciences 18 (1982) 99–116
North-Holland Publishing Company

INTEGER PROGRAMMING MODEL AND ALGORITHMIC EVOLUTION: A CASE FROM SALES RESOURCE ALLOCATION

Prabhakant SINHA

Rutgers University

and

Andris A. ZOLTNERS

Northwestern University

The evolutionary change in an integer programming model and resulting algorithmic modifications are traced for an actual sales force time allocation application. The need to solve problems quickly dictated a special purpose structure-exploiting algorithm. But as new practical considerations arose and were incorporated into the model, algorithmic modifications were needed.

1. Introduction

Successful normative models are frequently the result of an evolutionary process involving both the model builder and the model user. The process may start with an initial model formulation which is subsequently revised several times before a final steady state model becomes available to the model user. Refinement to the initial model may be the result of imprecise initial problem definition, environmental (or market) shifts and/or emerging modeling, algorithmic and computational advancement.

Mathematical programming models occasionally require customized algorithms for their efficient solution. This is especially true in an area such as integer programming where many customized algorithms have been developed. The impact of model evolution on the implementation of models requiring customized algorithms can be significant. For example, a minor change in a model formulation can render a customized algorithm ineffectual. Thus, algorithmic evolution must parallel model evolution in those cases where the model relies upon customized algorithms. This paper presents an integer programming customized algorithmic evolution which parallelled an actual sales resource allocation model evolution and implementation. The model evolution is described in the next section. This will be followed by the algorithmic evolution.

2. A sales resource allocation model evolution

The management of a large U.S. firm was re-examining the allocation of its sales effort across its served markets and among its products. The study was motivated by several factors. First, the firm's sales costs were escalating rapidly. In fact, the average cost of a single sales call for U.S. firms is now over $100 [2]. Second, a recent marketing research study conducted by the firm revealed that almost 90% of its sales came from 40% of the served market. Third, the firm was planning to introduce several new products. Due to the continuing increase in sales force related costs, the firm had decided to maintain the current sales force size, at least in the short run. Consequently, the new product introductions would require reallocating sales force resources among markets as well as among existing and the new products. However, in view of the marketing research results, the firm believed that effective redeployment of the sales force would enable the existing sales force to handle the enlarged product line with improved sales performance.

The initial sales effort allocation model determined the allocation of the firm's aggregate sales resource (product mentions) across the firm's products and markets. The allocations sought to maximize the firm's aggregate expected profit utilizing disaggregate profit response functions estimated for each product–market combination.

The total available sales force resource, R_0, was defined as the total expected number of product mentions or product messages delivered by the sales force. R_0 was determined by multiplying the average number of annual product mentions per sales person by the current sales force size. The firm's customers and prospects formed natural market segments based upon each customer's business and annual volume. In other applications, the markets may be defined in terms of industry, geography, channels of distribution, product benefits, etc. Most of the firm's products served all of the markets. The remaining products served all but one or two of the markets.

For each product–market combination, a discrete profit response function links the expected profit to various feasible sales effort allocation levels. Specifically, if an average of m_{jk} product mentions per year (e.g. $m_{j1} = 0$, $m_{j2} = 1$, $m_{j3} = 2$, $m_{j4} = 4$, $m_{j5} = 6$, $m_{j6} = 12$) are allocated to customers and prospects in market i, then c_{ijk} represents the expected profit derived from sales of product j to this market. Profit response estimates were made using a combination of survey data, experimental data, sales representative judgment, and managerial judgment. The total sales force resource required to realize c_{ijk} is $a_{ijk} = m_{jk} n_i$, where n_i is the number of customers and prospects in market i.

The following model (Ml) allocates the firm's available sales resource across its products and markets:

$$\max \sum_{i=1}^{n} \sum_{j \in P_i} \sum_{k \in N_{ij}} c_{ijk} x_{ijk} \qquad (1)$$

$$\text{s.t.} \sum_{i=1}^{n} \sum_{j \in P_i} \sum_{k \in N_{ij}} a_{ijk} x_{ijk} \leq R_0, \tag{2}$$

$$\sum_{k \in N_{ij}} x_{ijk} = 1, \quad \text{for each } j \in P_i \text{ and } i = 1, 2, \ldots, n, \tag{3}$$

$$x_{ijk} = 0 \text{ or } 1, \quad \text{for each } k \in N_{ij}, j \in P_i \text{ and } i = 1, 2, \ldots, n, \tag{4}$$

where

i is an index for each of the n markets,

j is an index for each product,

k is an index for the feasible product mention levels,

P_i is an index set of products which can be sold to market i,

N_{ij} is an index set of feasible product mention levels for product j in market i,

c_{ijk} is the expected profit realized if the kth product mention level is applied to product j in market i,

a_{ijk} is the number of product j mentions required to service market i using call strategy k,

R_0 is the available sales force resource measure in terms of total product mentions,

$$x_{ijk} = \begin{cases} 1, & \textit{if the kth product mention level is used for product j in market i,} \\ 0, & \textit{otherwise.} \end{cases}$$

Model (M1) assumes separability across markets and products. It was felt that there were no appreciable demand interactions among markets. Some demand interaction probably did exist among products. However, it was felt that this demand interaction was too difficult to measure and that its effect could be adequately assessed via sensitivity analysis. No assumptions were made or needed regarding the shape of the profit response function.

Model (M1) is a multiple-choice knapsack problem. An efficient algorithm for its solution is developed in [3] and recapitulated in the next section. The algorithm was developed to solve the model interactively. The model user could input data, modify data and quickly re-solve the model under various market, competitive and environmental assumptions.

On examining the model results, it was noticed that some products received what was considered to be a disproportionate resource allocation when steep sales response functions were used. This shift was found to be problematic since it exposed some underallocated products to excessive competitive pressure. It was therefore decided that (M1) should have the extended capability to include product specific upper limits on the amount of sales resource which could be allocated to each product. This gave rise to a new model (M2) which was derived from (M1) by appending the following constraints:

$$\sum_{i=1}^{n} \sum_{k \in N_{ij}} a_{ijk}x_{ijk} \leqslant R_{j}, \qquad \text{for each } j \in P, \tag{5}$$

where P is an index set of products, i.e. $P = \cup_{i=1}^{n} P_{i}$, and R_{j} is the maximum number of product mentions to be allocated to product j.

The incorporation of these constraints required an algorithmic revision. The details of this revision are presented in the next section. The revised algorithm retained much of the computational efficiency of the original algorithm.

A final model revision surfaced prior to the development of the final marketing plan. It had been assumed that product mentions could be combined, if necessary, into sales calls of reasonable length. Product mention combinability became an issue because the sales force usually made several product mentions on each sales call. Table 1 illustrates the combinability issue. Consider a three product illustration in which two product mentions are made on each call. Strategies 1 and 2 each comprise twelve product mentions. Yet, they differ in terms of the minimum number of sales calls necessary to make the requisite product mentions without doubling mentions of a single product on the same call (table 2).

Model (M2) was refined to develop sales force resource allocations in which product mentions can be combined in such a way that the total number of

Table 1
Product mention allocation to products A, B and C

	Strategy 1	Strategy 2
Product A	1	1
Product B	8	6
Product C	3	5
Total product mentions	12	12

Table 2
Sales calls resulting from product pairing

Products mentioned on a sales call	Strategy 1	Strategy 2
A and B	1	1
A and C	–	–
B and C	3	5
B only	4	–
Total calls	8	6

sales calls is minimized. Specifically, if M distinct product mentions are to be made on each sales call then the total number of sales calls will be minimized when exactly M product mentions are made on each call. This can be accomplished by solving the following model (M3):

$$\max \sum_{i=1}^{n} \sum_{j \in P_i} \sum_{k \in N_{ij}} c_{ijk} x_{ijk} \tag{7}$$

$$\text{s.t.} \sum_{i=1}^{n} \sum_{j \in P_i} \sum_{k \in N_{ij}} kn_i x_{ijk} \leq R_0, \tag{8}$$

$$\sum_{i=1}^{n} \sum_{k \in N_{ij}} kn_i x_{ijk} \leq R_j, \quad \text{for each } j \in P, \tag{9}$$

$$M \sum_{k \in N_{ij}} k x_{ijk} \leq \sum_{j \in P_i} \sum_{k \in N_{ij}} k x_{ijk}, \quad \text{for each } j \in P_i \text{ and } i = 1, 2, \ldots, n, \tag{10}$$

$$\sum_{k \in N_{ij}} x_{ijk} = 1, \quad \text{for each } j \in P_i \text{ and } i = 1, 2, \ldots, n, \tag{11}$$

$$x_{ijk} = 0 \text{ or } 1, \quad \text{for each } k \in N_{ij}, j \in P_i \text{ and } i = 1, 2, \ldots, n, \tag{12}$$

where $N_{ij} = \{0, 1, 2, \ldots, m_{ij}\}$.

The addition of constraints (10) insures that product mention M-tuples can be formed. Explicit consideration of all of these constraints makes the final model (M3) difficult to solve with a general-purpose integer programming algorithm. Fortunately, since $a_{ijk} = kn_i$ for each $k \in N_{ij} = \{0, 1, 2, \ldots, m_{ij}\}$ in the actual sales resource allocation model formulation, the search strategy employed for (M1) and (M2) can be extended to implicitly account for these constraints. An algorithm for (M3) is presented in the next section.

3. The algorithmic evolution

The model evolution from (M1) to (M2) and from (M2) to (M3) consists of adding sets of constraints at each step. The objective function, the resource constraint, and the multiple-choice constraints are identical in all three models. This commonality in the models carries through, to a degree, to the algorithms used to solve them. The algorithms use the partial enumeration scheme of branch-and-bound, with candidate problem relaxations obtained by relaxing integrality restrictions on decision variables. In each case, the candidate problem relaxations, which are linear programs, are solved optimally using an ascent procedure. The added constraints in (M2) and (M3) are accommodated by adapting the ascent procedure for these cases.

For any candidate problem, the ascent procedure begins by setting the first free variable in each class to 1. Since branching eliminates variables from the problem, the first free variable in a class may not be the first variable in the original problem. The ascent procedure then proceeds by picking a new variable to be set to 1 adjacent to a variable currently at 1 such that it yields the largest contribution per unit of resource. It should be noted that the objective function and resource coefficients are monotonically increasing for each multiple choice class because the profit response functions are monotonically increasing. These ascents are made in a way such that the feasibility of all constraints is maintained at each step. For (M1), this implies that the algorithm terminates when the single resource (2) is exhausted. For (M2), the limit of expendable resource for a product (5) may be reached first. In this case, all multiple choice classes involving such a product are barred from further ascents, and the algorithm proceeds with ascents over multiple choice classes involving other products. For (M3), the ascent procedures ensures that M-tuples can be formed at each step. This insures that product mentions can be combined into the minimum number of sales calls.

3.1. An algorithm for (M1)

At any stage in the algorithm, the candidate problem relaxation is the following $(CM1_R)$:

$$\max \sum_{i=1}^{n} \sum_{j \in P_i} \sum_{k \in N'_{ij}} c_{ijk} x_{ijk}$$

$$\text{s.t.} \sum_{i=1}^{n} \sum_{j \in P_i} \sum_{k \in N'_{ij}} a_{ijk} x_{ijk} \leq R_0,$$

$$\sum_{k \in N'_{ij}} x_{ijk} = 1, \quad \text{for each } j \in P_i \text{ and } i = 1, 2, \ldots, n,$$

$$0 \leq x_{ijk} \leq 1, \quad \text{for each } k \in N'_{ij}, j \in P_i, \text{ and } i = 1, 2, \ldots, n,$$

where $N'_{ij} \subseteq N_{ij}$ because some variable may have been fixed by branching and others may be dominated by theorem 1:

Theorem 1. If

$$r, s, t \in N_{ij}, \quad \text{with } a_{ijr} < a_{ijs} < a_{ijt}, c_{ijr} < c_{ijs} < c_{ijt}$$

and

$$(c_{ijs} - c_{ijr}) / (a_{ijs} - a_{ijr}) < (c_{ijt} - c_{ijs}) / (a_{ijt} - a_{ijs}),$$

then

$x_{ijs} = 0$ in every optimal solution to (CM1_R).

Proof.   See [2].

Without loss of generality, it is assumed that variables in each multiple choice class have been reindexed, if necessary, such that the indices are contiguous and full. The following ascent procedure solves (CM1_R) optimally.

Step 1: For each discrete segment of each sales response function, define the incremental resource usage and slope:

$$y_{ijk} = a_{ijk} - a_{ijk-1},$$
$$r_{ijk} = (c_{ijk} - c_{ijk-1})/y_{ijk}, \qquad k \in N'_{ij}, k \neq 1, j \in P_i \text{ and } i = 1, 2, \dots, n.$$

Set solution pointers to the first active strategy for each market–product combination:

$$p_{ij} = 1 \text{ for each } j \in P_i \text{ and } i = 1, 2, \dots, n$$

If $\bar{R}_0 < 0$, no feasible solution exists; stop.
If $\bar{R}_0 = 0$, the optimal solution to (CM1_R) has been found, go to Step 5.
If $\bar{R}_0 > 0$, go to Step 2.

Step 2: Find the steepest ascent slope:

$$r_{sqp_{sq}+1} = \max_{i,j} \{r_{ijp_{ij}+1}\}.$$

If the maximum does not exist, the optimal solution to (CM1_R) has been found, go to Step 5.
If $\bar{R}_0 - y_{sqp_{sq}+1} \leq 0$, go to Step 4.
If $\bar{R}_0 - y_{sqp_{sq}+1} > 0$, go to Step 3.

Step 3: Update the remaining resource and solution pointers:

$$\bar{R}_0 \leftarrow \bar{R}_0 - y_{sqp_{sq}+1},$$

$$p_{sq} \leftarrow p_{sq} + 1.$$

Go to Step 2.

Step 4: An optimal solution to (CM1_R) has been found. The fractional variables are defined by:

$$x^*_{sqp_{sq}} = \frac{y_{sqp_{sq}+1} - \bar{R}_0}{y_{sqp_{sq}+1}},$$

$$x^*_{sqp_{sq}+1} = 1 - x^*_{sqp_{sq}}.$$

Go to Step 5.

Step 5: The integral variables are defined by:

$$x^*_{ijk} = \begin{cases} 1, & \text{for } j = p_{ij}, \ ij \neq sq, \\ 0, & \text{otherwise } ij \neq sq, \ k \neq p_{sq}, \ k \neq p_{sq} + 1. \end{cases}$$

Stop.

This algorithm for candidate problem relaxations is embedded in a branch-and-bound search. If the algorithm terminates with fractional variables, new candidate problems are generated by the multiple-choice dichotomy [1]:

$$\sum_{k \in R_{sq}} x_{sqk} = 1 \quad \text{or} \quad \sum_{k \in N_{sq} - R_{sq}} x_{sqk} = 1, \tag{13}$$

where $R_{sq} \subset N_{sq}$ is chosen so as to only include one of the fractional variables. The algorithm for (M1) is able to solve a typical 50-class sales resource allocation problem with ten possible strategies in each class in 100 ms on the CDC 6600. We have since solved 10,000-class, 35,000-variable problems for another sales resource allocation application on the same computer in about 10 s of computer time.

3.2. An algorithm for M2

Model (M2) is derived from (M1) by appending constraints (5). These added constraints have exactly the same coefficients as the total effort constraint (2). This permits the utilization of an ascent procedure to solve candidate problem relaxations. Two significant modifications to the ascent procedure used for (CM1_R) are necessary. First, since there are several constraints, the ascent procedure has to check for possible violations of each of the constraints. Second, whereas the algorithm for (CM1_R) stops as soon as the resource R_0 is consumed, a revised algorithm must continue until either the resource R_0 is exhausted or until all product limits R_i have been reached.

Unlike the algorithm for $(CM1_R)$, this will typically result in more than one pair of fractional variables.

At any stage in the algorithm for (M2), the candidate problem relaxation is as follows $(CM2_R)$:

$$\max \sum_{i=1}^{n} \sum_{j \in P_i} \sum_{k \in N'_{ij}} c_{ijk} x_{ijk}$$

$$\text{s.t. } \sum_{i=1}^{n} \sum_{j \in P_i} \sum_{k \in N'_{ij}} a_{ijk} x_{ijk} \leq R_0,$$

$$\sum_{j=1}^{n} \sum_{k \in N'_{ij}} a_{ijk} x_{ijk} \leq R_j, \quad \text{for each } j \in P,$$

$$\sum_{k \in N'_{ij}} x_{ijk} = 1, \quad \text{for each } j \in P \text{ and } i = 1, 2, \ldots, n,$$

$$0 \leq x_{ijk} \leq 1, \quad \text{for each } k \in N'_{ij}, j \in P, \text{ and } i = 1, 2, \ldots, n.$$

As before, we assume, without loss of generality, that variables in multiple-choice classes have been reindexed if necessary so that the indices are contiguous and full. The following ascent procedure yields an optimal solution to $(CM2_R)$:

Step 1: Set $x^*_{ijk} = 0$ for each i, j, k. For each discrete segment of each sales response function, define the incremental resource usage and slope:

$$y_{ijk} = a_{ijk} - a_{ijk-1},$$
$$r_{ijk} = (c_{ijk} - c_{ijk-1})/y_{ijk}, \qquad k \in N'_{ij}, k \neq 1, j \in P_i \text{ and } i = 1, 2, \ldots, n.$$

Set up solution pointers to the first active strategy in each class:

$$p_{ij} = 1 \quad \text{and} \quad x^*_{ijp_{ij}} = 1, \quad \text{for each } j \in P_i \text{ and } i = 1, 2, \ldots, n.$$

Define $P' = P$ to be products for which the resource limit has not been reached.

$$\bar{R}_0 = R_0 - \sum_{i=1}^{n} \sum_{j \in P_i} a_{ij1}$$

and

$$\bar{R}_\ell = R_\ell - \sum_{i:\ell \in P_i} a_{i\ell1}, \quad \text{for each } \ell \in P.$$

If $\overline{R}_\ell < 0$ for $\ell = 0$ or any $\ell \in P$, no feasible solution exists; stop. Otherwise, go to Step 2.

Step 2: Determine the steepest slope for ascent:

$$r_{sqp_{sq}+1} = \max_{i,j \in P'} \{r_{ijp_{ij}+1}\}.$$

If the maximum does not exist, the optimal solution to $(CM2_R)$ has been found, go to Step 6. Let

$$\Delta_1 = \overline{R}_q - y_{sqp_{sq}+1},$$

$$\Delta_0 = \overline{R}_0 - y_{sqp_{sq}+1}.$$

 If $\min\{\Delta_0, \Delta_1\} \geq 0$, go to Step 3.
  Otherwise, if $\min\{\Delta_0, \Delta_1\} = \Delta_1$, go to Step 4;
      and if $\min\{\Delta_0, \Delta_1\} = \Delta_0$, go to Step 5.

Step 3: No resource or product limits have been reached. Update resource and product slacks and solution pointer.

$$\overline{R}_0 \leftarrow \Delta_0,$$

$$\overline{R}_q \leftarrow \Delta_1,$$

$$x^*_{sqp_{sq}} \leftarrow 0,$$

$$p_{sq} \leftarrow p_{sq} + 1,$$

$$x^*_{sqp_{sq}} \leftarrow 1.$$

Go to Step 2.

Step 4: A product limit has been reached. Update resource and product slacks and solution pointer. Set

$$x^*_{sqp_{sq}} = \frac{-\Delta_1}{y_{sqp_{sq}+1}}.$$

$$x^*_{sqp_{sq}+1} = 1 - x^*_{sqp_{sq}},$$

$$P' \leftarrow P' - \{q\},$$

$$\overline{R}_0 \leftarrow \overline{R}_0 - \overline{R}_q,$$

$$p_{sq} \leftarrow 0.$$

Go to Step 2.

Step 5: An optimal solution has been found:

$$x^*_{sqp_{sq}} = \frac{-\Delta_0}{y_{sqp_{sq}+1}}$$

$$x^*_{sqp_{sq}} = 1 - x^*_{sqp_{sq}}.$$

Go to Step 6.

Step 6: The optimal solution is $x_{ijk} = x^*_{ijk}$ for each i, j, k. Stop.

As with (M1), this algorithm for candidate problem relaxation is embedded in a branch-and-bound search. If the algorithm terminates in fractional variables, new candidate problems are generated by dichotomizing on the multiple-choice class that became fractional first. It may be noted that model (M2) subsumes (M1).

Solutions to (M2) were obtained with approximately a twofold increase in computational time over (M1) for problems of the same size. For example, the sales resource application described earlier involving 50 classes and 10 potential strategies in each class was usually solved in less than one-quarter of a second on the CDC 6600.

3.3. An algorithm for (M3)

Model (M3) is derived from (M2) by adding constraints which insure that product mention M-tuples can be formed from the product mention allocations to each market. The algorithm is developed for the case where $M = 2$, i.e. product mentions are paired to form sales calls. This is done to make the exposition simpler. The necessary changes for the case where $M > 2$ are discussed below.

Three basic modifications to the algorithm for (M2) are made. First, variables dominated by theorem 1 are retained. Second, pairability of product mentions is preserved at each step of the ascent procedure by making ascents simultaneously on pairs of products in a market. A double ascent on a single product is permitted if pairability is preserved after the ascent. Fractional variables can result when a resource limit on a product is reached or when the overall resource limit is reached.

Third, an approximation-relaxation is solved at each branch of the search since it is easier to solve than its relaxation counterpart. The objective function of each multiple-choice class (market–product combination) of the relaxation of (M3) is approximated by the piecewise-linear concave function which deviates the least from the original function. Fig. 1 displays a typical profit response function with the dotted line showing the concave approximation used to obtain the objective function coefficients for the approximation-relaxation. In view of the ascent procedure described above, the following approximation-relaxation is used ($CM3_{AR}$):

$$\max \ \sum_{i=1}^{n} \sum_{j \in P_i} \sum_{k \in N'_{ij}} c'_{ijk} x_{ijk}$$

$$\text{s.t.} \ \sum_{i=1}^{n} \sum_{j \in P_i} \sum_{k \in N'_{ij}} k n_i x_{ijk} \leq R_0, \tag{14}$$

$$\sum_{i=1}^{n} \sum_{k \in N'_{ij}} k n_i x_{ijk} \leq R_j, \quad \text{for each } j \in P, \tag{15}$$

$$M \sum_{k \in N'_{ij}} k x_{ijk} \leq \sum_{j \in P_i} \sum_{k \in N'_{ij}} k x_{ijk}, \quad \text{for each } j \in P_i \text{ and } i = 1, 2, \ldots, n,$$

$$\sum_{k \in N'_{ij}} x_{ijk} = 1, \quad \text{for each } j \in P_i \text{ and } i = 1, 2, \ldots, n,$$

$$0 \leq x_{ijk} \leq 1, \quad \text{for each } k \in N'_{ij}, j \in P_i \text{ and } i = 1, 2, \ldots, n,$$

where c'_{ijk} is the approximated objective function.

Since concavized profits are always greater than actual profits, the optimal solution to ($CM3_{AR}$) provides a valid upper bound to the solution of (M3), and since no changes have been made to the constraints, the objective function of (M3) evaluated for integer solutions to ($CM3_{AR}$) provides a valid lower bound for (M3). The algorithm presented below solves approximation-relaxations and recreates the original functions via the branching process during the search.

Step 1: Set $x^*_{ijk} = 0$ for each $k \in N'_{ij}, j \in P_i$ and $i = 1, 2, \ldots, n$. Set up solution pointers to the first active strategy for each market–product combination:

$$p_{ij} = \min_{q \in N'_{ij}} \{q\},$$
$$x^*_{ijp_{ij}} = 1, \qquad \text{for each } j \in P_i \text{ and } i = 1, 2, \ldots, n.$$

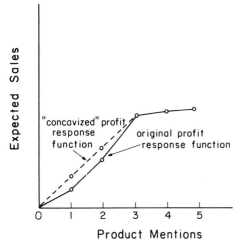

Fig. 1. A typical profit response function and its concavized form for the approximation-relaxation $(\mathrm{CM3_{AR}})$.

Define the slopes of the response function in each discrete segment:

$$r_{ijk} = \left(c'_{ijk} - c'_{ijk-1}\right)/n_i, \quad \text{for each } k \in N'_{ij},\, k \neq p_{ij},\, j \in P_i, \text{ and } i = 1, 2, \ldots, n.$$

Define the active product set and the remaining resources:

$$P' = P,$$

$$\bar{R}_0 = R_0 - \sum_{i=1}^{n} \sum_{j \in P_i} P_{ij} n_i,$$

$$\bar{R}_\ell = R_\ell - \sum_{i:\ell \in P_i} P_{i\ell} n_\ell, \quad \text{for each } \ell \in P.$$

Define the total number of product mentions to a market:

$$T_i = \sum_{j \in P_i} p_{ij}, \quad \text{for each } i = 1, 2, \ldots, n.$$

If $\bar{R}_\ell < 0$ for $\ell = 0$ or any $\ell \in P$, no feasible solution exists; stop. Otherwise, go to Step 2.

Step 2: Find the best pair of ascents for two different products. Determine

$$\theta_1 = \max_{\substack{j,t \in P' \\ p_{ij}, p_{it} \leq T_i/2 \\ j \neq t}} \left\{ r_{ijp_{ij}+1} + r_{itp_{it}+1} \right\}.$$

The condition $p_{ij}, p_{it} \leq T_i/2$ insures that the ascents remain pairable or move toward pairability if this has not already been achieved. The only case when an intermediate solution is not pairable, and this condition affects a move, is when some variables have been fixed, and a candidate problem approximation-relaxation is being reoptimized.

Find the best pair of ascents for the same product. Determine

$$\theta_2 = \max_{\substack{j \in P' \\ p_{ij} < T_i/2}} \left\{ r_{ijp_{ij}+1} + r_{ijp_{ij}+2} \right\}.$$

The condition $p_{ij} < T_i/2$ insures that an ascent in thes multiple choice class does not destroy pairability.

If neither θ_1 nor θ_2 is defined, $(CM3_{AR})$ is solved. Go to Step 11.

If $\theta_1 \geq \theta_2$, go to Step 3.

Otherwise, go to Step 6.

Step 3. Ascents are on two different products. Let

$$r_{sqp_{sq}+1} + r_{shp_{sh}+1} = \max_{\substack{j,t \in P' \\ p_{ij}, p_{it} \leq T_i/2 \\ j \neq t}} \left\{ r_{ijp_{ij}} + r_{itp_{it}+1} \right\}.$$

Let

$$\Delta = \min\left\{ \left(1 - x^*_{sqp_{sq}+1}\right), \left(1 - x^*_{shp_{sh}+1}\right) \right\}.$$

Δ defines the magnitude of the potential ascent. Usually $\Delta = 1$. But if a product limit was reached on a prior ascent, one of the variables determining Δ may be a nonzero:

$$\Delta_0 = \bar{R}_0 - 2n_s \Delta,$$

$$\Delta_1 = \bar{R}_q - n_s \Delta,$$

$$\Delta_2 = \bar{R}_h - n_s \Delta.$$

If $\min\{\Delta_0, \Delta_1, \Delta_2\} \geq 0$, i.e. the ascent is not limited by any constraints, go to Step 4.

If $\min\{\Delta_0, \Delta_1, \Delta_2\} = \Delta_0$, i.e. the resource will be exhausted during this ascent, go to Step 9.

Otherwise, go to Step 5.

Step 4: Reset resource slack and product slacks:

$$\bar{R}_0 \leftarrow \Delta_0,$$

$$\bar{R}_q \leftarrow \Delta_1,$$

$$\bar{R}_h \leftarrow \Delta_2.$$

Reset total number of product mentions for market s:

$$T_s \leftarrow T_s + 2n_s \Delta.$$

Adjust variable values to reflect ascent:

$$x^*_{sqp_{sq}} \leftarrow x^*_{sqp_{sq}} - \Delta,$$

$$x^*_{sqp_{sq}+1} \leftarrow x^*_{sqp_{sq}+1} + \Delta,$$

$$x^*_{shp_{sh}} \leftarrow x^*_{shp_{sh}} - \Delta,$$

$$x^*_{shp_{sh}+1} \leftarrow x^*_{shp_{sh}+1} + \Delta.$$

Solution pointers point to the first nonzero variable in each class. Reset them if a variable $x_{sqp_{sq}}$ or $x_{shp_{sh}}$ is now zero.

If $x^*_{sqp_{sq}} = 0$, $p_{sq} \leftarrow p_{sq} + 1$.
If $x^*_{shp_{sh}} = 0$, $p_{sh} \leftarrow p_{sh} + 1$.
If $\bar{R}_0 = 0$, go to Step 11.
Otherwise, go to Step 2.

Step 5: This ascent has reached a product limit. Redefine Δ to be the magnitude of the actual ascent:

$$\Delta = \min\{\bar{R}_q, \bar{R}_h\}/n_s,$$

$$\Delta = \bar{R}_0 - 2n_s \Delta,$$

$$\Delta_1 = \bar{R}_q - n_s \Delta,$$

$$\Delta_2 = \bar{R}_h - n_s \Delta.$$

If $\Delta_1 = 0$, remove product q from active product. Set:

$$P' \leftarrow P' - \{q\}.$$

If $\Delta_2 = 0$, remove product h from active product. Set:

$$P' \leftarrow P' - \{h\}.$$

Go to Step 4.

Step 6: Both ascents are on the same product. Let

$$r_{sqp_{sq}+1} + r_{sqp_{sq}+2} = \max_{\substack{j \in P' \\ p_{ij} < T_i/2}} \{r_{ijp_{ij}+1} + r_{ijp_{ij}+2}\}.$$

Δ defines the magnitude of the potential ascent:

$$\Delta = \min\left\{(2 - x^*_{sqp_{sq}+1}), \ T_s - 2\left[p_{sq}x^*_{sqp_{sq}} + (p_{sq}+1)x^*_{sqp_{sq}+1}\right]\right\}$$

The second term in the above expression insures that the ascent preserves pairability:

$$\Delta_0 = \overline{R}_0 - n_s \Delta,$$

$$\Delta_1 = \overline{R}_q - n_s \Delta.$$

If $\min\{\Delta_0, \Delta_1\} \geq 0$, i.e. the ascent is not limited by constraints (14) or (15), go to Step 7.
If $\min\{\Delta_0, \Delta_1\} = \Delta_0$, go to Step 10.
Otherwise, go to Step 8.

Step 7: Reset constraint slacks and product mention total for the case of double ascent on same market–product combination:

$$\overline{R}_0 \leftarrow \Delta_0,$$

$$\overline{R}_q \leftarrow \Delta_1,$$

$$T_s \leftarrow T_s + n_s \Delta.$$

Reset variable values and solution pointers.
If $\Delta = 1 - x^*_{sqp_{sq}+1}$, set $x^*_{sqp_{sq}} = x^*_{sqp_{sq}+1} = 0$, and $x^*_{sqp_{sq}+2} = 1$. Also, $p_{sq} \leftarrow p_{sq} + 2$.

Otherwise, if $\Delta < (1 - x^*_{sqp_{sq}})$, $x^*_{sqp_{sq}+1} \leftarrow x^*_{sqp_{sq}+1} + \Delta$ and $x^*_{sqp_{sq}} \leftarrow x^*_{sqp_{sq}} - \Delta$,

and if $\Delta \geqslant (1 - x^*_{sqp_{sq}})$, $x^*_{sqp_{sq}+2} = \Delta - (1 - x^*_{sqp_{sq}})$,
$x^*_{sqp_{sq}+1} = 1 - x^*_{p_{sq}+2}$ and $x^*_{sqp_{sq}} = 0$.

Also, $p_{sq} \leftarrow p_{sq} + 1$.

If $\bar{R}_0 = 0$, go to Step 11.

Otherwise, go the Step 2.

Step 8: The double ascent on the same market–product combination is limited by the product resource. Redefine Δ to be the magnitude of actual ascent:

$$\Delta = \bar{R}_q / n_s,$$

$$P' \leftarrow P' - \{q\},$$

$$\Delta_0 = \bar{R}_0 - n_s \Delta,$$

$$\Delta_1 = 0.$$

Go to Step 7.

Step 9: Resource will be exhausted during this ascent on two different products. Redefine Δ to be the magnitude of the actual ascent:

$$\Delta = \bar{R}_0 / 2n_s,$$

$$\Delta_1 = \bar{R}_q - n_s \Delta,$$

$$\Delta_2 = \bar{R}_h - n_s \Delta.$$

To to Step 4.

Step 10: Resource will be exhausted during this double ascent on the same product. Redefine Δ to be the magnitude of the actual ascent:

$$\Delta = \bar{R}_0 / n_s,$$

$$\Delta_0 = 0,$$

$$\Delta_1 = \bar{R}_q - \bar{R}_0.$$

Go to Step 7.

Step 11: If

$$2 \sum_{k \in N'_{ij}} kx^*_{ijk} \leqslant \sum_{j \in P_i} \sum_{k \in N'_{ij}} kx^*_{ijk}, \quad \text{for each } j \in P_i \text{ and } i = 1, 2, \ldots, n,$$

the optimal solution is $\{x^*_{ijk}\}$.
Otherwise, the candidate problem has no feasible solution; Stop.

This algorithm for candidate problem approximation-relaxations is embedded in a branch-and-bound search. New candidate problems are created using dichotomy (13) if the algorithm terminates with fractional variables or if the solution lies on an approximated portion of the response curve.

Solutions to (M3) were obtained with less than a twofold increase in computation time over (M2) for problems of the same size. Sales resource allocation problems with four products, 50 classes and ten variables per class were usually solved in less than one-half second on the CDC 6600.

To accommodate the case where more than two product mentions comprise a sales call, the ascent procedure must be modified to make M ascents as each step instead of just two.

References

[1] E.M.L. Beale and J.A. Tomlin, Special facilities in a general mathematical programming system for non-convex problems using ordered sets of variables, in: J. Lawrence, ed., Proceedings of the Fifth International Conference of Operational Research (Tavestock Publications, London, 1969) pp. 821–828.
[2] Marketing observer, Business Week (11 September 1978) 121.
[3] P. Sinha and A.A. Zoltners, The multiple-choice knapsack problem, Operations Research 27, no. 3 (1979) 503–515.

TIMS/Studies in the Management Sciences 18 (1982) 117–140
North-Holland Publishing Company

A DISCRETE MAXIMUM PRINCIPLE APPROACH TO A GENERAL DYNAMIC MARKET RESPONSE MODEL

Thomas E. MORTON, Andrew A. MITCHELL
Carnegie-Mellon University

and

Eitan ZEMEL
Northwestern University

Modeling the effect of marketing control variables frequently involves dynamic or carryover effects. Two types of carryover effects have been discussed in the literature, a Brand Loyalty Effect and a Buildup Effect. A general discrete time dynamic market response model which includes both types of carryover effects, and allows for interproduct effects and/or interacting market segments or territories is considered. Most dynamic market response models that have appeared in the literature are special cases of this model. This model and the special cases of it are generally too large to be solved exactly by conventional optimization methods. An approximate solution procedure utilizing the discrete maximum principle is developed which has desirable properties when a specified portion of the model is concave. Like the Srinivasan procedure, the solution of a T-period problem is decomposed into a sequence of one-period problems, so that very large problems may be handled. Like Little–Lodish, successive iterations produce monotonically increasing values of the objective function. In addition, each iteration yields successively improving upper bounds on the value of the optimal solution, and consequently, on the value of continuing the procedure. Computational results confirm Srinivasan's finding that for the type of five-period problem he considered, his procedure is near-optimal, and considerably superior to Little–Lodish. The new procedure outperforms Srinivasan slightly for these problems. For similar 10 and 20-period problems, however, Srinivasan's procedure deteriorates, becoming inferior to Little–Lodish for $T=20$. The new procedure strongly outperforms both older procedures for $T=10$ and $T=20$; it never deviates by more than 2% from the upper bound on optimality. The appendix discusses improved but more complicated versions of the new procedure, as well as suggested methodology for adapting it to problems with relaxed concavity requirements.

1. Introduction

It is generally believed that the effects of some marketing control variables (e.g. advertising) affect market response not only in the time period in which they occur, but also in future time periods. These dynamic or carryover effects are well documented in the literature on both a theoretical (i.e. [9,10,15,17]) and an empirical basis (i.e. [3,8,11,12,18,21]). In building normative models of market response, therefore, it is frequently necessary to include dynamic or carryover effects.

Two different types of dynamic or carryover effects have previously been identified [1,10,17,27]. The first is a *Brand Loyalty Effect* which occurs when consumers have a tendency to purchase the same brands in future time periods. This effect is generally modeled with the following structural equation:

$$m_{t+1} = \alpha_t m_t + f(x_t). \tag{1}$$

Here m_t is a measure of market response (e.g. sales) in time t, x_t is the level of the control variable in time t, α_t is a constrained parameter ($0 < \alpha_t < 1$) and f is generally a monotonic increasing function. Models of this general form include ADBUDG [13] and the reduced form of the Koyck model [21].

The second type of dynamic effect is a *Buildup Effect* which occurs when the current effect of a marketing control variable depends on the level of this control variable in previous time periods. This effect is generally modeled with the following structural equations:

$$m_t = h(y_t), \tag{2}$$

$$y_t = \gamma y_{t-1} + f(x_t). \tag{3}$$

Here y_t is a measure of "goodwill" or the current effect of control variable decisions in the current and previous time periods, γ is a constrained parameter ($0 < \gamma < 1$) and h is a monotone increasing function. Models of this general form include DETAILER [19] and MEDIAC [16].

These two types of carryover effects can be combined into the following general model:

$$m_{t+1} = \alpha_t m_t + h(y_t), \tag{4}$$

$$y_t = \gamma y_{t-1} + f(x_t). \tag{5}$$

An example of this general model is BRANDAID [14].

1.1. Parameterization

In estimating the parameters of these models, model builders have generally relied on either statistical techniques or judgmental estimates by managers. For instance, Little [13] developed procedures for using managerial judgements to obtain parameter estimates for a model of the form given by eq. (1), while econometric procedures have also been used to estimate the parameters of this type of model (e.g. [3,21]). Models of the buildup effect (eqs. (2) and (3)) and the general model (eqs. (4) and (5)) usually rely exclusively on managerial judgment (i.e. [16,19]) since goodwill is generally treated as an unobserved variable.

Chakravarti, Mitchell and Staelin [5,6] have demonstrated that the use of managerial judgments may result in biased parameter estimates, and when this occurs the resulting models may *not* improve managerial decision-making. These effects appear to be most pronounced with dynamic market response models [7]. If managerial judgment is used for estimating these parameters, the anchoring bias found by Chakravarti, Mitchell and Staelin [6] suggests that the estimated response function may be "flatter" than it should be. If this occurs, conservative solutions will occur if optimization procedures are applied to the resulting model.

In an attempt to circumvent these problems Chakravarti, Mitchell and Staelin [7] have suggested the use of both statistical procedures and managerial judgments in estimating the parameters of these models. This suggested procedure essentially involves estimating the brand loyalty effect (the parameter α in eq. (1)) with statistical procedures and then the use of either managerial judgment or statistical procedures for estimating the parameters of the response function f.

Similar procedures might be applied to estimating the parameters of buildup effect models or the general model; however, their effectiveness on these types of models have not yet been examined. Alternatively, econometric procedures might be used to estimate these parameters. Avery, Mitchell and Winer [1], for instance, discussed estimation procedures for the general model when h and f are linear. The reduced form of this model is underidentified; however, if a contemporaneous variable is also included in the model, the resulting equation is overidentified. In this case, constraints may be added to obtain estimates of the parameters.

1.2. Optimization procedures

Once parameterized, the resulting models may be used as "what if" models to assess alternative decisions. However, the models are most useful if optimization procedures are available. In some cases the effects of decisions in one time period are independent of the effects of decisions in previous time periods. In these situations the model is separable and may be solved by applying nonlinear programming procedures on a time period by time period basis. The brand loyalty effect model (eq. (1)), for instance, is separable if the carryover parameter (α) is constant through time [17,27].

In general, however, the buildup effect models and the general market response model are not separable. In these cases it is necessary to determine the optimal solution for each time period simultaneously. Although the resulting problem is formally a dynamic programming problem, it is impractical to solve such a model exactly unless the number of time periods is small (i.e. one or two time periods). Consequently, heuristic procedures are required.

Two heuristic procedure have been developed for solving the buildup effect model (eqs. (2) and (3)). Little and Lodish [16] use a heuristic search procedure in their MEDIAC model which starts with any media schedule and then adds insertions that produce a high incremental response per dollar and deletes those insertions that produce a low decremental response per dollar until the budget is expended. Srinivasan [25] later developed a solution procedure based on the discrete maximum principle that, for 12-sample, 5-period problems, yielded solutions that were closer to the optimal than the Little–Lodish procedure for nine of the problems.

In this paper we present an optimization procedure that is also based on the discrete maximum principle. As we show, it may be used to obtain solutions for either the buildup effect model or the general market response model. In the next section the general market response model is expanded to include interacting market segments or products. In most applied situations the problems involved in estimating the additional parameters will preclude the use of this expansion. It is included here to demonstrate the generalizability of the proposed optimization procedure.

Section 3 gives the necessary and sufficient conditions for obtaining the optimal solution to this model using the discrete maximum principle. These conditions suggest an iterative solution procedure which may be directly interpreted as the maximization of successive linear approximations to the concave portion of the model. Like the procedures developed by Srinivasan [25] for special cases of the general model, the solution of a T-period problem is decomposed into a sequence of one-period problems, so that very large problems may be handled. In addition, the procedure has the advantage that each successive iteration produces a strictly better approximate solution than the previous solution. The Little–Lodish procedure also has this property; however, the Srinivasan procedure does not. Finally, the new procedure also calculates an upper bound to the optimal solution on each iteration, which provides a measure of the value of continuing the procedure. While it is not clear that the upper bounds improve monotonically with each iteration, one may simply save the best upper bound to date for comparison purposes.

Section 4 gives the computational results comparing the three procedures on a media model with 5, 10 and 20 time periods, 5 and 10 market segments and 10, 20 and 40 media vehicles. The results indicate that for the 5-period problem the new procedure outperforms the Srinivasan procedure slightly which, in turn, yields solution values that are 17–47% better than the Little–Lodish procedure. However, for problems of 10–20 time periods the new procedure consistently outperforms both the Srinivasan and the Little–Lodish procedures. For these longer problems, the Srinivasan procedure deteriorates progressively. For 20-period problems the Srinivasan procedure performed *worse* than the Little–Lodish procedure in 7 of the 8 problems and actually achieved a negative profit in 3 of these 7 instances. Finally, the new procedure averages within 0.8%, 0.7% and 1.8% of the upper bound on optimality for problems of 5, 10 and 20 periods, respectively.

In the appendix stronger sufficiency conditions for the optimality of the discrete maximum principal are obtained. While these conditions do not share the convenient period by period decomposition property of the original procedure, an approximate decomposition which does is suggested. Finally, methods for adapting the iterative procedure to situations when the incremental market response functions is nonconcave are explored.

2. The general model

In this section the general model is extended to include interacting product/market segment/territories. In this expanded model, the scalar variables defined earlier become vectors. The x_t variable becomes an m-dimensional vector whose elements are the "effort levels" in time t. For instance, in the media selection problem, the elements would be the number of insertions in m different media. The set of constraints on the vector x_t will vary depending on the problem. In some cases, non-negativity will be required ($x_t \geq 0$), while in other cases both non-negativity and upper bounds will be required ($0 \leq x_t \leq b$). In still other cases, x_t will be required to take on integer values. In general, we will require $x_t \in \Omega_t$ and note that in some cases Ω_t may not be convex.

The model allows for n different product/market segment/territory conditions. In some situations we may be interested in modeling one product and a number of different market segments and/or territories (e.g. MEDIAC), in other situations one market segment and/or territory and a number of different products (e.g. DETAILER), while in still other situations a number of different products and market segments/territories. The m different effort levels may or may not be common to all product/market segment/territories.

The y_t variable becomes an n-dimensional vector that gives the size of the buildup effect or "goodwill" in each product/market segment/territory. The buildup effect is modeled in the following equation:

$$y_{t+1} = C_t y_t + f_t(x_t). \tag{6}$$

Here C_t is an $n \times n$ "carryover effect" matrix. The diagonal elements of C_t indicate the amount of forgetting that occurs between time periods within a product/market segment/territory. If spillover effects occur between product/market segments/territories, then C_t will also contain off-diagonal elements.

The n-dimensional vector function f_t translates the m-dimensional "effort levels" into "goodwill" for each product/market segment/territory. In some cases, f_t may be a complicated function, as in the media selection problem where this function must account for duplication between media. In other cases, the function may be very simple as in the advertising budgeting problem where "effort levels" may simply equal the addition to "goodwill" or $f_t(x_t) = x_t$.

The transfer of "goodwill" into market response is contained in the following equation modeling the "brand loyalty effect":

$$m_{t+1} = A_t m_t + B_t h_t(y_t).\tag{7}$$

The m_t variable becomes an n-dimensional vector whose elements give the amount of market response, sales or market share, in each product/market segment/territory. The diagonal elements of the $n \times n$ matrix A_t gives the proportion of sales response that is repeated between time periods. Depending on the particular problem being modeled, A_t and B_t may either be diagonal matrices or contain off-diagonal elements. The n-dimensional vector function h_t defines the amount of market response generated from a particular level of "goodwill".

In most situations, the off-diagonal elements of the A_t, B_t, and C_t matrices will be close to zero and the diagonal elements will be fairly stable through time. Consequently, for all intentional purposes, these matrices may be treated as stationary diagonal matrices. In these situations, as discussed above, econometric techniques or a combination of judgmental and statistical procedures may be used to obtain estimates of these diagonal elements.

Next, let the function $\pi_t(m_t)$ give the level of profit generated from a particular level of market response. All costs associated with the product, except the costs specifically tied to the "effort levels", x_t, are included in the profit function. The costs associated with a particular "effort level" x_t are modeled in the function $g_t(x_t)$.

The problem then is to determine the optimal "effort levels" x_t for a time horizon of T time periods. Mathematically, this is

$$\max_x V = \sum_{t=0}^{T-1} \{\pi_t(m_t) - g_t(x_t)\} + \pi_T(m_T, y_T) \qquad (X = (x_0,...,x_{T-1})),\tag{8}$$

$$\left.\begin{aligned}
m_{t+1} &= A_t m_t + B_t h_t(y_t) \\
y_{t+1} &= C_t y_t + f_t(x_t) \\
x_t &\in \Omega_t
\end{aligned}\right\} \quad \text{for } t = 0,...,T-1, \qquad \begin{aligned}&(9)\\&(10)\\&(11)\end{aligned}$$

$$m_t, y_t \geq 0, \quad \text{for } t = 1,...,T-1 \text{ and } m_0, Y_0 \text{ given},\tag{12}$$

$$\pi_t(0) = h_t(0) = f_t(0) = g_t(0) = 0.\tag{13}$$

Here, 0 is the null vector of the appropriate dimension. The function $\pi_T(m_T, y_T)$

gives the residual profit from future time periods from leaving the system in state m_T and y_T. Finally, it should be noted that the nonstationarity of the π and g functions allows discounting to be handled automatically.

3. Analysis

In developing a solution procedure for the model presented in the previous section, the discrete maximum principle is formally applied [4]. This principle is the discrete version of the continuous maximum principle first set forth by Pontryagin et al. [23]. Basically, this approach obtains a solution to a dynamic model by maximizing a function called the Hamiltonian in each time period. This allows the problem to be decomposed into a series of one-period problems and provides a method for the solution of problems that would be too large to be solved by dynamic programming methods. This decomposition of the problem, however, comes at a price since the Hamiltonian in each time period is a function of the control variables (in our case the x_t vector) and costate variables or adjoint functions. These costate variables are similar to the dual variables in mathematical programming and their values must be determined in each time period in order to maximize the Hamiltonian. Generally, an iterative procedure is required to obtain the values of the costate or adjoint functions.

In this section we first provide an intuitive explanation of the adjoint functions and the Hamiltonian. Then a set of conditions for an optimal solution based on the discrete maximum principle will be set forth and a lemma based on these conditions will be proven. Next the necessary and sufficient conditions will be proven.

3.1. Intuitive explanation

An intuitive understanding of the Hamiltonian and the adjoint functions are now provided since they form the basis of the suggested solution procedure. First, we define two sets of adjoint functions, z_t and w_t, for each time period. These functions are n-component row vectors which provide measures of the marginal carryover value of current sales or market share and goodwill, respectively. For instance, the jth component of z_t is the marginal contribution to total profits in periods t through T from one additional unit of sales or market share from product/market segment/territory j in time period t. Similarly, the jth component of w_t is the marginal contribution to total profit in periods t through T from one additional unit of goodwill in product/market segment/territory j.

Next, we define the Hamiltonian:

$$H_t(m_t, x_t, z_{t+1}, w_{t+1}) = \pi_t(m_t) - g_t(x_t) + z_{t+1}\left[A_t m_t + B_t h_t(y_t)\right]$$

$$+ w_{t+1}\left[C_t y_t + f_t(x_t)\right], \tag{14}$$

$$H_t(m_T, y_T) = \pi_T(m_T, y_T). \tag{15}$$

The Hamiltonian can be interpreted as a measure of the total profit for period t and future profits derived from leaving the system in state m_{t+1} and y_{t+1}. This can be seen by noting that the first term in eq. (14) gives the direct profit in period t and the second term gives the direct costs of setting the "effort levels" x_t in that time period. The final two terms of eq. (14) give the future profits derived from leaving the system in state m_{t+1} and y_{t+1}. This follows from eqs. (9) and (10) and the definition of the adjoint function.

It should be noted that the sum of the Hamiltonians for all periods does *not* represent total profits since the latter two terms in eq. (14) measure the total carryover from sales and goodwill in that time period instead of just the carryover effects of the sales and goodwill generated in that time period by "effort levels" x_t. This means that summing the Hamiltonians will result in double counting and will consequently overstate the total profits generated in the planning horizon. Nevertheless, *changes* in "effort levels" x_t which improve the Hamiltonian in that time period may be used as a surrogate for changes that will improve total profits. Geometrically, the Hamiltonian is equivalent to a linear approximation of the concave part of the model around a current solution and will, therefore, overestimate the value to be obtained from a change.

Now, a set of conditions that an optimal solution to the problem defined by eqs. (8)–(13) should satisfy are discussed. First, however, we define the following n-dimensional gradient functions:

$$\nabla h_t(y_t) = \left\{\partial h_t(y_t)/\partial y_t^j\right\}, \tag{16}$$

$$\nabla \pi_t(m_t) = \left\{\partial \pi_t(m_t)/\partial m_t^j\right\}, \tag{17}$$

$$\nabla_1 \pi_t(m_T, y_T) = \left\{\partial \pi_T(m_T, y_T)/\partial m_T^j\right\}, \tag{18}$$

$$\nabla_2 \pi_T(m_T, y_T) = \left\{\partial \pi_T(m_T, y_T)/\partial y_T^j\right\}. \tag{19}$$

The set of conditions is:

$$z_t^* = z_{t+1}^* A_t + \nabla \pi_t(m_t^*), \tag{20}$$

$$z_T^* = \nabla_1 \pi_T(m_T^*, y_T^*),$$ (21)

$$w_t^* = w_{t+1}^* C_t + z_{t+1}^* B_t \nabla h_t(y_t^*),$$ (22)

$$w_T^* = \nabla_2 \pi_T(m_T^*, y_T^*),$$ (23)

$$w_{t+1}^* D_t f_t(x_t^*) - g_t(x_t^*) \geqslant w_{t+1}^* f_t(x_t) - g_t(x_t), \quad \text{for all } x_t \in \Omega_t.$$ (24)

The optimal solution in the above equations is denoted by asterisks. Under certain additional assumptions, which will be presented in the next section, these conditions become the necessary conditions for the problem.

The above conditions can be intuitively interpreted in the following way. First, the interpretation of eqs. (21) and (23), called the transversality conditions, follow immediately from the definition of the adjoint function and the residual profit function. Eq. (20), which is called an adjoint condition, gives the total effect from time t through $T-1$ of an additional unit of market response in time t. The right-hand side of (20) decomposes this into the marginal profit in time t, $\nabla \pi_t(m_t^*)$ and the marginal profit from periods $t+1$ through $T-1$, $z_{t+1}^* A_t$. This follows from the definition of the adjoint function, z_{t+1}^*, and eq. (7). A similar interpretation can be given to eq. (22). The first term in this equation, $w_{t+1}^* C_t$, gives the marginal effect of goodwill from periods $t+1$ through $T-1$, while the second term, $z_{t+1}^* B_t \nabla h_t(y_t^*)$, gives the marginal value of goodwill in time t. Finally, eq. (24), called the Hamiltonian condition, may be interpreted as follows. Given a decision x_t, $w_{t+1}^* D_t f_t(x_t)$ is the total value of goodwill created over all future periods, from which the cost $g_t(x_t)$ must be deducted. Choose x_t^* to maximize this net value.

3.2. Central lemma

Using the conditions stated above, we now define the linear approximation of the incremental value of changing from a current solution to an alternative solution.

Definition. Given a current solution $X' = \{x_0', \ldots, x_{T-1}'\}$ and an alternative solution $X = \{x_0, \ldots, x_{T-1}\}$, define $L(X, X')$ to be the "linear approximation of the incremental value of moving to X from X'". It is formally defined by the system

$$z_t' = z_{t+1}' A_t + \nabla \pi_t(m_t'),$$ (25)

$$z_T' = \nabla_1 \pi_T(m_T', y_T'),$$ (26)

$$w_t' = w_{t+1}' C_t + z_{t+1}' B_t \nabla h_t(y_t'),$$ (27)

$$w'_T = \nabla_2 \pi_T(m'_T, y'_T),$$
(28)

$$\ell_t(x_t, x'_t) = \{w'_{t+1} f_t(x_t) - g_t(x_t)\} - \{w'_{t+1} f_t(x'_t) - g_t(x'_t)\},$$
(29)

$$L(X, X') = \sum_{t=0}^{T-1} \ell_t(x_t, x'_t).$$
(30)

We now show, in the following lemma, that $L(X, X')$ overestimates the incremental value of moving from the current solution, X', to an alternative solution, X. The lemma does not depend on the feasibility of either X' or X and is, therefore, useful for considering various upper bound solutions when the constraint set is relaxed. The lemma, however, does require $\pi_t(m_t)$, $h_t(y_t)$ and $\pi_T(m_T, y_T)$ to be concave.

Lemma 1. Suppose π_t, h'_t, and π_t are concave. Then
(a) $V(X') + L(X, X') \geq V(X)$
(b) If π_t and h_t are linear for all t, $V(X') + L(X, X') = V(X)$

Proof.
(a) By definition (eq. (8)):

$$V(X') - V(X) = \sum_{t=0}^{T-1} \{\pi_t(m'_t) - g_t(x'_t) - \pi_t(m_t) + g(x_t)\}$$

$$+ \pi_T(m_T, y_T) - \pi_T(m'_T, y'_T).$$

Since $\pi_t(m_t)$ and $\pi_T(m_T, y_T)$ are concave

$$V(X') - V(X) - \sum_{t=0}^{T-1} \{g_t(x_t) - g_t(x'_t)\} \geq \sum_{t=0}^{T-1} \{\nabla \pi'_t(m'_t - m_t)\}$$

$$+ \nabla_1 \pi'_T(m'_T - m_T) + \nabla_2 \pi'_T(y'_T - y_T).$$

From eqs. (25), (26) and (28), we have

$$V(X') - V(X) - \sum_{t=0}^{T-1} \{g_t(x_t) - g_t(x'_t)\}$$

$$\geq \sum_{t=0}^{T-1} (z'_t - z'_{t+1} A_t)(m'_t - m_t)$$

$$+ z'_T(m'_T - m_T) + w'_T(y'_T - y_T).$$

Rearranging terms and since $z_0 = z_0'$:

$$V(X') - V(X) - \sum_{t=0}^{T-1} \{g_t(x_t) - g_t(x_t')\}$$

$$\geq \sum_{t=0}^{T-1} \{z_{t+1}'[(m_{t+1}' - A_t m_t')$$

$$- (m_{t+1} - A_t m_t)]\} + w_T'(y_T' - y_T).$$

From eq. (27):

$$\geq \sum_{t=0}^{T-1} \{z_{t+1}' B_t[h_t(y_t') - h_t(y_t)]\} + w_T'(y_T' - y_T).$$

Since $h_t(y_t)$ is concave:

$$\geq \sum_{t=0}^{T-1} \{z_{t+1}' B_t \nabla h_t' \cdot (y_t' - y_t)\} + w_T'(y_T' - y_T).$$

From eq. (15):

$$\geq \sum_{t=0}^{T-1} \{w_t' - w_{t+1}' C_t)(y_t' - y_t)\} + w_T'(y_T' - y_T).$$

Rearranging terms and since $y_0 = y_0'$:

$$\geq \sum_{t=0}^{T-1} \{w_{t+1}'[f_t(x_t') - f_t(x_t)]\}.$$

Therefore, from eq. (29):

$$V(X') - V(X) \geq \sum_{t=0}^{T-1} \{[w_{t+1}' f_t(x_t') - g_t(x_t')]$$

$$- [w_{t+1}' f_t(x_t) - g_t(x_t)]\} = -L(X, X'),$$

$$V(X') + L(X, X') \geq V(X).$$

(b) In the proof for part (a), the steps producing inequalities for the general concave case are equalities for the linear case.

3.3. Necessary and sufficient conditions

In lemma 1 it was shown that a linear approximation of the incremental value of moving from a solution X' to X, $L(X, X')$ overestimated the actual incremental value. We now use these results to determine the sufficient conditions for an optimal solution in terms of the linear approximations.

Definition. A linear estimated optimum, given a previous solution X', is a solution X'' which satisfies

$$L(X'', X') = \max_{X \in \Omega} L(X, X') = \sum_{t=0}^{T-1} \max_{x_t \in \Omega_t} l_t(x_t, x_t'). \tag{31}$$

Theorem 1. Let X^* represent an optimum solution to the problem, then
    (a) $V(X') + L(X'', X') \geqslant V(X^*)$.
    (b) Equality holds for part (a), if π_t and h_t are linear.
    (c) $L(X'', X') = 0$ implies $V(X'') = V(X^*)$.

Proof.
    (a) The proof follows directly from lemma 1. Since lemma 1 holds for any X, it must also hold for a specific X:

$$V(X') + L(X, X') \geqslant V(X),$$

$$V(X') + \max_{X \in \Omega} L(X, X') \geqslant \max_{X \in \Omega} V(X) = V(X^*).$$

    (b) Follows immediately from lemma 1.
    (c) Follows immediately from (a).

Part (c) is simply the discrete maximum principle. It says that if there is a point which is its own linear estimated optimum, then it is optimal. Part (a), however, tells us considerably more. The maximum linear estimation of any point X' provides an *upper bound* on the optimal solution. Furthermore, the estimated solution X'' bears careful investigation, for it can only depart from optimality by the amount of deviation of π_t and h_t from linearity in a region around X' containing X''.

This suggests the following iterative procedure.
    (1) Find an initial solution.
    (2) Given a current solution X' find the feasible solution X'' which maximizes $L(X'', X')$.
    (3) If this leads to an improved value of the objective function, let $X'' \rightarrow X'$ and go back to (2).

(4) Otherwise consider the feasible solutions X_t'' where all but k of the successive x_j's; $x_j, \ldots, x_{j+k}$ are held at their values in x_t' and $x_1 \ldots x_{1+k}$ are set to their value in x_t''.

(5) If any of these solutions lead to an improved value of the objective function let X_t'' be the best such solution, $X_t'' \rightarrow X'$, and go back to (2).

(6) Otherwise halt.

Theorem 1 is especially useful since the computation of X'' and $L(X'', X')$ decomposes the problem into $T-1$ separate problems. Theorem 1(c) provides a sufficiency condition for optimality. We now provide a necessary condition which is stronger than Srinivasan's necessary condition.

Theorem 2. If f_t is concave and g_t and Ω_t are convex, then there exists at least one optimal solution, X^*, satisfying

$$\max_{x \in \Omega} L(X, X^*) = 0,$$

provided π_t and h_t possess continuous first partials.

Proof. By hypothesis, the functions $\ell_t(x_t, x_t^*)$ are concave, and hence possess a unique local optimum which is the global optimum. But at any optimum point $X^* = \{x_t^*\}$, each $\ell_t(x_t, x_t^*)$ must be at least a local optimum since by assumption there is an asymptotically accurate linear approximation to the function there. Hence, the global maximum for each $\ell_t(x_t, x_t^*)$ must be zero.

4. Computational results

At this point, it is probably helpful to compare the procedure suggested here to the one used by Srinivasan [15] and in the process, compare both with Little–Lodish. Although the Srinivasan procedure and the Little–Lodish procedure were applied to a special case of the model proposed here, we can, in general, compare the approaches.

Under the Srinivasan procedure, one starts with an initial estimate of the value of the adjoint functions and the known value of the state variable at $t = 0$. The value of the adjoint functions at time $t = 1$ are determined using the adjoint equation which is equivalent to eqs. (20) and (22) of our problem. Then the Hamiltonian is maximized to obtain a solution for the first time period. Once the solution is known for a given time period, the value of the state variable and the adjoint function can be computed for the next time period using the adjoint equation. This procedure is repeated until a solution is obtained for each time period and a solution for the adjoint function and the state variable at time T is determined. Knowledge of the state variable in time T provides another estimate of the value of the adjoint function in time T by using the transversality conditions, our eqs. (21) and (23). If these two estimates of the adjoint function at time T are "close" then the procedure terminates. If not, the procedure is repeated with a new estimate of the adjoint functions at $t = 0$. The new estimate of the adjoint function is essentially obtained by changing the previous estimate by the difference between the two adjoint functions at time T, weighted by the product of the carryover matrices for each time period.

Our procedure and the Srinivasan procedure decompose a multi-period problem into a sequence of one-period optimizations. Srinivasan's procedure uses successive approximations in matching the adjoint variables, while the new procedures uses successive linear approximations to the concave portion of the model. Srinivasan's procedure has the disadvantage that successive iterations may not provide improved solutions: there is no monotonicity guarantee. Furthermore, the termination condition and other parameters may have to be adjusted for different types of problems to avoid instability and premature termination. By contrast, the new procedure provides monotonicity of successive iterations, requires no parameter settings, and possesses a natural criterion, i.e. when two successive iterations produce no improvement in the objective functions. Finally, the new procedure provides upper bounds on the optimal solution to provide an immediate check as to how good the current solution is.

In contrast, the Little–Lodish procedure does *not* decompose the multi-period problem into a sequence of one-period optimizations. Instead, the procedure starts with any solution and examines the marginal effect of changing the solution for each time period. It then makes the change that yields the greatest marginal effect iteratively. This continues until the budget is exhausted. Once this occurs, the procedure then checks to determine if any changes in the solution might lead to an improvement.

4.1. Computational test results

Srinivasan was gracious enough to provide the authors with the computer programs that he used for comparing his procedure with the Little–Lodish procedure for the media scheduling problem. This was easily modified to include the new procedure as well.

Srinivasan solved 12 5-period multi-media problems. These 12 problems varied the number of market segments (5 and 10), number of media options (10, 20, and 40) and whether or not interaction terms were used (problems with interaction terms were solved by branch-and-bound techniques). One problem was solved for each combination of factors. To provide direct comparability, we ran similar problems with 5, 10 and 20 time periods, 5 and 10 market segments, and 10, 20, 30 or 40 media options, all without interaction terms. The problems were randomly generated by the same method used by Srinivasan [25]. Four different problems were generated for each of the eight different 5-period problems, leading to 32 test problems. Because of increased cost, only 2 different problems were generated for the 8 different 10-period problems, leading to 16 test problems, and only 1 problem was generated for the 20 period problems, leading to 8 test problems. A total of 54 test problems were, therefore, generated.

A summary of the solution values obtained by the Little–Lodish, the Srinivasan, and the new procedure, as well as the final upper bound on optimality obtained by the new procedure for each problem type, averaged over replications, are presented in table 1. While the average does not contain all the information, it was not deemed worthwhile to present more complicated

Table 1
Comparison of solution values for the three procedures

T	m	n	Little–Lodish procedure	Srinivasan procedure	M.M.Z. procedure	Upper bound on optimum
5	5	10	1.18	1.52	1.54	1.57
		20	1.23	1.61	1.63	1.65
		30	1.97	2.50	2.52	2.53
		40	2.04	2.38	2.38	2.38
	10	10	2.34	3.44	3.44	3.45
		20	2.40	3.30	3.42	3.48
		30	3.58	4.68	4.80	4.84
		40	3.49	4.44	4.59	4.62
10	5	10	2.58	2.93	3.50	3.54
		20	1.94	2.20	2.78	2.78
		30	3.02	3.81	4.02	4.04
		40	2.90	3.47	3.97	4.07
	10	10	6.65	8.16	8.63	8.65
		20	4.80	5.16	6.90	6.92
		30	6.24	6.14	8.81	8.88
		40	6.52	6.13	8.48	8.60
20	5	10	2.21	2.69	3.22	3.42
		20	4.23	1.57	7.38	7.52
		30	5.10	0.98	6.62	6.70
		40	3.55	1.54	6.06	6.15
	10	10	9.22	1.06	13.80	13.84
		20	7.36	−4.92	12.67	12.83
		30	10.17	−7.89	16.53	16.53
		40	7.86	−4.76	13.63	13.93

Note: T = number of periods, m = number of market segments, n = number of media options. For $T = 5$ each case is the average of 4 different problems, for $T = 10$ an average of 2 different problems, for $T = 20$ a single problem.

statistics for such a limited number of sums. A very brief summary of the computation times for the three procedures, averaged over all problems for each time horizon length, are given in table 2.

The results indicate that for time horizons of 5 periods ($T = 5$), the Srinivasan procedure yields solutions that are always within 5% of the upper bound on optimality obtained from the new procedure. Since this 5% difference may be a considerable overestimate of the deviation from optimality, this confirms the findings of Srinivasan [25] that his procedure produces solutions that are very close to optimal for time horizons of this length. His procedure yields solutions that are 17–47% better than the Little–Lodish solutions. The computation time, however, is four times longer. The new procedure yields solutions that are only 0–4% better than the Srinivasan procedure; however, it should be noted that there is little room for improvement. At the same time, the new procedure only requires about one-half the computation time.

With longer time horizons, the new procedure yields progressively better solution values than the other two procedures for the problems. For problems with time horizons of 10 periods ($T = 10$), the new procedure yields solution values that are 6–44% better (median about 23%) than the Srinivasan procedure and its computation time is about one-third faster. The new procedure outperforms the Little–Lodish procedure by 30–44% (median about 36%); however, its computation time is about twice as long. Finally, the new procedure is never more than 2.5% away from the optimal solution as evidenced by the upper bound to optimality.

With time horizons of 20 periods ($T = 20$), the Srinivasan procedure performs much worse than the Little–Lodish procedure for 7 of the 8 problems. In 3 of the 7 problems, the Srinivasan procedure yielded a negative profit. The new procedure outperforms the Little–Lodish procedure by 30–74%, with a median of about 65%. Its computation times are slightly longer than the Srinivasan procedure and not quite twice as long as the Little–Lodish procedure.

In general the results indicate that the new procedure is much more robust

Table 2
Comparison of computation times for the three procedures

T	Little–Lodish procedure	Srinivasan procedure	M.M.Z. procedure
5	3	13	7
10	11	41	26
20	44	72	79

Note: T = number of periods. Computation times (in seconds) are on the CDC 6600. The three procedures were programmed in FORTRAN IV.

than either the Srinivasan or the Little–Lodish procedure and achieves near optimal results for multi-media problems. Out of the 54 problems tested, it yield the best solution 52 times and the second best twice. The differences in computation times are not extreme enough to differentiate between procedures. Clearly, additional testing of the three procedures would be desirable, both for this problem and for other problems encompassed by the general dynamic market response model.

Appendix

In this appendix, stronger sufficiency conditions will be presented which generally will not have the decomposition property. However, an approximate decomposition which does will be suggested. In addition, methods for extending the procedure to situations in which incremental market response functions is nonconcave will be considered.

More powerful sufficiency condition

It is possible to provide a more powerful sufficiency condition for optimality than theorem 1. However, the use of this condition generally does not allow the problem to be decomposed in a period-by-period manner. Basically, this procedure involves using k different feasible solutions (e.g. satisfying eqs. (3)–(8)) and using the linear evaluation of moving between these solutions to form a piecewise linear approximation to the concave part of the model. Since increasing the number of linear evaluations will, in general, improve the "fit" to the concave part of the model, the bounds and the sufficiency condition obtained are asymptotically "perfect". These results are now stated more formally as theorem 3.

Theorem 3. Let $X^{(1)}, \ldots, X^{(k)}$ be k feasible solutions to the T period problem defined by eqs. (3)–(8) and generate a new solution $\tilde{X}$ by

$$V(X^{(ii)}) + L(X, X^{(ii)}) = \max_{x \in \Omega} \min_i \left\{ V(X^{(i)}) + L(X, X^{(i)}) \right\},$$

where i represents the minimizing values of i. Then
(a) $V(X^{(ii)}) + L(\tilde{X}, X^{(ii)}) \geqslant V(X^*)$,
(b) $L(\tilde{X}, X^{(ii)}) \leqslant 0 \Rightarrow L(\tilde{X}, X^{(ii)}) = 0 \Rightarrow X^{(ii)}$ is optimal.

Proof.
(a) From the central lemma

$$V(X^{(i)}) + L(X, X^{(i)}) \geqslant V(X),$$

$$\min_{i} \left\{ V(X^{(i)}) + L(X, X^{(i)}) \right\} \geq V(X),$$

$$\max_{x \in \Omega} \min_{i} \left\{ V(X^{(i)}) + L(X, X^{(i)}) \right\} \geq \max_{x \in \Omega} V(X) = V(X^*).$$

(b) This follows from (a) and simply means that if a piecewise linear approximation from the current solution to any other feasible solution produces an estimated increment that is not greater than zero, then the current solution must be optimal.

A decomposable approximation

Since the approach presented as theorem 3 generally will not be decomposable into periods, we now investigate an approximation which is decomposable. First, we define the following term.

Definition. Let $X^{(1)} \dots X^{(k)}$ be k feasible solutions to the problem defined by eqs. (3)–(8). Define a linear evaluation of the decomposable approximation to the problem at the point x as

$$M(X, X^{(j)}) = \sum_{t=0}^{T-1} \left\{ \min_{i} \left[c_t^{(i)} + w_{t+1}^{(i)} f_t(x_t) \right] - g_t(x_t) \right\},$$

where $c_t^{(i)} = \pi_{t+1}^{(i)} - w_{t+1}^{(i)} f_t(x_t^{(i)})$.

Proposition.

$$M(\tilde{X}, X^{(j)}) = \max_{x \in \Omega} M(X, X^{(j)}) \leq \max_{x \in \Omega} \min_{i} \left\{ V(X^{(i)}) + L(X, X^{(i)}) \right\}.$$

Proof.

$$\max_{x \in \Omega} \min_{i} \left\{ V(X^{(i)}) + L(X, X^{(i)}) \right\} = \max_{x \in \Omega} \min_{i} \sum_{t=0}^{T-1} \left\{ \pi_{t+1}^{(i)} - g_t(x_t^{(i)}) \right.$$

$$\left. + w_{t+1}^{(i)} \left[f_t(x_t) - f_t(x_t^{(i)}) \right] + g_t(x_t^{(i)}) - g_t(x_t) \right\}$$

$$\geq \max_{x \in \Omega} \sum_{t=0}^{T-1} \left\{ \min_{i} \left[c_t^{(i)} + w_{t+1}^{(i)} f_t(x_t) \right] - g_t(x_t) \right\}$$

$$\geq \max_{x \in \Omega} M(X, X^{(j)}).$$

In the above formulation, $M(X, X^{(j)})$ may be maximized on a period-by-period basis. The proposition shows that the separable linear evaluation is less than the linear evaluation for all time periods, so $M(X, X^{(j)})$ no longer provides an upper bound on the optimal solution. From the above proposition we have the following relationship between the linear evaluation of the entire problem and the linear evaluation to the separable approximation:

$$M(\tilde{X}, X^{(j)}) \leqslant V(X^{(ii)}) + L(\tilde{X}, X^{(ii)}) \geqslant V(X^*). \tag{32}$$

If the piecewise linear approximation provides a fairly good fit to the concave part of the model, we would expect that

$$\min_i \left\{ V(X^{(i)}) + L(X, X^{(i)}) \right\} \approx V(X), \tag{33}$$

which would imply that

$$M(\tilde{X}, X^{(j)}) \leqslant V(\tilde{X}). \tag{34}$$

Therefore, if

$$M(\tilde{X}, X^{(j)}) \geqslant \max_i V(X^{(i)}), \tag{35}$$

we would expect that

$$V(\tilde{X}) \geqslant \max_i V(X^{(i)}). \tag{36}$$

This would mean that X would represent an improvement over the current best feasible solution. However, to achieve this last result, two conflicting objectives are required:

(a) many wide spaced linear evaluations so that the piecewise linear fit is good, then theorem 3 is powerful; and

(b) few closely spaced linear evaluations so that the process of finding a new solution does not destroy eq. (35).

Whether these conflicting objectives can be accomplished in practice must be tested empirically.

Solution procedure

Here a solution procedure based on the central lemma for solving the problem defined by eqs. (3)–(8) is suggested. The procedure is divided into the following four phases: (1) Phase I—Relaxed Solution; (2) Phase II—Initial Feasible Solution; (3) Phase III—Rapid Improvement; (4) Phase IV—Slow

Improvement/Termination. A flow chart of the first three phases is presented in fig. 1. Each phase will now be discussed in detail.

Phase I: In this phase, the relaxed concave problem is solved. First transform the problem so that $g_t(x_t)$ is linear. Each f_t (and Ω_t) is replaced by its concave (convex) envelope.

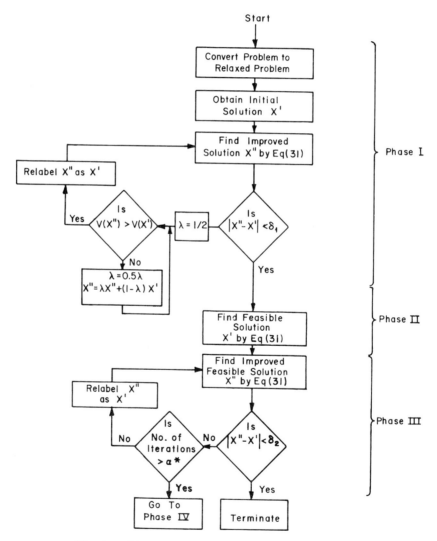

*Number of iterations since last improvement in V(X)

Fig. 1. Solution procedure for first three phases.

The relaxed problem will be relatively easy to solve and should provide an excellent upper bound on the objective value of the optimal solution and a policy that is "close" to the optimal policy in the policy space.

The relaxed problem may be solved in the following manner. First, pick an initial solution X' and apply the iterative procedure implied by eq. (24) to obtain an improved solution X''. If $V(X'') \geqslant V(X')$, then repeat the procedure using the point X''. If $V(X'') < V(X')$, search the space between X'' and X' to obtain a better solution. More formally, for some $0 \leqslant \lambda \leqslant 1$, $V(\lambda X'' + (1 - \lambda)X') \geqslant V(X')$. By successively reducing λ the improved point will be obtained. The procedure is terminated when $|X'' - X'| < \delta$. Since this solution only represents a starting point for the procedure, it is not necessary to obtain it to a fine degree of tolerance. The relaxed problem is a concave problem and a gradient method is being used to search for a solution, hence the optimum to the relaxed problem should be achieved.

The relaxed problem will provide an upper bound to the optimal solution and should provide a *good* upper bound. To demonstrate this, consider the following common case. The constraint set Ω_t represents the positive orthant and f_t is "S"-shaped. Suppose, as illustrated in fig. 2, that f_t does not change over time and that the relaxed optimal solution is $x_t^r = 0.30$, with the relaxed function f^r equal to f at $x = 0$ and $x = 0.90$. Since we only seek a solution that is close to the optimal in this phase, $f^r(0.30)$ may not be obtained directly, but it would be available in expectation if $x_t = 0$ is chosen two-thirds of the time and $x_t = 0.90$ one-third of the time. This solution should give approximately the same solution value as the optimum solution, $x_t = 0.30$ in each time period, due to the smoothing provided by the cumulative nature of "goodwill", if seasonal correction factors are ignored. The same argument suggests that the relaxed solution may be relatively good in policy space.

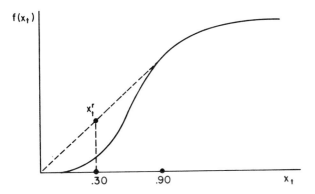

Fig. 2. Solution for the relaxed problem.

Phase II: The proof of the central lemma does not depend on using the same f_t for the two points x_t or x_t' or an even using the same g_t. Therefore, theorem 1(a) remains true if we use the relaxed problem for all terms with a prime, the original problem for nonprimed terms and maximize over the true constraint set.

The first maximizing feasible solution x_t^0 will provide an upper bound on the optimal solution that is strictly better than the one provided by the relaxed solution. This is because a linear approximation with the same slope as the relaxed problem is being used; however, since the constraint set is smaller and the relaxed solution overestimates the actual value of a solution, the solution value at x_t^0 will be less than the solution value of the relaxed problem. For reasons given in Phase I, the initial feasible solution may be expected to provide a solution that is "close" to the optimal and a policy that is "close to the optimal policy".

Phase III: Once a feasible solution is obtained, the iterative procedure suggested by theorem 1 is used. A new solution obtained by finding the feasible point that is the linear estimated optimum. Since there is no guarantee of monotonicity, both the best feasible solution to date, in terms of objective value, and the best upper bound to date, are saved. If at any point two successive X', X'' differ by no more than some allowed tolerance, then the procedure terminates. Otherwise, the procedures move to Phase IV if an iteration brings no improvement in the solution.

Phase IV: In this phase all periods but the first are fixed and the procedure is applied to obtain a solution for the first period. Then a solution is obtained for each period sequentially with all other periods remaining fixed. The procedure is then repeated for pairs of adjacent periods and then triads of adjacent periods. If at any point an improvement is obtained, return to Phase III.

If no improvement is obtained then repeat the above procedure using the best solution to date and the separable approximation method of the proposition following theorem 3. In other words, this method is used to obtain a solution for each period sequentially and for adjacent pairs and triplets sequentially. If an improvement is obtained return to Phase III, otherwise terminate the procedure.

Extension to nonconcave h_t

In many problems of interest, h_t will not be concave, which is required in the central lemma, but "S"-shaped. In these situations it would be possible to relax the problem and apply Phase I as before; however, the solution and policy obtained from the relaxed problem generally will not be as close to the optimal solution and policy as if h_t were concave. This is because, while the control variable x_t can be pulsed arbitrarily over a short span of two or three periods to approximate a randomization procedure, the state variable y_t is a smoothed average of past advertising and cannot.

The very stability of the state variable y_t, however, suggests that a linear approximation of h_t may be quite satisfactory in the region around the optimal. Therefore, if a good initial solution is obtained, the application of Phases III and IV should lead to improvements even though bounding and sufficiency conditions are no longer available.

The question is, of course, how to obtain a "good" initial solution. One approach would be to use Phase I as before, to obtain the relaxed solution, but to modify Phase II so that more caution is used in moving to a feasible solution. One such modification might be to simply choose the "nearest" feasible solution to the relaxed solution ignoring the linear approximation to the objective function. Alternatively, another heuristic procedure might be developed for obtaining an initial feasible solution that would be "close" to the optimal.

References

[1] R. Avery, A.A. Mitchell and R. Winer, Issues in modelling the carry-over effects of advertising, in: K.L. Bernhardt, ed., Marketing: 1776–1976 and Beyond (American Marketing Association, Chicago, Ill., 1976) 473–477.

[2] R.L. Ackoff and J.R. Emshoff, Advertising research at Anheuser-Busch, Inc., Sloan Management Review 16 (1975) 1–16.

[3] F.M. Bass and D.G. Clarke, Testing distributed lag models of advertising effect, Journal of Marketing Research 9 (1972) 298–308.

[4] M.D. Canon, C.D. Cullum, Jr. and E. Polak, Theory of Optimal Control and Mathematical Programming (McGraw-Hill Book Company, New York, 1976).

[5] D. Chakravarti, A.A. Mitchell and R. Staelin, A cognitive approach to model building and evaluation, in: B. Greenberg and D. Ballinger, eds., Contemporary Marketing Thought (American Marketing Association, Chicago, Ill., 1977) 213–218.

[6] D. Chakravarti, A.A. Mitchell and R. Staelin, Judgment based marketing decision models: An investigation of the decision calculus approach, Management Science 25 (1979) 251–263.

[7] D. Chakravarti, A.A. Mitchell and R. Staelin, A procedure for parameterizing decision calculus models of market response, in: R. Leone, ed., Proceedings of the Second TIMS/ORSA Conference on Market Measurement and Analysis (TIMS College on Marketing and the Institute of Management Sciences, Providence, R.I., 1981) 135–146.

[8] R.I. Haley, Sales effects of media weight, Journal of Advertising Research 18 (1978) 9–18.

[9] R.W. Jastram, A treatment of distributed lags in the theory of advertising expenditures, Journal of Marketing 20 (July 1955) 36–46.

[10] P. Kotler, Marketing Decision Making: A Model Building Approach (Holt, Rinehart and Winston, New York, 1971).

[11] J. Lambin, Measuring the profitability of advertising: An empirical study, Journal of Industrial Economics 17 (1969) 86–103.

[12] J. Lambin, Optimal allocation of competitive marketing efforts: An empirical study, Journal of Business 43 (1970).

[13] J.D.C. Little, Models and managers: The concept of a decision calculus, Management Science 16 (1970) B466–B485.

[14] J.D.C. Little, BRANDAID: A marketing-mix model, Parts 1 and 2, Operations Research 23 (1975) 628–673.

[15] J.D.C. Little, Aggregate advertising models: The state of the art, Operations Research 27 (1979) 629–667.

[16] J.D.C. Little and L.M. Lodish, A media planning calculus, Operations Research 17 (1969) 1–35.

[17] A.A. Mitchell and T.E. Morton, Toward a general dynamic model of market response, in: K.L. Bernhardt ed., Marketing: 1776–1976 and Beyond (American Marketing Association, Chicago, Ill., 1976) 639–643.

[18] D.B. Montgomery and A.J. Silk, Estimating dynamic effects of market communications expenditures, Management Science 18 (1972) B485–501.

[19] D.B. Montgomery, A.J. Silk and C.E. Zaragoza, A multi-product sales force allocation model, Management Science 18, Part II (1971) 3–24.

[20] M. Nerlove and K.J. Arrow, Optimal advertising policy under dynamic conditions, Econometrica 22 (1962) 129–142.

[21] K.S. Palda, The Measurement of Cumulative Advertising Effects (Prentice-Hall, Englewood Cliffs, N.J., 1964).

[22] D. Pekelman and E. Tse, Experimentation and budgeting in advertising: An adaptive control approach, Operations Research 28 (1980).

[23] L.S. Pontryagin, V.G. Boltyanskii, R.V. Gamkrelizde and E.F. Mishchenko, The Mathematical Theory of Optimal Processes (John Wiley and Sons, New York, 1962).

[24] S.P. Sethi, Dynamic optimal control models in advertising: A survey, SIAM Review 19 (1977) 685–725.

[25] V. Srinivasan, Decomposition of a multi-period media scheduling model in terms of single period equivalents, Management Science 23 (1976) 349–360.

[26] D.S. Tull, The carryover effect of advertising, Journal of Marketing 29 (1965) 46–53.

[27] C.B. Weinberg, Dynamic correction in marketing planning models, Management Science 22 (1976) 677–687.

TIMS Studies in the Management Sciences 18 (1982) 141–160
© North-Holland Publishing Company

OPTIMAL STRATEGIC BUSINESS UNITS PORTFOLIO ANALYSIS

Marcel CORSTJENS and David WEINSTEIN
INSEAD

The development of product-portfolio models has become an important research area in marketing strategy. This paper describes a normative strategic business unit portfolio model. It is based on recent development in strategic planning and the finance portfolio model. Special emphasis is put on the formal specification of the model and its implementation. The proposed model is evaluated in an application: (marketing–product policy; strategic planning–portfolio analysis).

1. Introduction

Two basic approaches to portfolio design have been put forward to date: the one derived from the field of finance, and the other developed by strategic planners. The different origins of these approaches have made integration difficult. In this paper we propose to combine these approaches into a normative strategic business unit (SBU)[1] portfolio model. Such integration, although proposed by others (e.g. [24]) has not yet been rigorously developed. The majority of strategic planners who prefer intuitive decision-making feel more at ease with descriptive conceptual frameworks than with formal optimization procedures. In addition, data requirements and estimation problems have also postponed a formal integration. The shortening of product life cycles has progressively reduced the data available and the estimation of the variance–covariance structure of the returns and risk aversion coefficients have proven extremely difficult. The proposed model deals with both types of problems. First, it not only provides "optimal solutions" for the portfolio problem but also tests the sensitivity of the results to marginal changes in some key parameters. Both should be extremely useful to strategic planners who prefer the more intuitive decision-making approaches. Second, it provides a methodology to cope with the important data and estimation problems.

In section 2 we discuss the appropriateness of existing finance and strategic

---

[1] A strategic business unit designates the smallest individual entity which is considered as a self-contained programme for resource allocation purposes. It may be a single combination of served markets, the function the product performs and its technology [1].

planning models for the SBU portfolio problem. The proposed model is specified in section 3 and potential implementation problems are discussed in section 4. The final part of the paper is devoted to an application of the model and an assessment of its contributions and shortcomings.

2. The two approaches to portfolio decisions

In the finance portfolio model the return on various investments (the ratio of annual profits after tax to investment) and the risk involved (measured by the variance and covariance structure of the returns) define an efficient set of portfolios. Management would then select the portfolio yielding maximum expected utility given their risk–return objectives (e.g. [17,23]). Several authors have suggested a straightforward application of the standard finance model to strategic decisions. Kotler [15], Kahane [12] and Wind [24] considered this in product-line decisions; Cardozo and Wind [4] and Salter [21] in product–market combinations and Abell [1] in SBU portfolios.

The strategic planning approach differs greatly. It incorporates two major concepts: (1) the "company–product–market fit", aimed at matching interest, skills and resources of the company to the needs of various market segments, while considering competition within them [13]; and (2) the "product–market portfolio", directed at balancing short and long-run profitability, given cash-flow constraint (e.g. [1,6,9,20,25]). This framework provides the criteria to determine the two basic dimensions of the product market portfolio: competitive position and market attractiveness. The Boston Consulting Group (BCG) concept is one of the operationalizations which allows analytical treatment. Their framework is derived from applications of the concepts of "experience curve" (e.g. [5]) and product life cycle (e.g. [19]) yielding four categories of SBUs: "cash-cows"; "stars", "question marks" and "dogs". Focus is placed on "relative market share" and "market growth" as indicators of competitive position and market attractiveness, respectively. An "effective" portfolio should be well balanced in terms of its cash-generating power (high relative market share and low growth) and its cash consumption needs (low relative market share and high market growth; e.g. [6]).

The applicability of the finance model to strategic portfolio decisions is limited in several respects. External lending and borrowing are a vital element in the finance framework, whereas internal financing of cash-consuming SBUs by cash-generating ones is a major contemporary constraint in product management. Hence, while strategic decisions require consideration of "cash flow", the finance model still revolves around "return". The finance model neither considers the dynamics of the real market situation, which often forces managers into trade-offs between short and long-term profitability, nor does it fully take into account the strategic determinants of competitive success, competitive position entry barriers and market opportunities [3,22], which determine the SBU investment pattern. These factors impede its immediate integration into strategic planning.

The strategic planning approach is equally open to criticism. Although a multi-factor strategic approach (e.g. [20]) may handle the risk directly to balance the proportion of SBUs at different stages of competitive advantage and market attractiveness, it does not explicitly incorporate the financial implications. Financial risk, as expressed by the variance–covariance of the returns, is not explicitly taken into consideration.

The usefulness of these two methods has been limited to situations for which they are normally employed. The finance model was developed for the formulation of investment strategies in the securities market, where issues such as risk–return preferences and uncertainty of return must be dealt with. The SBU portfolio framework, on the other hand, was designed to help managers create a more loosely defined "appropriate mix" of businesses. While the conceptual framework and measurement scales of the finance model may be treated analytically, the language and graphical representations of the strategic model are difficult to quantify. The model we propose in the next section is a first step towards the integration of both these approches.

Summarizing, our goal is to develop a more comprehensive strategic planning model to assist management in determining the composition of the desired portfolio of strategic business units for allocating scarce resources. To accomplish this task the analytical optimization approach to returns, variability and covariability of returns suggested by the finance model is integrated with the strategic and cash-flow balance considerations proposed by strategic planning models.

3. The proposed model

In their planning process management has to decide on the allocation of scarce resources (e.g. production capacity, personnel, working capital) to the set of available SBUs. The proposed model determines target levels for each SBU in such a way that management's expected utility is maximized, subject to several strategic and operational constraints. The expected utility function is assumed to be a quadratic function of the expected returns and the variance–covariance structure of the returns. This specification, which is borrowed from the finance portfolio model, is intuitively appealing since it implies that for a given risk level management will select the portfolio with the highest expected return and that, for a given expected level of returns, management will opt for the portfolio that minimizes the risk dimension. In addition, the quadratic utility function is concave and smooth since first derivatives exist at all points. Since portfolio decision-makers usually are risk averse the quadratic function will still be a good approximation to their actual expected utility function even if it is not actually quadratic [16].

This objective function can be expressed more formally as:

$$\max \mathrm{E}(U) = \sum_{i=1}^{n} x_i \,\mathrm{E}(R_i) + \theta \sum_{i=1}^{n} \sum_{j=1}^{n} x_i x_j \sigma_{ij}, \qquad (1)$$

where

$\mathrm{E}(U)$ = expected utility;

n = the number of SBUs;

x_i = target number of units for SBU$_i$;

$\mathrm{E}(R_i)$ = the expected return (profit after tax) per unit sold of SBU$_i$ for the relevant decision period;

σ_{ij} = the covariance between the expected rate of return of SBU$_i$ and SBU$_j$;

θ = a measure of risk aversion which may vary between $+\infty$ (infinite risk taking) and $-\infty$ (infinite risk aversion), with 0 for risk neutrality.

The following two assumptions specify the realm of the applicability of our model.

(1) There exist no cost interdependencies between SBUs.

(2) Experience effects due to learning and economies of scale occur at discrete points. Thus, $\mathrm{E}(R_i)$ is a function of the cumulative production of SBU$_i$ up to the beginning of the decision period. However, no experience effects are included during the decision period.

The objective function may be optimized subject to several constraints: (1) operational constraints, (2) system inflexibilities, (3) demand constraints, (4) strategic constraints, (5) *ad hoc* constraints, and (6) non-negativity constraints.

The resulting model is used by management to determine the optimal target SBU portfolio for the coming period. The specific time frame used may be varied depending on the planning horizon of the firm (typically one year). This process is then repeated periodically.

3.1. Operational constraints

Existing production facilities, human and other material resources (machine capacity, sales force) may create bottlenecks in implementing a strategy. This may be expressed as follows:

$$\sum_{i=1}^{n} \alpha_{ki} x_i \leqslant \alpha_k, \quad \text{for all } k, \qquad (2)$$

where k = designates a scarce resource, $k = 1, \ldots, K$; α_{ki} = usage rate of resource k for one unit of SBU$_i$; and α_k = the upper bound (capacity) of resource k.

3.2. System inflexibilities

(a) Changes in an ongoing portfolio are usually limited by inertia. Short-run changes may not be possible in view of, for example, the need to act as a secure supplier for one's clients, and thus prevent from dropping an undesirable SBU:

$$\mu_{i\ell} \leq x_i \leq \mu_{iu}, \quad \text{for all } i, \tag{3}$$

where $\mu_{i\ell}$ = lower bound for x_i, and μ_{iu} = upper bound for x_i.

(b) A product may be part of a "bundle" bought by a customer or produced jointly by a given technological process. More formally, product complementarity or joint production may be expressed as follows:

$$\gamma_{ij\ell} \leq x_i/x_j \leq \gamma_{iju}, \quad \text{for the relevant } i, j, \tag{4}$$

where $\gamma_{ij\ell}$ = lower bound for x_i/x_j, and γ_{iju} = upper bound for x_i/x_j.

3.3. Demand constraint

The demand structure of the various SBUs is an important strategic input for the resource allocation process and the target levels for each SBU. This may be introduced in two alternative ways. An elaborate demand schedule may be used which takes into account both the effects of the price charged by an SBU on its quantity demanded and the cross elasticities with related SBUs. However, as explicit demand schedules are usually difficult to obtain, a more realistic (though also more restrictive) approach would be to estimate the most "pessimistic" and "optimistic" demand levels for each SBU at a given price level.

$$\delta_{\ell(p_i)} \leq x_i \leq \delta_{u(p_i)}, \tag{5}$$

where $\delta_{\ell(p_i)}$ = lower bound for the demand in SBU$_i$ at price p_i, and $\delta_{u(p_i)}$ = upper bound for the demand in SBU$_i$ at price p_i.

A number of the constraints (3) and (5) may be redundant. To make the model more parsimonious, both these constraints may be combined into

$$a_i \leq x_i \leq b_i,$$

where $a_i = \max[\mu_{i\ell}, \delta_{\ell(p_i)}]$, and $b_i = \min[\mu_{iu}, \delta_{u(p_i)}]$.

It should be noted that optimization may be performed subject to the SBUs' "prevailing prices", thus assuming prices to be exogenously determined. The impact of different price schedules on the optimum may be subsequently tested by a sensitivity analysis of the price variable. It would be computationally more efficient to build the price variable directly into the model as a decision variable. Furthermore, the model could be made more complete by introducing additional marketing support variables (advertising, sales force) to specify the response function for each SBU. Further research related to these issues is under way.

3.4. Strategic constraints

3.4.1. The exposure constraint

The objective function takes into account the risk of the variability of the returns of the portfolio. There are, however, other types of risk [2] which the manager has to face simultaneously. For example, the higher the dependency on success in a single market, the higher the investment risk to which the portfolio is exposed. More formally:

$$\sum_{i \in I_j} x_i c_i \bigg/ \sum_{i=1}^{n} x_i c_i \leq \omega_{I_j}, \tag{6}$$

where

c_i = cost per unit sold in SBU$_i$;
$x_i c_i$ = total costs for SBU$_i$;
I_j = category j, grouping several SBUs for risk exposure purposes ($j = 1, \ldots, J$);
ω_{I_j} = upper limit of the proportion of category I_j in the total outlays for all SBUs.

Notice how this notion of exposure is fundamentally different from the "covariance of returns" concept in the objective function of our model. While the expected utility function deals with individual SBUs and the portfolio as a whole, this constraint treats specific clusters of SBUs as designated by management. For example, the sale of four products to five countries might imply twenty different SBUs. Concern with overexposure in one of the countries will place four individual SBUs in this cluster (I_j) for which we would aggregate the total costs and limit the proportion of the total outlay. This constraint deals directly with downside risk, which is a major consideration in portfolio management and has not so far been explicitly taken into account in portfolio optimization models.

---

[2] Some information on other types of risk might be included in the moment-generating function of the portfolio's returns. However, since the finance model takes into account only the first two moments, other types of risk are dealt with as constraints. Moreover, the estimation of the parameters of the moment-generating function of the returns of the SBUs would pose insurmountable problems to the implementation of our model.

3.4.2. Strategic balance of cash flow

A second contingency, conceptually different from the risk–return considerations of the objective function, is based on the strategic balance of the cash inflows and outflows of the portfolio. As outside debt or equity financing become more difficult to obtain at a reasonable cost, self-financing becomes a major concern and promotes an ensuing interest in cash-flow considerations. In line with BCG's "market share/market growth" framework, this notion of the strategic balance of the cash-flow may be expressed by two constraints: (i) the configurations of the portfolio's SBUs in the market share/market growth matrix (proportion of SBUs per quadrant), and (ii) the portfolio's center of gravity.

(i) Proportion of SBUs per quadrant. The criterion of "balance" of cash flows is determined by the firm's internally sustainable growth in a given return-on-equity structure. A financial structure permitting, for instance, greater debt financing should engender a concentration of cash-using SBUs, whilst a conservative structure would call for more cash generating SBUs. Thus, short, medium and long-term financial resources would be assured by sufficient "cash-cows", "stars" and "question marks" (naturally, one would like to minimize the number of "dogs").

To implement this concept, we need an operational typology of the four mutually exclusive categories of SBUs (dogs, cash-cows, stars and question marks). This is somewhat arbitrary as the lines between high and low relative market share and growth relate to the cash generation experience of the company [6]. Since the latter varies across businesses, we allow management to develop its own classification scheme, as the definition of business units is largely a subjective and *ad hoc* process [1]. The following constraints express the above concern:

$$\lambda_{k\ell} \leqslant \sum_{i \in \lambda_k} x_i F_i \bigg/ \sum_{i=1}^{n} x_i F_i \leqslant \lambda_{ku}, \quad \text{for all } k, \tag{7}$$

where

F_i = net cash per unit generated by SBU_i;

λ_k = index set of the number of SBUs in quadrant k; this index set becomes a decision variable if the model is extended from a single period to a multi-period model;

k = quadrant k, $k = 1,\dots,4$;

$\lambda_{k\ell}$ = lower bound of the proportion of total cash generated in quadrant k; and

λ_{ku} = upper bound of the proportion of total cash balance in quadrant k.

(ii) Center of gravity. Various SBU configurations might satisfy the previous constraints and still have different financial implications for the short and longer terms; for example, for the present aggregate cash balance and outlook for the future. There are two alternative sets of constraints which may be used. Whereas short-term balance specifications might be treated by an aggregate cash-balance constraint only, the outlook for the future cash balance depends on the strategic configuration of the portfolio. To help select the most appropriate constraint we introduce a summary measure of the relative market share/growth matrix, i.e. an index of the center of gravity of the portfolio.

The location of the center of gravity represents both the aggregate cash-balance profile of the portfolio and the cash-balance outlook. More specifically, a portfolio configuration with gravity center in the "dog" quadrant may represent a cash balance, yet the outlook would not be as attractive as one with a gravity center in the "star" quadrant which also represented a similar short-term balance.

A difficulty which arises in this context is that in reality SBUs do not always follow the theoretically expected cash-flow pattern as specified by the strategic planning framework. For example, a "cash-cow" may fail to deliver cash because of depressed market prices, unexpected working capital requirements, or equipment replacement needs. Thus, the value of sales may not be proportional to the cash generated. There are two alternatives for treating such "Pyrrhic victories" [7]: (a) use a center of gravity specification based on sales value and add a cash-balance constraint, or (b) use the actual cash-flow values of the SBUs and specify a corresponding center of gravity. The alternatives would entail the following respective sets of constraints.

(a) Separate center of gravity and cash-balance constraints:

$$\pi_\ell \leqslant \sum_{i=1}^{n} x_i p_i \rho_i \bigg/ \sum_{i=1}^{m} x_i p_i \leqslant \tau_u, \tag{8}$$

$$\chi_\ell \leqslant \sum_{i=1}^{n} x_i p_i \eta_i \bigg/ \sum_{i=1}^{n} x_i p_i \leqslant \chi_u, \tag{9}$$

$$\xi_\ell \leqslant \sum_{i=1}^{n} x_i F_i \leqslant \xi_u, \tag{10}$$

where

ρ_i	= the growth coordinate of SBU$_i$;
η_i	= the relative market share coordinate of SBU$_i$;
π_ℓ, π_u	= lower and upper bounds, respectively, of the growth coordinate of the center of gravity based on SBU sales;
χ_ℓ, χ_u	= lower and upper bounds, respectively, of the relative market share coordinate of the center of gravity based on SBU sales; and
ξ_ℓ, ξ_u	= lower and upper bounds for the overall cash-flow balance of the portfolio.

(b) Center of gravity based on cash generation per unit:

$$\rho_\ell \leqslant \sum_{i=1}^{n} x_i F_i \rho_i \Big/ \sum_{i=1}^{m} x_i F_i \leqslant \rho_u, \tag{11}$$

$$\eta_\ell \leqslant \sum_{i=1}^{n} x_i F_i \eta_i \Big/ \sum_{i=1} x_i F_i \leqslant \eta_u, \tag{12}$$

where

ρ_i	= the growth coordinate of SBU$_i$;
η_i	= the relative market share coordinate of SBU$_i$;
ρ_ℓ, ρ_u	= lower and upper bounds, respectively, of the growth coordinate of the center of gravity based on SBU cash flows; and
η_ℓ, η_u	= lower and upper bounds, respectively, of the relative market share coordinate of the center of gravity based on SBU cash flows.

3.5. Ad hoc constraint

In addition to operational and strategic constraints there may be other considerations which, while bearing on the portfolio, are idiosyncratic or transitory. For example, management might impose other constraints on the model to minimize their commitment to a certain market because of a potential temporary political instability in the market.

3.6. Non-negativity constraints

For the optimizing algorithm not to reach a negative solution for any SBU, we should add the following constraints:

$$x_i \geqslant 0, \quad \text{for all } i. \tag{13}$$

Some of the latter constraints may be redundant in light of (3) and (5).

4. Implementation

We have presented the formal structure of our model in which the decision variable is x_i, i.e. the optimal number of units for SBU$_i$ for all i. The model includes several parameters which are directly measurable (i.e. α_{ki}, c_i, ρ_i and η_i) and some which management must supply (i.e. α_k, $\mu_{i\ell}$, μ_{iu}, $\gamma_{ij\ell}$, γ_{iju}, $\delta_{\ell(p_i)}$, $\delta_{u(p_i)}$, ω_{I_j}, λ_k, ρ_ℓ, ρ_u, η_ℓ, η_u, π_ℓ, π_u, χ_ℓ, χ_u, ξ_ℓ, ξ_u, $\lambda_{k\ell}$, and λ_{ku}). The latter might be more difficult for management to specify. However, since the concepts are implicitly used for strategic decisions, the manager, after some training, should be able to provide the necessary inputs. Because he has to specify these parameters he will have to consider important strategic issues—an indirect benefit of using the model. The third category of inputs (R_i, σ_{ij} and θ) must be estimated. The following estimation procedure is proposed.

4.1. Estimation of returns (R_i) and variance–covariance structure of returns (σ_{ij})

There are three basic approaches to this estimation problem. Early financial portfolio models suggested the use of historical records of SBU performance on the basis of which the expected return and variance for each SBU as well as the covariance matrix between returns on all activities could be extrapolated [17]. This procedure requires that the number of observations on each SBU in the portfolio be greater than N (the number of different SBUs) in order to avoid singularity of the variance–covariance matrix. In addition, such data may not be available especially as SBUs enter and leave the portfolio.

Some of these problems may be overcome by using a single or multi-index approach which assumes that the returns of each element in the portfolio are linearly related to one or several common-market indices, which are readily available (GNP, Dow–Jones, etc.). However, in rapidly changing environments, projecting such historical statistical relationships into the future is highly questionable.

To avoid these difficulties, we propose a different estimation procedure which is based on the evidence that the variability of returns may be explained, on a cross-sectional basis, by a set of strategic characteristics of the relevant SBUs: relative market-share, growth, capital intensity, extent of differentiation and the like [3,8,13,22].[3] This relationship is expressed in the following regression model:

$$R = y\beta + e, \tag{14}$$

where

R = the vector of returns ($N \times 1$);
y = the matrix of observations of the strategic characteristics of the SBUs ($N \times M$);
β = the vector of regression coefficients ($M \times 1$); and
e = the random error term ($N \times 1$).

Since this should express a reliable theoretical relationship we may have the

---

[3] The PIMS project, using a similar linear model, claims to have captured 80% of the variation in profitability of more than 1,000 businesses across industries [22].

option of estimating the returns as follows:

$$E(\hat{R}) = y\hat{\beta}. \tag{15}$$

More important, the expression in (14) facilitates the estimation of the variance–covariance structure of the return in the following way:

$$\hat{\Sigma}_{(R)} = y\hat{\Sigma}_{(\beta)}y + \hat{\Sigma}_{(e)}, \tag{16}$$

where $\hat{\Sigma}_{(\beta)}$ = the estimated variance–covariance structure of the parameter estimates, and $\hat{\Sigma}_{(e)}$ = the estimated variance–covariance structure of the random error term.

Although statistically exact there are two limitations to our procedure: (1) the relationship assumes identical impact of strategic characteristics for new and existing SBUs; and (2) various scaling and heteroscedasticity problems may be present in addition to the standard reliability and validity problems of measurement. The advantages of our procedure are significant: (1) reduced data requirements; (2) simplicity; and (3) no dependence on historical data beyond one period before the decision.

4.2. Estimating q, the risk aversion parameter

Management's trade-off between risk and expected return can be determined by conjoint analysis, [4] a frequently used estimation technique in marketing. Following the conjoint method, management can be confronted with a set of SBU portfolios for which levels of risk and expected returns vary systematically. Management's stated preferences (e.g. a rank-order over the portfolios) are then used to estimate the relative importance attributed by management to risk and expected return. In practice, this method implies the following procedures.

Step 1: Define three to four discrete levels of risk and three to four discrete levels of expected returns, under the following conditions: (i) the levels should be specific and numerical as opposed to "high", "medium" and "low", and should be within a reasonable range for the portfolios in hand; (ii) all possible risk–return combinations (nine to sixteen) have to be feasible.

Step 2: Management would be asked to rank-order each of the risk–return combinations, assigning the number "1" to the combination most preferred, "2" to the next, etc. By using a monotone analysis of variance type procedure, utilities will be assigned to each of the levels of risk and return in such a way that there is a monotone relationship between the computed utility values for

---

[4] Other methods, e.g. Von Neumann–Morgenstern type procedures [11], can also be used to estimate the risk aversion parameter.

the risk–return combinations and the stated rank-orders over the same risk–return combinations. Based on our experience, management feels comfortable with this risk–return trade-off procedure since it is somehow an extension of their intuitive reasoning.

5. An illustration

A numerical application of the model shows the necessary data collection method and computational procedures involved. The data presented were simulated, based on a real company situation. The firm, which has been managed in a decentralized style, has ten strategic business units, each autonomously pursuing its own sales objectives with operational coordination at headquarters. Environmental pressures, i.e. higher interest rates and a growing risk aversion in the financial community, create a shortage of cash, which prompts management to reconsider the method by which cash has been allocated. With the data available (see table 1) headquarters' analysts constructed a BCG SBU portfolio chart in which they felt that 5% and 1.0 are reasonable borderlines between "high" and "low" market growth and relative market share, respectively.

Discussions of the location of the SBUs on the BCG chart (two "question marks", three "stars", four "cash-cows" and one "dog") were inconclusive since some staff members advocated "divesting", "milking" and "growing" SBUs as the chart implies, while others argued that this approach considered neither the risk involved nor all of the "realities" of the business. The following illustrates the implementation of our model for this particular problem. In order to evaluate the specific contribution of this complex model its results will

Table 1
Basic data for 10 product markets

SBU	Sales price	Average cost	Cash flow per unit	Relative M.S.	Market growth
1	100	90	8	1.5	0.10
2	100	88	10	1.0	0.03
3	100	87	11	1.1	0.02
4	100	92	6	0.4	0.09
5	100	93	5	0.2	0.04
6	100	94	4	0.2	0.15
7	100	86	12	1.1	0.01
8	100	91	7	1.1	0.06
9	100	96	2	1.1	0.01
10	100	97	1	1.1	0.28

be compared to the results of alternative model specifications: with and without the constraints on exposure, gravity center, and strategic balance. The sensitivity of the model to the risk aversion parameter is tested with risk aversion (quadratic programming) and risk neutrality (linear programming).

Data requirements

5.1. Expected returns and their variance–covariance structure

The expected returns per unit at prevailing prices for each SBU are jointly determined by SBU managers and corporate staff following market reviews and cost analyses. The staff also prepares a set of three strategic factors which have been major determinants of success of SBUs in the staff's experience. Utilizing the three strategic indices in a regression model and transforming the results according to eq. (16) we obtain the estimated variance–covariance structure of the returns (see table 2).

5.2. The set of constraints

In addition to non-negativity constraints, the constraints extracted from management discussions were as follows.

(1) Operational constraints. Production and sales-force capacities are retained. Each, with its limits, are presented in the first and second rows in the matrix below:

$$\begin{bmatrix} 0.1 & 0.5 & 0.7 & 1.3 & 0.6 & 0.9 & 2.1 & 0.9 & 0.1 & 1.1 \\ 1.7 & 0.9 & 0.5 & 0.7 & 0.3 & 0.8 & 1.1 & 0.2 & 1.3 & 0.9 \end{bmatrix} \begin{bmatrix} x_1 \\ x_{10} \end{bmatrix} \leq \begin{bmatrix} 100 \\ 100 \end{bmatrix}.$$

(2) System inflexibilities. Due to its ongoing activities the following limits are considered to be important by management:

$$x_1 \leq 20; \quad x_4 \leq 10; \quad x_6 \leq 20,$$
$$x_2 \leq 15; \quad 1 \leq x_5 \leq 15; \quad x_7 \leq 10.$$

Two joint production restrictions had to be taken into account:

$$0.5 \leq x_1/x_2 \leq 1.5 \quad \text{and} \quad 0.8 \leq x_8/x_7 \leq 1.5.$$

(3) Demand constraints. The maximum sales which could be expected at prevailing prices for each SBU are as follows:

$$x_1 \leq 30; \quad x_4 \leq 12; \quad x_7 \leq 12; \quad x_{10} \leq 5.$$
$$x_2 \leq 20; \quad x_5 \leq 17; \quad x_8 \leq 15;$$
$$x_3 \leq 20; \quad x_6 \leq 22; \quad x_9 \leq 5;$$

Table 2
Variance–covariance structure of return

	R_1	R_2	R_3	R_4	R_5	R_6	R_7	R_8	R_9	R_{10}
R_1	4.24									
R_2	3.11	4.11								
R_3	−0.89	1.13	4.28							
R_4	2.75	2.77	−0.96	3.29						
R_5	0.21	0.95	1.9	0.13	2.86					
R_6	1.44	0.35	−0.61	0.17	0.98	2.67				
R_7	−3.62	−4.08	2.95	3.07	−2.29	0.27	17.35			
R_8	−4.08	−3.08	1.43	−1.28	−2.01	−1.36	11.76	12.69		
R_9	3.93	2.29	−1.68	2.51	2.37	2.92	−8.03	−7.28	7.37	
R_{10}	0.01	0.28	−0.31	1.37	1.92	0.86	−3.28	−0.08	2.53	3.37

Table 3
Strategic cash-flow balance

	Quadrant 1	Quadrant 2	Quadrant 3	Quadrant 4
Proportion of total cash generated:				
● Minimum (%)	25	15	35	5
● Maximum (%)	35	35	60	15

Taken together with the system inflexibility constraints, some of the demand constraints may become redundant and vice versa.

(4) Strategic constraints.

(a) Exposure. Management prefers not to allocate more than 50% of all SBU related costs on a combination of SBU_2 and SBU_3. Similarly, a limit of 30% would be maintained for the combination of SBU_7 and SBU_9.

(b) Strategic cash-flow balance. The relative roles for the cash-flow generation of each quadrant of the BCG matrix is represented in table 3. In this specific application all quadrants generate positive cash flows. This might be surprising but is reasonable for technology-based industries, e.g. electronics, pharmaceutics.

(c) In addition, the desired center of gravity of the matrix has the following specification:

(i) market growth gravity center, using constraint (11):

$$0.04 \leqslant [(0.1)(8)x_1 + (0.03)(10)x_2 + (0.02)(11)x_3 + (0.09)6x_4$$
$$+ (0.04)(5)x_5 + (0.15)4x_6 + (0.01)(12)x_7 + (0.06)(7)x_8$$
$$+ (0.01)(2)x_9 + (0.28)(1)x_{10}]/[8x_1 + 10x_2 + 11x_3 + 6x_4$$
$$5x_5 + 4x_6 + 12x_7 + 7x_8 + 2x_9 + x_{10}] \leqslant 0.06;$$

(ii) relative market share/gravity center, using constrain (12):

$$0.9 \leqslant [(1.5)(8)x_1 + (1.0)(10)x_2 + (1.1)(11)x_3 + (0.4)(6)x_4$$
$$+ (0.2)(5)x_5 + (0.2)(4)x_6 + (1.1)(12)x_7 + (1.1)(7)x_8(1.1)(2)x_9$$
$$+ (1.1)(1)x_{10}]/[8x_1 + 10x_2 + 11x_3 + 6x_4 + 5x_5 + 4x_6 + 12x_7$$
$$+ 7x_8 + 2x_9 + x_{10}] \leqslant 1.1.$$

5.3. The risk–return trade-off preferences

Within the range of expected returns and their variability (the diagonal in table 2), three discrete levels are chosen in each, yielding nine possible risk–

Table 4
Risk–return trade-off matrix

Risk (σ)	Return		
	300	600	900
30	4	2	1
60	7	6	3
90	9	8	5

return combinations. Table 4 represents management's rank-order preferences over the various return–risk combinations, where 1 designates the most preferred risk–return alternative. Estimation based on a monotone analysis of variance procedure yields the following utility functions.

● For returns $U = 1.066 + 0.0733R$.
● For variance $U = 1.533 - 0.0100\sigma^2$.
  (These two linear utility functions may then be combined to fit the structure of the objective function of the proposed model which is linear in the return and risk components.)
● For risk-return $U = 6.3 + R_i - 0.13\sigma^2$.

Thus, the estimate of θ in this case is -0.13, representing management's risk aversion.

Several authors have pointed out the assumptions underlying this estimation procedure (e.g. [10,18]). We feel, however, that its simplicity and intuitive appeal to the managers make it, though a technically imperfect estimation procedure, a very useful and acceptable implementation tool in practice.

Reliable inputs for the trade-off depend on management's comprehension of the levels of risk (variances of returns) and returns and their trade-off combinations. For this, some basic explanation of the feasible range of returns and risks and the trade-off concept is required. These inputs, however, are a natural extension of their intuitive information processing framework and therefore will not be completely new to them.

6. The efficient portfolio

The model lends itself to optimization using standard quadratic programming techniques because the objective function is concave (variance–covariance matrix is positive semi-definite) and all constraints are (or can be) linear [2]. Table 5 column 2, presents the solution after 39 iterations yielding a total utility of 430.8. The dual solution pointing at the critical constraints indicates: (1) a 1.36 increase in utility if we relax the second joint production constraint

Table 5
Comparative solutions of (x_i) of quadratic (QP) and linear programming (LP) approaches under different sets of constraints

Present position in BCG chart	Predicted		Without exposure, grav. center and strategic balance		Upper bound
	All constraints				
(1)	QP (2)	LP (3)	QP (4)	LP (5)	(6)
X_1 ★	15.2	20.0	20.0	20.0	20
X_2 $	15.0	15.0	15.0	15.0	15
X_3 $	8.6	10.8	13.7	20.0	20
X_4 ?	1.9	2.8	0.0	0.0	10
X_5 ⊗	13.7	15.0	8.6	15.0	15
X_6 ?	19.4	20.0	11.3	2.8	20
X_7 $	6.8	6.0	6.8	10.0	10
X_8 ★	10.2	10.0	10.2	15.0	15
X_9 $	0.0	5.0	0.0	5.0	5
X_{10} ★	0.6	0.0	5.0	0.0	5
Total	430.8	963.4	457.8	1056.7	
	Y7=1.36 (joint product.)	Y1=9.2 (oper. constr.)	Y7=0.25 (joint product.)	Y1=6.67 (oper. constr.)	
	Y17=0.016 (exposure)	Y7=2.6 (joint product.)			
	Y22=0.66 (prop. "star")	Y17=0.05 (exposure)			
	Y27=1.43 (center of grav.)	Y22=0.34 (prop. "star")			

marginally; (2) an 0.016 increase in utility if the first exposure constraint is relaxed marginally; (3) an increase of 0.66 if management allows the proportion of "star" businesses to exceed the limit marginally; and (4) an increase of 1.43 if the center of gravity in the BCG chart is allowed to exceed the limit on the growth dimension marginally of cash flow coming from an SBU in the "high growth" quadrants.

To illustrate the importance of the two key dimensions of the proposed model, risk aversion and strategic constraints, the results of the model without these two parameters are presented in table 5. The neutral attitude of management towards the risk of the returns is captured by the linear programming solution (i.e. $\alpha = 0$). The model was also optimized without the strategic constraints, i.e. without the exposure and strategic balance constraints.

6.1. Strategic constraints

In comparing columns 2 with 4 and 3 with 5 it appears that the emphasis on "cash-cows" and "stars" (SBUs 1, 3 and 10) is reduced when introducing strategic constraints. This emphasis is taken up primarily by SBU 6. This is intuitively acceptable since SBU 6 is in a relatively high-growth market, thus potentially an important activity for the company. Had the strategic constraints not been present, the growth of SBU 6 would have been financed by external sources (borrow, issue stock). However, the inclusion of these constraints in the model represents the basic needs for internal financing in a scarcity of cash environment. Thus, the model indicates the direction of a trade-off in a situation where the "stars" and "cash cows" are traded off in favor of question-mark SBUs which have to capture a high relative market share if they are to turn into "stars" or eventually "cash cows".

6.2. Risk aversion

This parameter seems to have two important effects which may be seen by comparing columns 2 and 3 on the one hand and 4 and 5 on the other. It appears that risk aversion implies lower production levels for almost all SBUs. This is not surprising given the fact that the risk aversion decision-maker penalizes those SBUs that have more risky returns. In this light one can understand the second effect which shows that SBU 6 has a low risk profile in addition to its growth potential. This indeed explains its increased relative attractiveness under the risk aversion scenario.

7. Conclusion

The model presented in this paper fills a gap in the theoretical analysis of product portfolio planning. It combines the elegance and robustness of the financial portfolio model with the more practical Boston Consulting Group portfolio framework.

The proposed model is open to further development. For example, the exogenously determined upper and lower bounds in most of the constraints can be made endogenous. The operational capacity constraints can be handled by incorporating explicit production functions. Similarly, the more explicit treatment of demand schedules as proposed in the paper would further enrich the model and would show the effect of price elasticities for the different SBUs on the optimal portfolio.

Given management's willingness to provide the model inputs and using the proposed estimation procedure for the variance–covariance structure of the returns, the model should prove to be a powerful tool for aiding the analysis and determination of a company's product policy.

Acknowledgment

The authors wish to thank Professor Andris Zoltners for his helpful comments and suggestions on earlier drafts of the paper.

References

[1] D. Abell, Defining the Business: The Starting Point of Strategic Planning (Prentice-Hall, Englewood Cliffs, N.J., 1980).

[2] M. Avriel, Nonlinear Programming: Analysis and Method (Prentice Hall, Englewood Cliffs, N.J., 1976).

[3] R.D. Buzzel, B.T. Gale and R.G.M. Sultan, Market share—a key to profitability, Harvard Business Review 53, no. 1 (1975) 97–106.

[4] R. Cardozo and Y. Wind, Portfolio analysis for strategic product market planning, University of Pennsylvania, Wharton School, Working Paper (1980).

[5] P. Conley, Experience Curves as a Planning Tool: A Special Commentary (The Boston Consulting Group, Boston, Mass., 1970).

[6] G.S. Day, Diagnosing the product portfolio, Journal of Marketing 41, no. 2 (1977) 29–38.

[7] W.L. Fruhan, Jr., Pyrrhic victories in fights for market share, Harvard Business Review 50, no. 5 (1972) 100–107.

[8] B. Gale, Market share and the rate of return, Review of Economics and Statistics 54, no. 4 (1972) 412–423.

[9] B. Gale and B. Branch, Concentration versus market share: Which determines performance and why does it matter?, Strategic Planning Institute Staff Paper (1979).

[10] P.E. Green and Y. Wind, Multi-Attribute Decisions in Marketing: A Measurement Approach (The Dryden Press, New York, 1973).

[11] J. Hauser and G. Urban, A normative methodology for modelling consumer response to innovation, Operations Research 25 (1977) 574–619.

[12] Y. Kahane, Determination of the product mix and the business policy of an insurance company—A portfolio approach, Management Science 23, no. 10 (1977) 1060–1069.

[13] J. Kivoka, The effect of market share distribution on industry performance, Review of Economic and Statistics (forthcoming).

[14] P. Kotler, Marketing Management Analysis Planning and Control (Prentice-Hall, Englewood Cliffs, N.J., 1980).

[15] P. Kotler, Marketing Decision Making: A Model Building Approach (Holt, Rinehart and Winston, New York, 1971).

[16] H. Levy and H. Markowitz, Approximating expected utility by a function of mean and variances, American Economic Review 69, no. 3 (1979) 308–317.

[17] H.M. Markowitz, Portfolio Selection: Efficient Diversification of Investments (John Wiley and Sons, New York, 1959).

[18] D. Pekelmen and S. Sen, Improving prediction in conjoint measurement, Journal of Marketing Research (May 1979) 211–220.

[19] R. Polli and V. Cook, Validity of the product life cycle, Journal of Business 42, no. 4 (1969) 385–400.

[20] W.E. Rothchild, Putting It All Altogether: A Guide to Strategic Thinking (AMACOM, New York, 1976).

[21] M.S. Salter and W.A. Weinhold, Diversification Through Acquisition (The Free Press, New York, 1979).

[22] S. Schoeffler, Cross-sectional study of strategy structure and performance: Aspects of the PIMS programme, in: Hans B. Thorelli, ed., Strategy + Structure = Performance (Indiana University Press, 1977).

[23] W.F. Sharpe, A simplified model for portfolio analysis, Management Science 9, no. 2 (1963) 277–283.

[24] Y. Wind, Product portfolio analysis: A new approach to the product mix decision, in: R.C. Curhan, ed., Combined Proceedings (American Marketing Association, 1974).

[25] Y. Wind and H.J. Claycamp, Planning product line strategy: A matrix approach, Journal of Marketing 40, no. 1 (1976) 2–9.

TIMS Studies in the Management Sciences 18 (1982) 161–183

STOCHASTIC DOMINANCE RULES FOR PRODUCT PORTFOLIO ANALYSIS

Vijay MAHAJAN, Yoram WIND

University of Pennsylvania

and

John W. BRADFORD

Columbia University

The role of financial portfolio approaches, particularly the stochastic dominance (SD) rules in product portfolio analysis, is discussed. The SD rules identify the efficient or admissible sets of alternatives under specific stated assumption on the nature of the underlying utility functions without the subjective estimation of the utility functions. The application of the SD rules to the product (business) portfolio decisions of a firm is illustrated by analyzing the product portfolio of an insurance company. The adaptability of the SD approach to a marketing oriented product portfolio approach is outlined and directions for future marketing applications of the SD approach are suggested.

1. Introduction

One of top management's major tasks is the determination of the desired composition of the firm's product (business) portfolio and the allocation of resources among the various products (and businesses). Product portfolio models have been proposed, and implemented, to help management make this decision. Yet, most of the frequently used, standardized product portfolio models, [1] such as the Boston Consulting Group's growth/share matrix, the McKinsey/GE business assessment array, the A.D. Little business profile matrix, and the Shell International directional policy matrix, can help classify the current products (businesses) on a structured set of dimensions, but can offer little guidance as to the composition of the best *portfolio* of products and how management should allocate its resources among the various products.

---

[1] "Standardized" portfolio models are defined as those which offer management a structured set of dimensions, without allowing them to change the dimensions. The standardized models include both models with a univariate dimension such as the BCG model and models which use composite dimensions such as the GE/McKinsey model. For a detailed discussion of this classification of portfolio models, see [48].

Consider, for example, the popular BCG model. Whereas it allows management to classify its products (or businesses) in a simple and attractive manner, it offers only vague suggestions on the allocation of cash from "cash cows" to "problem children". It offers no guidelines for the construction of the desired portfolio of products. In fact, the BCG terminology is dysfunctional for portfolio management since many managers are hesitant to have "dogs" in their portfolio, whereas there are a number of situations that might call for a portfolio which includes current "dogs". [2]

To surmount the shortcomings of the standardized product portfolio models, a number of firms such as GE have used the results of the product portfolio analysis stage (which, in the case of the GE model, results in a classification of products on the two dimensions of business attractiveness and business strength) as inputs to other resource allocation models. An alternative approach has been the development of "customized" product portfolio models which allow management greater freedom in selecting the portfolio dimensions, weighting them, and evaluating the current and prospective products (or businesses) on these dimensions and inputing these judgments and data to a resource allocation model. These approaches include both a conjoint analysis based approach with a resource allocation simulator [47] and the Analytic Hierarchy Process [49].

These newer product portfolio approaches allow for an explicit resource allocation procedure; however, they tend to rely primarily on management's subjective judgment. [3] Furthermore, these approaches do not take full advantage of the concepts underlying the more traditional financial portfolio models, particularly their ability to identify an efficient frontier of products among which management can select their preferred target portfolio.

The potential contribution of financial portfolio models has long been recognized. Wind [46] suggested the application of the Markowitz risk/return model to the product portfolio area, and more recently Cardozo and Wind [7] suggested how the conventional risk–return model can be operationalized for product portfolio analysis. These developments have been quite isolated, however, from the major developments in the product portfolio area and have further ignored the developments in financial portfolio analysis relating to the stochastic dominance (SD) approach. The purpose of this paper is, therefore, to suggest the applicability of the SD rules to the product portfolio decision, illustrate its applicability, and outline an approach for its integration with the more conventional product portfolio approaches.

More specifically, the paper is divided into four parts: (a) a brief review of

---

[2] For a discussion of the limitations of the various portfolio models, see [47] and [50].

[3] Both the conjoint analysis and AHP approaches to portfolio analysis allow the integration of data with management's subjective judgment. Yet, in a number of applications, expediency has led to the almost exclusive reliance on subjective judgment.

the financial portfolio approach to product portfolio analysis and decisions, (b) a brief summary of the stochastic dominance rules (versus the more conventional mean–variance approach), (c) an illustrative application of the SD rules for the selection of the efficient frontier for an insurance company, and (d) a conclusions section which discusses the adaptability of the SD rules to a marketing oriented product portfolio analysis and decision, and suggested directions for future research concerning the applicability of the SD approach to marketing decisions.

2. The financial portfolio approach to product portfolio analysis

The financial approach to the portfolio selection problem assumes that the profits from portfolio items (such as product lines, stocks, bonds, etc.) are random variables, and estimates concerning their distribution (subjective or objective) are known. Furthermore, the rates of profit for different items may be correlated and hence the need to examine the portfolio items collectively. The expected rate of return on a portfolio is simply the weighted average of the expected rates of return of the items contained in that portfolio, i.e.

$$\bar{R}_p = \sum_{i=1}^m w_i R_i \quad \text{and} \quad \sum_{i=1}^m w_i = 1, \tag{1}$$

where w_i is the portion of funds invested in item i, R_i is the expected value of return for item i, m is the total number of items in the portfolio, and $\bar{R}_p$ is the expected rate of return for the portfolio. If variance is used as the measure of risk associated with a portfolio, it may be obtained by

$$V_p = \sum_{i=1}^m \sum_{j=1}^m w_i w_j \sigma_{ij}, \tag{2}$$

where V_p is the portfolio variance, w_i and w_j are the portion of funds invested in items i and j, respectively, and σ_{ij} is the covariance between returns of items i and j.

Fig. 1 represents a schematic diagram of the portfolio selection problem. The systematic steps which characterize the portfolio selection decision may be stated as follows.

(1) *Determine all possible items to be considered in the portfolio and generate all feasible portfolios.* Central to the portfolio selection decision is the identification of possible items to be considered as candidates for inclusion in the portfolio. This would involve an extensive search for and evaluation of potential items which might be included. The major objective of this step is to specify a finite number (m) of items and generate a set of feasible portfolios.

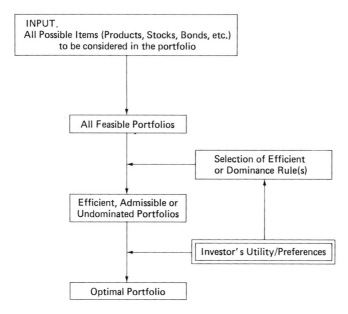

Fig. 1. Schematic diagram of the financially oriented portfolio selection process.

As explained below, the number of feasible portfolios can be determined by generating combinatorial solutions to the equation $\sum_{i=1}^{m} w_i = 1$ within the constraints imposed on the values of w_i.

(2) *Generate the admissible (efficient or undominated) portfolios.* This is probably the most critical step in the portfolio selection problem. The objective here is to reduce the large number of feasible portfolios to a smaller number using certain "efficient" rules. These rules are derived by making certain stated assumptions on the nature of the investor's underlying utility function. The reduced number of portfolios are termed as efficient, admissible, or undominated portfolios. The most popular-efficient rule for generating the efficient portfolios is the mean–variance rule (see, for example [25]). This paper, in addition to this conventional rule, will concentrate on the stochastic dominance (SD) rules for generating efficient product portfolios.

(3) *Determine the optimal portfolio from the admissible portfolios.* The efficient rules provide a mechanism to divide the feasible portfolios into two groups: those dominated by others and those not dominated by others. The undominated or admissible portfolios provide a smaller set of alternatives from which the optimal choice can be made by obtaining further information on the investor's utility function (risk/return tradeoff).

The adaptation of financial portfolio to product portfolio analysis assumes that an organization's products and markets can be considered investments that together comprise a portfolio.[4] These product-market investments can be measured in terms of both return and risk. Furthermore, the efficiency of each portfolio can be determined based on the return and risk patterns for all the product-market investments with the portfolio. The objective of managers (i.e. investors) at the profit center, division (or SBU) or corporate level is to evaluate the desired target portfolio from the alternative efficient portfolios and to determine the allocation of resource efforts (i.e. each w_i) across the product-market investments. (For further discussion on the adaptability of the financial approach to product portfolio analysis and the associated issues, see Cardozo and Wind [7] and Wind [47].)

3. The stochastic dominance rules (versus the mean–variance approach)

As summarized in fig. 1, the portfolio selection problem involves consideration of efficient or dominance rules to obtain the admissible set of portfolios. Furthermore, information about the investor's utility function is required to obtain this admissible set of portfolios and the optimal portfolio. It has been argued in the financial economics literature (e.g. [25,4]) that since in most situations complete information about an individual's utility function is not available, and assuming that the individual chooses an alternative in accordance with a consistent set of preferences which maximizes the expected utility expressed as a function of returns [43], efficient or dominance rules may be developed by considering certain restricted classes of utility functions. Thus, with only partial information that an individual's utility function belongs to a certain class of utility functions, these rules can be used to screen inferior alternatives from among the given set of alternatives. That is to say, these rules provide the efficient set of alternatives under specific stated assumptions on the nature of the underlying utility functions without the subjective estimation of the utility functions. Clearly, the stronger the restrictions assumed on admissible utilities, the smaller will be the admissible set in terms of the number of alternatives from which the optimal choice can be made.

The most widely used efficiency criterion for portfolio selection is the mean–variance (EV) rule suggested by Markowitz [28]. Since the decisions

---

[4] One has to recognize, however, the inherent differences between portfolio decisions for stocks/bonds and for products. In the case of stocks/bonds, the investor has (a) an almost unlimited number of options in terms of risk–return characteristics and (b) the cost, risk, and time lag with deletion/addition is minimal. In contrast, product portfolios are characterized by limited availability of options; product additions may be costly, involve longer time lags and higher risks. Product deletion decisions may not be based just on profit considerations. Yet, financial portfolio approaches (such as SD) can be used for *product* and *business* portfolios if they meet the following conditions: (a) they must include not only existing products but also new options; (b) the return data must incorporate the *costs* involved in developing or deleting a product; and (c) as suggested in the last section of this paper, product portfolios should not be guided solely by the results of the SD analysis but rather be considered in conjunction with other customized portfolio approaches such as the AHP.

about investment may be viewed as choices among alternative probability distributions of returns, the EV rule suggests that, for risk-averse individuals, the admissible set may be obtained by discarding those investments with a lower mean and a higher variance. That is, in a choice between two investments, designated by return distributions F and G, respectively, a risk-averse investor is presumed to prefer F to G, or to be indifferent between the two if the mean of F is as large as the mean of G and the variance of F (reflecting the associated risk) is not greater than the variance of G; i.e. if $\mu_F \geq \mu_G$ and $\sigma_F^2 \leq \sigma_G^2$. Furthermore, if at least one of these inequalities is strict, then some investors prefer F to G in the strict sense, and F is said to dominate G in the sense of EV. In this case, G can be eliminated from the admissible set. If only one of the inequalities holds, the selection depends on the individual's personal mean–variance tradeoff, and neither F nor G can be eliminated under the EV dominance rule [11]. The rule can be applied easily to the portfolio selection problem by ordering all portfolios by increasing means and excluding any portfolio i such that the variance of portfolio i is greater than or equal to the variance of portfolio j, where $i < j$.

In spite of its popularity, the mean–variance approach has been subject to serious criticisms. It has been argued (see, for example, [6,9,17]) that the EV rule is the optimal efficient rule only if the utility function is quadratic and the probability distributions of returns are normal. It has been further pointed out that both the assumptions are implausible since the first assumption implies increasing absolute risk aversion and the second excludes consideration of asymmetry or skewness in the probability distributions of returns. An important result of these criticisms of the EV approach has been the development of stochastic dominance rules. These rules have been derived, under differing restrictions on the utility functions, by Quirk and Saposnik [37], Fishburn [10], Hadar and Russell [14–16], Hammond [18], Hanoch and Levy [19], Whitmore [44], Bawa [4], and Vickson [39–41]. These rules involve pairwise comparison of the set of alternative probability distributions of returns. Efficient algorithms to implement these rules have been developed by Levy and Hanock [25], Levy and Sarnet [26], Porter, Wart and Ferguson [36], and Bawa, Lindenberg and Rasky [5]. In the financial economics literature, these rules have been tested empirically and examined by Levy and Hanock [25], Levy and Sarnat [26], Porter and Gaumnits [35], Porter [32,33], Porter and Bey [34], Vickson and Altman [42], and Perrakis and Zerbinis [31]. Attempts have also been made to extend these rules to multivariate distributions (see, for example, [21]) and to include borrowing and lending at a riskless interest rate (see, for example, [23]). (For a state-of-the-art review, see [45].)

Stochastic dominance is a relationship between pairs of probability distributions; in particular, it involves comparison of the relative positions of the cumulative distribution functions. Three types of stochastic dominance rules have been generally presented for decision-making under uncertainty: first-order stochastic dominance (FSD), second-order stochastic dominance (SSD), and third-order stochastic dominance (TSD). These rules have been derived by considering certain stated assumptions on the form of utility functions. If U, U', U'', and U''' stand for a utility function and its first, second, and third derivatives, respectively, the FSD rule assumes that $U' \geq 0$; the SSD rule assumes that $U' \geq 0$ and $U'' \leq 0$, and the TSD rule assumes that $U' \geq 0$, $U'' \leq 0$, and $U''' \geq 0$. That is to say, the FSD rule requires that the first derivative of the utility function be positive throughout; therefore, it allows risk preference, risk indifference, or risk aversion. The SSD rule eliminates risk preference by adding the restriction that the second derivative be everywhere nonpositive. Finally, the TSD rule requires that the third derivative of the utility function be everywhere non-negative. These assumptions are only necessary conditions; however, they are clearly more reasonable than the assumptions of a quadratic utility function with increasing absolute risk aversion implied by the EV rule [23]. To summarize, the admissible set of portfolios generated by:

(1) the FSD rule provides the efficient set for all decision makers with utility functions increasing in wealth;

(2) the SSD rule provides the efficient set for the *subset* of decision makers having increasing utility functions and risk-aversion; and

(3) the TSD rule provides the efficient set for the *subset* of risk-averse decision-makers with decreasing absolute risk.

The optimal portfolio for the investor can then be determined, based on his/her risk–return tradeoff, from among the relevant smaller set of admissible choices.

The three specific stochastic dominance rules were developed originally for continuous probability functions.[5] Yet, since the true form of the probability distributions is rarely known with complete certainty, to apply the three SD rules to portfolio selection, it is often necessary to estimate the underlying structures of the distributions using discrete sets of sample observations.[6] The first-, second-, and third-order stochastic dominance rules for *discrete* observations are defined as follows.

FSD. The distribution $f(x)$ is said to dominate the distribution $g(x)$ by FSD if and only if $F_1(x_n) \leq G_1(x_n)$ for all $n \leq N$ with at least one strict inequality, and N is the total number of discrete observations in both distributions, where

$$F_1(x_n) = \sum_{i=1}^{n} f(x_i), \qquad n = 1, 2, \ldots, N, \tag{3}$$

and $G_1(x_n)$ is similarly defined.

---

[5] For a discussion of the stochastic dominance rules for a continuous probability function, see [45].
[6] The effect of sampling errors on the portfolio efficient analysis has been examined by Levy and Kroll [27] and Kroll and Levy [24].

SSD. The distribution $f(x)$ is said to dominate the distribution $g(x)$ by SSD if and only if $F_2(x_n) \leq G_2(x_n)$ for all $n \leq N$ with at least one strict inequality, where

$$F_2(x_n) = \sum_{i=2}^{n} F_1(x_{i-1})(x_i - x_{i-1}), \qquad n = 2, 3, \dots, N, \tag{4}$$

and $F_2(x_1) = 0$. $G_2(x_n)$ is similarly defined.

TSD. The distribution $f(x)$ is said to dominate the distribution $g(x)$ by TSD if and only if $F_3(x_n) \leq G_3(x_n)$ for all $n \leq N$ with at least one strict inequality, and $F_2(x_N) \leq G_2(x_N)$, where

$$F_3(x_n) = \tfrac{1}{2} \sum_{i=2}^{n} [F_2(x_i) + F_2(x_{i-1})](x_i - x_{i-1}), \qquad n = 2, 3, \dots, N, \tag{5}$$

and $F_3(x_1) = 0$. $G_3(x_n)$ is similarly defined.

In addition, for the distribution $f(x)$ to dominate the distribution $g(x)$, it is necessary that the mean of the distribution $f(x)$ is at least as large as the mean of the distribution $g(x)$.

A simple example should help to clarify the calculations of the FSD, SSD, and TSD rules. Suppose a sample of k observations is taken from each of two distributions. This gives a total of $N = 2k$ observations. It is further assumed that each observation occurs with a sample relative frequency of $1/k$. Next, rank in ascending order the N observations such that $X_1 \leq X_2 \leq, \dots, \leq X_N$. If the ith observation belongs to the first distribution, $f(x)$, then $f(x_i) = 1/k$ and $g(x_i) = 0$; if it belongs to the second distribution, $g(x)$, then $g(x_i) = 1/k$ and $f(x_i) = 0$. Once these discrete distributions have been obtained, (3)–(5) can be easily applied.

To illustrate, consider the following example from Porter [32]. Two portfolios are observed to have the following historical returns:

Portfolio	Returns		
f	6.0, 2.0, 1.8, 7.0	$E(f) = 4.2$;	$\sigma_f^2 = 5.42$
g	6.0, 3.0, 1.0, 3.0	$E(g) = 3.25$;	$\sigma_g^2 = 3.18$

Since $k = 4$, the sample relative frequency is $1/k = 0.25$, and $N = 8$ ($2k$). Table 1 presents the calculations for the FSD, SSD, and TSD rules.

For FSD, the distributions $F_1(x_n)$ and $G_1(x_n)$ are simply the cumulative probability distributions for portfolios f and g, respectively. These are determined from (3). The calculations for SSD and TDS follow from (4) and (5).

Table 1
Illustrative calculations for the FSD, SSD, and TSD rules

		Observation number (n)							
		1	2	3	4	5	6	7	8
	x_n	1.0	1.8	2.0	3.0	3.0	6.0	6.0	7.0
	$f(x_n)$	0.0	0.25	0.25	0.0	0.0	0.25	0.0	0.25
	$g(x_n)$	0.25	0.0	0.0	0.25	0.25	0.0	0.25	0.0
FSD	$F_1(x_n)$	0.0	0.25	0.50	0.50	0.50	0.75	0.75	1.00
	$G_1(x_n)$	0.25	0.25	0.25	0.50	0.75	0.75	1.00	1.00
SSD	$F_2(x_n)$	0.0	0.0	0.05	0.55	0.55	2.05	2.05	2.8
	$G_2(x_n)$	0.0	0.2	0.25	0.50	0.50	2.75	2.75	3.75
TSD	$F_3(x_n)$	0.0	0.00	0.01	0.31	0.31	4.21	4.21	6.63
	$G_3(x_n)$	0.0	0.08	0.13	0.50	0.50	5.38	5.38	8.63
FSD	(Δ_n^1 of G with respect to F)	0.25	0.0	-0.25	0.0	0.25	0.0	0.25	0.0
SSD	(Δ_n^2 of G with respect to F)		0.20	0.20	-0.05	-0.05	0.7	0.7	0.95
TSD	(Δ_n^3 of G with respect to F)		0.08	0.12	0.19	0.19	1.17	1.17	2.00

For example,

$$F_2(x_6) = 0(1.8 - 1.0) + 0.25(2 - 1.8) + 0.5(3.0 - 2.0) \cdot$$

$$+ 0.5(3.0 - 3.0) + 0.5(6.0 - 3.0)$$

$$= 2.05,$$

and

$$G_3(x_6) = 1/2[(0.2 + 0.0)(1.8 - 1.0) + (0.25 + 0.20)(2.0 - 1.8)$$

$$+ (0.5 + 0.25)(3.0 - 2.0) + (0.5 + 0.5)(3.0 - 3.0)$$

$$+ (2.75 + 0.5)(6.0 - 3.0)]$$

$$= 5.38.$$

To evaluate the two portfolios by the three SD rules, it is necessary to define the differences between the two distributions for each rule. That is, each of the following must be calculated:

$$\text{FSD } \Delta_n^1 = [G_1(x_n) - F_1(x_n)], \qquad n = 1, 2, \ldots, N,$$
$$\text{SSD } \Delta_n^2 = [G_2(x_n) - F_2(x_n)], \qquad n = 2, 3, \ldots, N,$$
$$\text{TSD } \Delta_n^3 = [G_3(x_n) - F_3(x_n)], \qquad n = 2, 3, \ldots, N.$$

Having calculated the differences between the two distributions (which is summarized in the lower panel of table 1), the dominant distribution can be identified by simply observing the signs of the differences. Namely,

● If all Δ_n^i are zero and at least one difference is positive, portfolio f dominates portfolio g by ith-order SD.
● If all Δ_n^i are zero and at least one difference is negative, portfolio g dominates f by ith-order SD.
● If all Δ_n^i are mixed, i.e. some are zero, some positive, and some negative, neither portfolio dominates by ith-order SD.

For the example given in table 1, it is clear that the portfolio f dominates portfolio g by the TSD rule only.

Stochastic dominance provides a powerful tool for portfolio analysis since (a) no prior assumptions concerning the shape of the probability function are required and (b) every point in the probability distribution is utilized. The SD approach, however, is not without its limitations. The estimation of each probability function for each portfolio for a practical application may be very time-consuming in comparison to the EV approach, which requires estimation of only two parameters—mean and variance. For example, consider the computational requirements of generating the EV and SSD admissible set for 50 portfolios, each having 25 observations. To calculate either requires that each portfolio be compared with every other portfolio, thus there would be 1,225 comparisons. For the EV efficient set, each comparison involves two parameters (mean and variance) or a total of 2,450 paired comparisons. For the SSD comparison, each test requires 50 data points (25 from each portfolio) or a total of 61,250 paired comparisons. Since the FSD probabilities must be calculated prior to the calculation of the SSD probabilities, the total number of paired comparisons would be 122,500. As the number of portfolios and/or the number of sample data points increases, the number of calculations may become prohibitive.

Furthermore, the EV approach has been formulated as a quadratic programming problem.[7] This implies that it is not necessary to generate all the feasible portfolios since the algorithms determine the optimal allocation of resources across the product lines and hence the efficient portfolios. The SD approach, on the other hand, does not utilize an optimizing algorithm to determine the allocation of resources.[8] This necessitates the determination and examination of all feasible portfolios to identify the efficient ones. In the presence of a large number of portfolios, the implementation of SD again may be computationally prohibitive [12].

4. An illustrative application

The potential use of the SD rules in selecting a set of acceptable product options in a product portfolio is illustrated in this section using the published data of an insurance company—State Farm Fire and Casualty Company.[9] The return distributions were obtained from the firm's historical data as published in Best's *Property–Casualty Aggregates and Averages* (A.M. Best Co., New York, 1979). Rates of return were calculated by dividing annual underwriting profits (or losses) by the total premiums earned. This measure excludes investment income, which in a real world application should be considered in the evaluation of any insurance portfolio. The use of historical data is subject, of course, to the necessary assumptions about the use of *ex post* data as

---

[7] See, for example, [37] and [32] for the programming approaches to the portfolio selection problem.

[8] Markowitz [29] has suggested a linear programming formulation for the second stochastic dominance rule. However, the computational feasibility of this approach has not been established yet.

[9] Our analysis is limited to the products of State Farm Fire and Casualty Company. Similar analysis can be done for other State Farm SBUs or at the corporate level focusing on *all* the products of the various State Farm related companies and divisions.

estimators of *ex ante* expectations. Table 2 presents the return characteristics of state Farm Fire and Casualty Company's product lines and compares them to that of the entire industry.

Before constructing the efficient portfolios, the SD and EV rules were used to test the efficiency of State Farm's seven casualty product lines. [10] These results are summarized in table 3. Examination of this table suggests:

- Two products—Inland Marine and Work Compensation—were considered inefficient products by all four rules.
- Three products—Allied Lines, Homeowners, and Commercial—were identified by all four rules as efficient.
- Fire insurance was identified as an efficient product by the FSD rule only —the least restrictive SD rule.
- Liability Insurance was identified as an efficient product by the EV rule but was clearly inefficient even by the FSD rule. This suggests that the EV rule can result in erroneous selection of a product, as discussed earlier.

The results of the SSD dominance pattern are presented in table 4.

In order to illustrate the use of the SD rules for portfolio development, it is first necessary to generate all feasible portfolios. This requires generation of different sets of weights, $w_i s$ (see (1)) by considering combinatorial solutions to the following equation:

$$\sum_{i=1}^{m} w_i = 100, \tag{6}$$

where w_i now represents the percentage of funds allocation to product i. [11] The number of solutions of (6) in non-negative integers is $C(100 + m - 1, m - 1)$, where $C(100 + m - 1, m - 1)$ denotes the number of $(m - 1)$ combinations of a set of $(100 + m - 1)$ distinct numbers. The number of solutions of (6) in

---

[10] In an earlier study by Kahane [22], the aggregate industry data for 1956–1973 were used to illustrate the application of a single-index model to portfolio analysis. Kahane used, in addition to the 18 insurance lines, two assets (stocks and bonds). Owing to arbitrary restrictions imposed by Kahane on the weights, $w_i s$, of the product lines, the aggregation of certain product lines, and his focus on the data of the entire industry (which is not meaningful from a portfolio analysis standpoint), no comparison is made between the Kahane study and our analysis, which centers on the products of a single firm.

[11] This will result in solutions of $w_i s$ up to two decimal places. The values of $w_i s$ in three decimal places can be found by changing the right-hand side of eq. (6) to 1000 and so on.

Notes to table 2

[a] Total industry data refer only to stock companies (excluding mutual). State Farm data are also only for the stock company, excluding its major mutual firm which offers, among other products, its auto insurance.

[b] Includes earthquake for industry, 1973–1974; and extended coverage, 1968–1970.

[c] Includes miscellaneous P.D. and B.I. liability, 1968–1970.

[d] Includes automobile P.D. and B.I. liability, 1968–1970.

[e] Includes automobile collision, fire, theft, and comprehensive, 1968–1971.

Table 2

Return characteristics of State Farm and total industry [a]

Line number	Product Line	Total industry, 1968–1974	
		Mean rate of return	Variance
1	Fire	6.143	34.583
2	Allied Lines [b]	7.171	109.932
3	Homeowners	−1.600	31.890
4	Commercial	4.071	26.789
5	Ocean Marine	2.314	35.698
6	Inland Marine	5.457	36.920
7	Group Health	−2.600	5.040
8	Health	4.143	24.413
9	Work Compensation	2.986	18.721
10	Liability [c]	−11.571	56.822
11	Auto Liability [d]	−4.386	4.875
12	Auto Property [e]	1.557	23.373
13	Fidelity	0.386	29.431
14	Surety	7.200	127.267
15	Glass	−1.743	34.290
16	Burglary	8.914	151.775
17	Boiler	4.600	20.097
18	Credit	−17.300	1808.773

Line number	Product line	State Farm			State Farm, 1968–1974	
		Data for period	Mean rate of return	Variance	Mean rate of return	Variance
1	Fire	1963–78	6.069	62.777	5.314	54.841
2	Allied Lines [b]	1963–78	14.862	128.905	16.429	276.602
3	Homeowners	1963–78	3.469	18.876	2.386	13.295
4	Commercial	1963–78	−0.056	99.005	6.614	39.401
5	Ocean Marine	−	−	−	−	−
6	Inland Marine	1963–78	−3.487	58.573	−0.671	53.769
7	Group Health	−	−	−	−	−
8	Health	−	−	−	−	−
9	Work Compensation	1968–78	−1.336	135.100	−1.386	173.261
10	Liability [c]	1967–78	3.925	258.942	8.143	195.929
11	Auto Liability	−	−	−	−	−
12	Auto Property	−	−	−	−	−
13	Fidelity	−	−	−	−	−
14	Surety	−	−	−	−	−
15	Glass	−	−	−	−	−
16	Burglary	−	−	−	−	−
17	Boiler	−	−	−	−	−
18	Credit	−	−	−	−	−

Notes to table on facing page

Table 3

Results of EV and SD rules for individual product lines of State Farm (1968–1974)

Product line	Dominated Product Line [a]			
	EV	FSD	SSD	TSD
Fire	Work Compensation	Inland Marine	Inland Marine, Work Compensation	Inland Marine, Work Compensation, Liability
Allied Lines	None	Work Compensation, Liability	Work Compensation, Liability	Work Compensation, Liability
Home-owners	Inland Marine, Work Compensation	None	Inland Marine, Work Compensation	Inland Marine, Work Compensation
Commer-cial	Fire, Inland, Marine, Work Compensation	Inland Marine	Fire, Inland Marine, Work Compensation	Fire, Inland Marine, Work Compensation Liability
Inland Marine	Work Compensation	None	Work Compensation	Work Compensation
Work Compensation	None	None	None	None
Liabil-ity	None	Work Compensation	Work Compensation	Work Compensation
Un-dominated Products	Allied Lines, Homeowners, Commercial, Liability	Fire, Allied Lines, Homeowners, Commercial	Allied Lines, Homeowners, Commercial	Allied Lines, Homeowners, Commercial

[a] Row dominates column.

positive integers is $C(100 - 1, m - 1)$. If it is assumed that each $w_i > c_i$ (where c_i is the percentage constraint imposed on the value of w_i), the number of solutions of (6) in positive integers is $C(100 - c_1 - c_2, \ldots, -c_m - 1, m - 1)$. [12]

For the seven product lines under consideration, the following arbitrary

[12] In general, the number of solutions of $\Sigma_{i=1}^{m} w_i = n$ in positive integers is $C(n-1, m-1)$; in non-negative integers it is $C(n-m-1, m-1)$. Furthermore, if $w_i > c_i$, then the number of solutions in non-negative integers is $C[n - (\Sigma_{i=1}^{m} c_i) - 1, m - 1]$. For the derivations of these formulae, see [30, Ch. 4 and 5]. The formulae for the number of solutions to eq. (6) in the presence of less than or equal to constraints on the values of $w_i s$ can be found in [30, ch. 5].

Table 4
SSD dominance pattern [a]

	Fire	Allied Lines	Home-owners	Commer-cial	Inland Marine	Work Compen-sation	Lia-bility
Fire					√	√	
Allied Lines						√	√
Homeowners					√	√	
Commercial	√				√	√	
Inland Marine						√	
Work Compensation							
Liability						√	
Total no. of times a product is dominated	1	0	0	0	3	6	1

Undominated products

[a] Row dominates column.

constraints were imposed. For Fire, Allied Lines, Homeowners, and Commercial—identified by the FSD rules (table 3) as the "best" four products—the w_is were constrained to be greater than 10%, and only the solutions in increments of 5% were considered. Imposition of these constraints when applied to (6) resulted in the following:

$$\sum_{i=1}^{7} w_i = 20, \quad w_i > 2 \text{ for } i = 1, 2, 3, \text{ and } 4,$$

$$w_i \geq 1 \text{ for } i = 5, 6 \text{ and } 7.$$

Note here that $w_i = 1$ represents 5%, $w_i = 2$ represents 10%, and so on. The number of solutions in positive integers is $C(20\text{-}8\text{-}1, 7\text{-}1)$ or $C(11,6)$ and $C(11,6) = 11!/5!6! = 462$, i.e. there are 462 feasible portfolios to be considered.

The application of the FSD rule eliminated all but 43 portfolios from the feasible set of 462 portfolios. Table 5 summarizes the results for the EV, SSD, and TSD rules. The application of the SSD rule eliminated all but 14 portfolios. That is, by this rule these portfolios represent the "best" portfolios from which the optimal choice can be determined. The EV rule yielded 17 efficient portfolios, but only 7 of them are also included in the SSD set. Of importance to the decision whether to use the EV or SD rules are the findings

Table 5
Results of EV, SSD, and TSD for State Farm for the years 1968–1974

Portfolio Number	Mean return	Variance	Undominated set EV	Undominated set SSD	Undominated set TSD	Fire	Applied Lines	Home-owners	Commercial	Inland Marine	Work Compensation	Liability
33	8.532	45.410		X		0.15	0.35	0.15	0.20	0.05	0.05	0.05
42	9.023	56.593	X	X	X	0.15	0.40	0.15	0.15	0.05	0.05	0.05
49	8.042	35.932		X		0.15	0.30	0.15	0.25	0.05	0.05	0.05
71	6.952	22.717		X		0.15	0.15	0.15	0.15	0.05	0.05	0.30
125	7.627	26.309		X		0.15	0.25	0.15	0.25	0.05	0.05	0.10
207	7.289	20.813	X			0.15	0.20	0.15	0.20	0.05	0.05	0.20
220	6.246	15.035	X			0.15	0.15	0.15	0.30	0.05	0.10	0.10
251	6.813	18.667	X			0.15	0.20	0.15	0.20	0.05	0.10	0.15
300	8.194	31.558	X	X	X	0.15	0.30	0.15	0.15	0.05	0.05	0.15
305	5.769	13.885	X			0.15	0.15	0.15	0.30	0.05	0.15	0.05
306	6.722	17.548	X		X	0.15	0.15	0.15	0.30	0.05	0.05	0.15
312	7.780	24.783	X	X	X	0.15	0.25	0.15	0.15	0.05	0.05	0.20
318	6.799	18.548	X			0.15	0.15	0.15	0.25	0.05	0.05	0.20
333	7.704	25.184		X		0.15	0.25	0.15	0.20	0.05	0.05	0.15
351	7.213	20.514	X	X	X	0.15	0.20	0.15	0.25	0.05	0.05	0.15
366	7.304	23.330		X		0.15	0.25	0.15	0.15	0.05	0.10	0.15
377	5.846	14.232	X			0.15	0.15	0.15	0.25	0.05	0.15	0.10
378	6.322	15.708	X			0.15	0.15	0.15	0.25	0.05	0.10	0.15
384	7.366	21.836	X	X		0.15	0.20	0.15	0.15	0.05	0.05	0.25
396	8.609	42.161	X	X	X	0.15	0.35	0.15	0.15	0.05	0.05	0.10
402	6.646	17.273	X			0.15	0.15	0.15	0.35	0.05	0.05	0.10
414	6.889	19.363	X			0.15	0.20	0.15	0.15	0.05	0.10	0.20
441	8.118	33.383		X		0.15	0.30	0.15	0.20	0.05	0.05	0.10
462	6.434	17.080	X			0.15	0.15	0.20	0.30	0.05	0.05	0.10

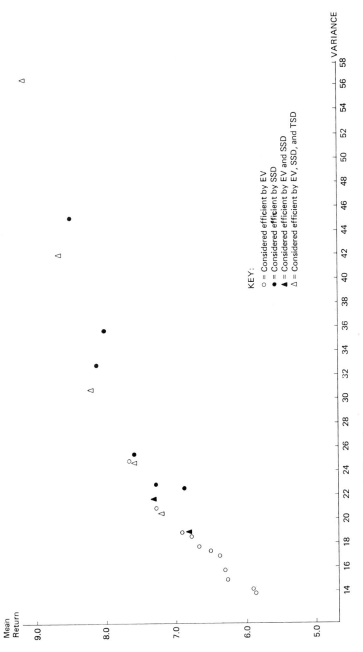

Fig. 2. Stochastic dominance-based efficient frontier.

KEY:

○ = Considered efficient by EV
● = Considered efficient by SSD
▲ = Considered efficient by EV and SSD
△ = Considered efficient by EV, SSD, and TSD

that portfolios 305, 377, 378 and 462 were identified as efficient by the EV rule but *not* by the FSD—the least restrictive rule. The TSD rule eliminated all but 5 portfolios, and these are also included in both the EV and SSD sets. The efficient portfolios identified by the various rules are depicted in fig. 2.

Given the conceptual advantages of the SSD and TSD rules (over the EV and FSD rules), management has to choose either the SSD or TSD rule and select a portfolio from those identified as efficient by each. The specific selection can be based on either the traditional risk–return tradeoff or, alternatively, other considerations, as discussed in the next section.

5. Discussion and conclusions

Increased recognition of the importance of product (business) portfolio analysis and decisions as an integral and central part of a firm's strategic planning efforts has had both positive and negative effects on marketing and corporate strategy. On the positive side, it has focused attention on the critical interdependencies among products and the critical need for a careful evaluation of product performance as input to the firm's marketing and resource allocation decisions. On the negative side, however, it has led to an increased reliance on a few oversimplified models such as the one propagated by the BCG, with little incentive to question the basic premises of these simplified models or attempt to improve them. In a sense, convergence on a model was reached much too early in the development of the field, to the detriment of the field's intellectual development. Symptomatic of this problem are recent strategy books such as Abell and Hammond's [1] which offers too much description of current usage of the BCG model and its related PIMS findings with no real effort to improve the current state of the art.

Given this need for re-examination of the current approaches to product portfolio analysis and finding ways of enriching them, this paper has proposed the utilization of the basic concepts of financial portfolio analysis, particularly those of the stochastic dominance rules, to product portfolio analysis. The advantages of this approach are:

● A focus on two conceptually desirable dimensions of any portfolio analysis —return and risk. These are especially relevant since most standardized portfolio models do not include them emplicitly.

● Whereas all other product portfolio approaches focus on *individual* product (product line or business) evaluation, financial portfolio analysis focuses on *portfolios* of products (product lines or businesses).

● The financial portfolio analysis clearly classifies products and portfolios into those dominated by others and those not dominated by others. The undominated or admissible set of product options provides a smaller set from which the optimal choice can be determined. In this respect, the stochastic dominance approach (as compared with the traditional risk–return (EV) approach) requires fewer restrictions on the nature of the underlying utility functions or return distributions. It thus provides an effective analytical tool to screen the available alternatives without the subjective estimation of the utility function.

- The SD approach allows the evaluation of alternative resource allocation plans. As shown in table 5, each of the portfolios is defined in terms of specific products and their proportion of the total portfolio. The return and risk (variance) of each portfolio is specified allowing management to choose among various portfolios not only in terms of their inclusion or exclusion of products, but in terms of the specific percentage of the total portfolio allocated to each product. Portfolio 312 differs, for example, from portfolio 351 (in table 5) in the allocation of its resources to three products—Allied Lines, 25% vs. 20%; Commercial, 15% vs. 25%; and Liability, 20% vs. 15%. These differences between the two portfolios result in different return and risk outcomes—7.78 mean return and 24.78 variance for portfolio 312 versus a lower return of 7.21 but also less variance of 20.51 for portfolio 351.

- Since the specific allocations to be examined are determined by the constraints imposed by management, the SD approach offers a convenient mechanism for testing the impact of various assumptions. For example, if management does not want to change its current portfolio by more than a certain percentage, this can be incorporated as a constraint.

The SD approach, at least in its simplest formulation, has a number of shortcomings when applied to the product portfolio:

- It is based on historical performance. Whereas this might be appropriate for the analysis of financial portfolios, product decisions should not be made based on historical performance, but rather based on projected performance. This can be corrected easily, however, by supplementing the historical performance with the projected performance. The projected performance can be based on time series, econometric analysis, or even subjective judgments. The expected returns (over the planning horizon) and their associated variances can then be used as the input data for the SD analysis.

- As compared to the EV approach, the SD approach does not include or utilize optimizing algorithms to determine the allocation of resources across product options. This necessitates the determination and examination of all feasible portfolios to identify the efficient portfolios and, hence, the determination of resource allocation. For a reasonable size product portfolio problem, the number of such feasible portfolios can be very large, prohibiting the implementation of the SD rules. Although efficient algorithms are currently available to implement the SD rules, there is a need to examine other possible approaches to combat the combinatorial nature of the portfolio problem. For example, Markowitz [29] has suggested a linear programming formulation for the second dominance rule. However, the computational feasibility of this approach has not been established yet. Future efforts to deal with this combinational problem may also consider the utilization certain approximation procedure such as the random sampling methods [2,8] and statistical designs [3].

Overcoming these limitations is the next research step. Yet, even if satisfactorily solved, stochastic dominance should *not* be used by itself as the sole product portfolio model. Rather, it should be incorporated with a customized approach which reflects other relevant management objectives (portfolio dimensions) in making the final selection among feasible portfolios. In this respect, the SD approach, especially if it includes the projected performance of both current and proposed products, is a valuable first step in a portfolio analysis system based on the analytic hierarchy process (AHP).

The AHP approach to portfolio analysis [49] offers a procedure for evaluating the various portfolios identified by the Stochastic Dominance approach on additional criteria deemed appropriate by management. By integrating the two approaches one avoids the problem inherent in the SD approach, namely the selection of a portfolio based only on its return and risk characteristics. At the same time, using the results of the SD analysis as input to the AHP improves the latter approach since it allows for an efficient, initial screening of portfolios and further allows for the evaluation of *portfolios* rather than individual products.

A first application of the SD approach coupled with the AHP framework is currently being implemented, but it is too early to evaluate it. The SD approach is not limited, however, to portfolio analysis. It can be applied to any marketing decision involving a combinatorial problem with a single objective and available time series data. It can be applied, for example, to the study of consumer behavior (using panel data). A considerable amount of effort has been devoted to the determination and estimation of consumer preference and utility functions [13,20]. The SD approach complements these efforts by delineating rules that provide the dominant or admissible set of alternatives under very plausible and prevalent restrictions on the form of utility functions without the subjective estimation of same.

Similarly, concepts underlying the SD approach are applicable to a number of marketing strategy variables such as media selection, product line pricing, sales force allocations, new product project selection, and other decision areas where the analyst is interested in comparing and evaluating the probabilistic response of different strategic alternatives. In these applications, the SD approach provides an additional analytical approach which might shed some light on the problem under study and, if incorporated with other appropriate procedures, improve the manager's odds of making better marketing decisions.

Our hope is that this paper will stimulate further examination of the appropriateness of the SD approach to product portfolios and other marketing decisions areas, and also encourage marketing scientists to explore the potential of other financial management approaches to the marketing area.

References

[1] D.F. Abell and J.S. Hammond, Strategic Market Planning: Problems and Analytical Approaches (Prentice-Hall, Englewood Cliffs, N.J., 1979).

[2] D.D. Achabal and V. Mahajan, An application of the multiplicative competitive interactive choice model to multiple store location decisions, Working Paper, Faculty of Marketing, The Ohio State University, Columbus, OH (1980).

[3] S. Addelman, Orthogonal main effect plans for asymmetrical factorial experiments, Technometrics 4 (February 1962) 21–46.

[4] V.S. Bawa, Optimal rules for ordering uncertain prospects, Journal of Financial Economics 2 (March 1975) 95–121.

[5] V.S. Bawa, E.B. Lindenberg and L.C. Rafsky, An efficient algorithm to determine stochastic dominance admissible sets, Management Science 25 (July 1979) 609–622.

[6] K. Borch, A note on uncertainty and indifference curves, Review of Economic Studies 36, 105 (January 1969) 1–4.

[7] R. Cardozo and Y. Wind, Portfolio analysis for strategic product-market planning, Wharton School Working Paper, University of Pennsylvania, Philadelphia, PA (1980).

[8] D.G. Dannenbring, Procedures for estimating optimal solution values for large combinatorial problems, Management Science 23, no. 12 (August 1977) 1273–1283.

[9] M.S. Feldstein, Mean–variance analysis in the theory of liquidity preference and portfolio selection, Review of Economic Studies 36 (January 1969) 5–12.

[10] P.C. Fishburn, Decision and Value Theory (John Wiley and Sons, New York, 1964).

[11] P.C. Fishburn and R.G. Vickson, Theoretical foundations of stochastic dominance, in: G.A. Whitmore and M.C. Findlay, eds., Stochastic Dominance (Lexington Books, Lexington, MA, 1978).

[12] G.M. Franfurter and H.E. Phillips, Efficient algorithms for conducting stochastic dominance tests on large number of portfolios: A comment, Journal of Financial and Quantitative Analysis 10 (March 1975) 177–179.

[13] P.E. Green and V. Srinivasan, Conjoint analysis in consumer behavior: Status and outlook, Journal of Consumer Research 5, no. 2 (September 1977) 103–123.

[14] J. Hader and W.R. Russell, Rules for ordering uncertain prospects, American Economic Review 59 (March 1969) 25–34.

[15] J. Hader and W.R. Russell, Stochastic dominance and diversification, Journal of Economic Theory 3, no. 3 (September 1971) 288–305.

[16] J. Hader and W.R. Russell, Decision making with stochastic dominance, Omega 2, no. 3 (June 1974) 365–376.

[17] N. Hakansson, Mean–variance analysis in a finite world, Journal of Financial and Quantitative Analysis 7 (September 1972) 1873–1880.

[18] J.S. Hammond, III, Simplifying the choice between uncertain prospects where preference is nonlinear, Management Science 20, no. 7 (March 1974) 1047–1072.

[19] G. Hanock and H. Levy, The efficiency analysis of choices involving risk, Review of Economic Studies 36 (July 1969) 335–346.

[20] J.R. Hauser and G.L. Urban, Assessment of attribute importances and consumer utility functions, Journal of Consumer Research 5, no. 4 (March 1979) 251–262.

[21] C.C. Huang, I. Vertinsky and W.T. Ziemba, On multiperiod stochastic dominance, Journal of Financial and Quantitative Analysis 13 (March 1978) 1–13.

[22] Y. Kahane, Determination of the product mix and the business policy of an insurance company—A portfolio approach, Management Science 23, no. 10 (June 1977) 1060–1069.

[23] Y. Kroll and H. Levy, Stochastic dominance with a riskless asset: An imperfect market, Journal of Financial and Quantitative Analysis 14, no. 2 (June 1979) 179–204.

[24] Y. Kroll and H. Levy, Sampling errors and portfolio efficient analysis, Journal of Financial and Quantitative Analysis 15 (September 1980) 655–688.

[25] H. Levy and G. Hanoch, Relative effectiveness of efficiency criteria for portfolio selection, Journal of Financial and Quantitative Analysis 5 (March 1970) 63–76.

[26] H. Levy and M. Sarnat, Alternative efficiency criteria: An empirical analysis, Journal of Finance 25 (December 1970) 1153–1158.

[27] H. Levy and Y. Kroll, Sample vs. population mean–variance efficient portfolios, Management Science 26 (November 1980) 1108–1116.

[28] H. Markowitz, Portfolio Selection: Efficient Diversification of Investments (John Wiley and Sons, New York, 1970).

[29] H. Markowitz, An algorithm for finding undominated portfolios, in: H. Levy and M. Sarnat, eds., Financial Decision Making Under Uncertainty (Academic Press, New York, 1977) 3–10.

[30] I. Niven, Mathematics of Choice (The Mathematical Association of America, New York, 1965).

[31] S. Perrakis and J. Zerbinis, Identifying the SSD portion of the EV frontier: A note, Journal of Financial and Quantitative Analysis 13 (March 1978) 167–171.

[32] R.B. Porter, An empirical comparison of stochastic dominance and mean variance portfolio choice criteria, Journal of Financial and Quantitative Analysis 8 (September 1973) 587–608.

[33] R.B. Porter, A comparison of stochastic dominance and stochastic programming, Omega 2, no. 1 (February 1974) 105–117.

[34] R.B. Porter and R. Bey, An evaluation of the empirical significance of optimal seeking algorithms in portfolio selection, Journal of Finance 29 (December 1974) 1479–1490.

[35] R.B. Porter and J.E. Gaumnitz, Stochastic dominance vs. mean–variance portfolio analysis: An empirical evaluation, American Economic Review 62 (June 1972) 438–446.

[36] R.B. Porter, J.R. Wart and D.L. Ferguson, Efficient algorithms for conducting stochastic dominance tests on large numbers of portfolios, Journal of Financial and Quantitative Analysis 8 (January 1973) 71–81.

[37] J.P. Quirk and R. Saposnik, Admissibility and measurable utility functions, Review of Economic Studies 29 (1962) 140–146.

[38] B.K. Stone, A linear programming formulation of the general portfolio selection problem, Journal of Financial and Quantitative Analysis 8 (September 1973) 621–636.

[39] R.G. Vickson, Stochastic dominance for decreasing absolute risk aversion, Journal of Financial and Quantitative Analysis 10 (December 1975) 799–811.

[40] R.G. Vickson, Stochastic dominance tests for decreasing absolute risk aversion I: Discrete random variables, Management Science 21, no. 12 (August 1975) 1438–1496.

[41] R.G. Vickson, Stochastic dominance tests for decreasing absolute risk aversion II: General random variables, Management Science 23, no. 5 (January 1977) 478–489.

[42] R.G. Vickson and M. Altman, On the relative effectiveness of stochastic dominance rules: Extension to decreasing risk-averse utility functions, Journal of Financial and Quantitative Analysis 12 (March 1977) 73–83.

[43] J. Von Neumann and O. Morgenstern, Theory of Games and Economic Behavior (John Wiley and Sons, New York, 1967).

[44] G.A. Whitmore, Third order stochastic dominance, American Economic Review 60 (June 1970) 457–459.

[45] G.A. Whitmore and M.C. Findlay, Stochastic Dominance (Lexington Books, Lexington, MA, 1978).

[46] Y. Wind, Product portfolio analysis: A new approach to the product mix decisions, in: R.C.

Curhan, ed., Combined Proceedings (American Marketing Association, Chicago, IL, 1974) 460–464.

[47] Y. Wind, Product Policy: Concepts Methods and Strategies (Addison-Wesley, Reading, MA, 1981).

[48] Y. Wind and V. Mahajan, Portfolio Analysis and Strategy (Addison-Wesley, Reading, MA, forthcoming).

[49] Y. Wind and T. Saaty, Marketing applications of the analytic hierarchy process, Management Science 26 (July 1980) 641–658.

[50] Y. Wind and V. Mahajan, Designing product and business portfolios, Harvard Business Review 59 (January–February 1981).

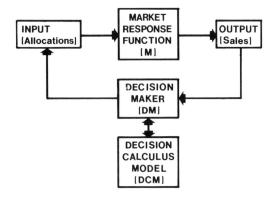

Where: M = Market Reaction to the Firm's Marketing
             Mix (i.e., Market Response Function)

         DM = The Decision Maker

         DCM = Decision Calculus Model (or model based
               representation of market response)

Fig. 1. The decision environment.

output measures such as profits, sales, consumer satisfaction, etc. it may be helpful to assess the effect of a decision calculus model on other important aspects of decisions. For example, the use of a decision calculus model may lead to radical shifts in allocation from one usage occasion to another for only minor improvements in profit. Such an occurrence would lead to organizational difficulties. Thus, there is need to assess the decision calculus impact on resource volatility (an input measure). As another example, managerial use of such a model could also lead to greater confidence in sales forecasts. The confidence aspect of a decision is important with regard to the vigor with which model recommendations will be implemented. The multiplicity of possible impacts due to the use of a decision calculus model warrants multiple measures of decision quality or model usefulness. [2] The multiple measures may not be strictly independent. For example, assume that two output-related objectives are (a) higher average profits and (b) fewer very low profit periods. Higher average profit would probably be associated with fewer low profit

[2] Even without multiple objectives, measurement of decision "quality" is a very difficult task. This difficulty arises due to the fact that there can be no absolute definition of optimality. All conceptions of optimality are contingent on the type of problem involved, the decision-maker's purpose, ability and needs and on the context of the problem [14].

periods. Nevertheless, multiple measures are interesting, even in this instance, because it would be possible to achieve the same profit level in two cases, one of which contained a greater number of low profit periods compensated for by a few periods of high profits. Therefore it is preferable to develop several measures.

3. Multiple measures of decision quality

In attempting to evaluate judgment-based models by operationalizing measures of decision quality, McIntyre [25] adopted the term "leverage". [3] This term was used to identify aspects of decision quality that might be impacted upon by a decision calculus system. Multiple measures were defined, some of which were input and output focused, while others were related to the decision-maker's understanding of market response or to his/her confidence in the decisions made. While it might be possible to develop many such measures, the following set captures some key aspects of decision quality. Below these measures are grouped into three categories.

I. Output related measures.

   L1: Impact on average profit (AP),
   L2: Impact on number of low profit periods (LP).
   L3: Impact on profit volatility (PV).
   L4: Impact on rate of profit improvement (PI).

II. Input related measures.

   L5: Impact on resource volatility (RV).
   L6: Impact on over-reaction (OR).
   L7: Impact on confidence in allocation (CA).

III. Understanding of response function measures.

   L8: Impact on ability to forecast sales (FS).
   L9: Impact on confidence in sales forecasts (CF).

In the next section these measures are made explicit for a specific setting and the measures are more thoroughly discussed.

---

[3] This term was used to suggest an analogy between physical leverage which is a mechanical advantage and mental leverage which is a judgmental advantage or way of improving upon the usefulness of fundamental judgment. In the multiple measures context, leverage becomes a vector.

3.1. Measure development

Our measures are developed for a static model being used in several time periods (e.g. CALLPLAN [21]). However, these measures could be extended for evaluating dynamic models (e.g. ADBUDG [16]). The measures are primarily designed for laboratory use wherein the true market response function (or "truth generating process") is known. However, some of these measures can be extended, in certain cases, to the evaluation of field tests. The measures were developed, for example, to assess model use by regional brand managers who reassess their marketing strategy at specified intervals (e.g. simulated quarters) based on updated knowledge of the market. The situation thus involves multiple episodes of use with a static model. The key decision left to the regional brand manager may be, for instance, how to allocate a regional promotional budget across several marketing control areas or territories, perhaps key cities in the region. It would then be possible to assess the model's impact by randomly assigning it to some of the managers and employing the nonusers as a control group.

Since one objective is to assess the profit performance impact from model use, it is helpful, when possible, to control for certain idiosyncratic aspects of the regions which might affect that part of profit performance which relates specifically to the budget allocation decision. One key aspect of a region, in this respect, is its profit improvement potential due to better budget allocation decisions. To measure this potential it is necessary to have (a) a naive basis against which improvement can be measured and (b) the optimal profit that could be achieved under the best possible allocation. One such basis is the profit achieved from a naive strategy of splitting the budget equally across the control areas or cities. When the profit from such a splitting is known (probably only in a laboratory situation), then the actual profit achieved by the manager can be compared to this naive strategy. Also, in laboratory settings (and in certain field settings) the true optimal allocation and corresponding profit can be determined which allows for the construction of the measures listed above as developed in the next sections.

3.2. Output related measures

Output measures are usually thought of as the most central aspect of decision quality. For this reason, our first set of measures deal with profits: average profits, frequency of low profit periods, volatility of profits, and rate of improvement in profits.

3.2.1. L1: Impact on average profit (AP)
One objective of model use is to achieve higher profits on the average. Period profit, for the purposes of this research, is defined as gross contribution

margin less marketing expense. This is equivalent to maximizing cumulative profits. Assume that each of R regional managers is allocating his/her promotional budget for a total of T periods. In order to assess the impact of model use it is essential to accumulate observations across decision-makers who deal with different decision problems so as to increase the number of observations when making statistical comparisons. In order to achieve that end, the measure must be appropriately comparable across decision-makers. Therefore, it is necessary to normalize across the decision situations for the relative degree of profit improvement that could be achieved (relative to the basis of naive or equal splitting, as discussed above). The following measure accomplishes such normalization. The average profit measure for manager r is:

$$AP_r = \frac{1}{T} \sum_{t=1}^{T} \left(\frac{\pi_{tr} - \pi_{br}}{\pi_{tr}^* - \pi_{br}} \right) \quad \text{or} \quad \frac{1}{T} \sum_{t=1}^{T} L_{tr},$$

where

$\pi_{tr}=$ expected value of profit from the promotional allocation decision in period t for regional manager r;

$\pi_{br}=$ expected value of profit from the basis (e.g. equal splitting of the budget across control areas in region r);

$\pi_{tr}^*=$ expected value of profit from the optimal splitting of the budget for regional manager r in period t;

$L_{tr}=$ normalized profit achievement obtained by manager r in period t.

The measure may be thought of as the average fraction of attainable profit improvement actually achieved during the T periods because improvement is constrained to $(\pi_{tr}^* - \pi_{br})$.

3.2.2. L2: Impact on number of low profit periods (LP)

Maximizing profits may not be the only goal of the brand manager. Reduction in the risk associated with decision-making may also be important. The brand manager may want to reduce the occurrence of poor profit performance periods. If this is true, then it is interesting to assess the model's impact on the occurrence of such periods.

Using a model may not lead to higher average profits, but could nevertheless reduce the number of low profit periods for users as compared to nonusers of such a decision aid. One way to operationalize this measure is to designate a period as a "low profit period" if a model-using manager experiences a normalized profit performance measure more than one standard deviation below the mean across all managers (users and nonusers) for that period. The objective is to minimize $LP_r = (\Sigma_t I_{tr})$, where I_{tr} is an indicator function which takes on a value of 1 if period t is a low profit period for manager r and zero otherwise. Period t is defined to be a low profit period if

$$\frac{L_{tr} - L_{t \cdot}}{\sigma_{L_{t \cdot}}} < -1, \quad \text{for regional manager } r,$$

where

$$L_{tr} = \frac{\pi_{tr} - \pi_{br}}{\pi_{tr}^* - \pi_{br}},$$

$$L_{t \cdot} = \frac{1}{R} \sum_{r=1}^{R} \left(\frac{\pi_{tr} - \pi_{br}}{\pi_{tr}^* - \pi_{br}} \right)$$

and

$$\sigma_{L_{t \cdot}} = \sqrt{\left(\frac{1}{R} \sum_{r=1}^{R} (L_{tr} - L_{t \cdot})^2 \right)}.$$

3.2.3. L3: Impact on profit volatility (PV)

Another important measure of risk is simply profit volatility. Financial theory suggests that profit volatility (as distinct from just low profit occurrences) is important. If a regional brand manager is risk averse, a reduction in profit volatility at any given average profit level is preferred. A reduction in the total variation in profit performance, therefore, is our third output related measure of decision quality. Note that this profit volatility measure is calculated as a within-user as opposed to an across-users measure. In addition, this measure is formed on the basis of the variation in normalized profit performance as compared to actual profit performance. Again, the reason for using normalized profit performance is to control for variations in the problems (e.g. number of control areas, profit improvement potential, etc.) confronted by different users. The measure is represented as $(\sigma_{L \cdot r})$ which model use might be expected to affect.

$$pv_r = \sigma_{L \cdot r} = \sqrt{\left(\frac{1}{T} \sum_{t=1}^{T} (L_{tr} - L_{\cdot r})^2 \right)},$$

Where

$$L_{\cdot r} = \frac{1}{T} \sum_{t=1}^{T} L_{tr}.$$

3.2.4. L4: Impact on rate of profit improvement (PI)

A fourth index of decision quality is the learning effect that might be exhibited through faster profit improvement over time with repeated use of the model. The issue here is whether the decision calculus model is useful only on its first application or whether relative profit improvement continues to increase with repeated model use. This is simply denoted as: [4]

$$\text{PI}_t = L_t.$$

According to the measure, if $(L_t) > 0$ in the first period then there is a "learning effect" in that period. For continued improvement, $(L_{t'}) > (L_t)$ for $t' > t$. This is a stringent test of the model's impact. If the model provides any improvement on the first use, then in a subsequent period model users will start from a higher profit level and the model must exhibit faster improvement even from that higher base to impact on this measure of decision quality. This is made more difficult by the fact that there is a natural constraint on the upper limit of profit at (π_t^*).

3.3. Input related measures

In addition to the above output criteria (measures), the objective of a decision calculus model may be input related. For example, it may be of interest to assess whether using the model has an influence on the volatility of resource allocation. Secondly, in certain situations (e.g. competitive bidding), the manager is apt to over-react to the outcome of the last decision [27]. The benefit of a model in such a situation may be to reduce over-reaction to recent outcomes. A third input related measure is the manager's confidence that the allocation being used is "optimal".

3.3.1. L5: Impact on resource volatility (RV)

When S-shaped response functions are involved, slight modifications in these functions, implied by the user through his/her answer to the parameterization questions, could lead to rather large shifts in suggested allocations, but for only minor profit improvements. Such shifts would have obvious intra-organizational problems in implementation. Thus, it is important to assess this potential aspect of model impact over repeated use.

It is relatively simple to measure the total amount of resource shifting that the manager does. This reallocation is divided by twice the budget because: (a) in budget constrained problems what is moved to one territory must be taken

---

[4] Note that the r (or manager) subscript is now dropped for this and all subsequent measures. This is because beyond measure L3 all calculations are carried out within manager. These within-manager measures are then to be used for comparison across managers. This simplifies the notation.

from another and (b) in order to make the measure comparable across regional managers the measure must be normalized for each manager's budget level. The resource volatility for regional manager r is represented as:

$$RV = \frac{1}{2B} \sum_{t=2}^{T} \sum_{k=1}^{K} |C_{kt} - C_{kt-1}|,$$

where B = budget level for regional manager r, and C_{kt} = allocation to territory k in period t by regional manager r.

3.3.2. L6: Impact on over-reaction (OR)

The motivation for this measure comes from the work of Edelman [10] who found that his competitive bidding model seemed to help managers prepare better bids by eliminating their tendency to over-react to the outcome of the last bid; they seemed to over-correct when working on their own.

The problem in measuring this aspect of decision quality is in defining what is meant by over-reaction. Obviously some reaction is beneficial, as long as it moves in the direction of greater profit. However, when testing judgment models by using a truth generating process for the market response function, the profit cannot increase over the optimum. Thus, over-reaction in allocation problems is measured at the input level and is defined as the amount to which a manager first under-allocates and then over-allocates to a given control area relative to the true optimum (or vice versa). The measure is then summed over areas and time periods (omitting the first use period). To make the measure comparable across managers, it needs to be normalized by expressing it as a percentage of the budget. Over-reaction for manager r is represented as:

$$OR = \frac{1}{B} \sum_{t=2}^{T} \sum_{k=1}^{K} |C_k^* - C_{kt}|,$$
$$\text{if } (C_k^* - C_{kt})(C_k^* - C_{k(t-1)}) < 0,$$
$$= 0, \text{ otherwise,}$$

where C_k^* = the optimum allocation to territory k of manager r, and C_{kt} = the allocation to territory k at time t.

3.3.3. L7: Impact on confidence in allocation (CA)

This measure is an indirect indication of how close the manager feels that he/she is to the optimum allocation. If model users (as compared to nonusers) believe that their profits are higher (e.g. closer to the true optimum) as compared to nonusers, then we define them to have greater confidence that their allocation is appropriate. Managers measuring high on this index are in essence indicating that there is little more profit to be gained from some reallocation of the budget.

This aspect of decision-making is important because the greater the confidence in model-aided decisions, the more likely that the recommendations will be implemented. If model users make better decisions than nonusers but do not realize this fact, then they will not be likely to implement the model recommendations with much vigor in practice.

In order to operationalize this measure, the manager is asked to estimate what the maximum possible profit would be under the true optimal (but unknown) allocation. Confidence in allocation is then measured as the difference between this estimate of true optimal profit and the actual profit achieved by the manager at that time.

This is normalized by dividing by π_t^* to make it comparable across regions. Confidence in allocation for regional manager r, then, is represented as:

$$CA = \frac{1}{\hat{\pi}_{t'}^*} \sum_{t'=1}^{T'} |\hat{\pi}_{t'}^* - \pi_{t'}|,$$

where

$\hat{\pi}_{t'}^* =$ manager r's estimate of the optimal expected profit in periods t',

$t' =$ periods in which the manager is asked to estimate the optimal profit, and

$T' =$ number of periods in which the manager is asked to make the estimate.

3.4. Market response function related measures

Another impact of a decision calculus model may be to improve the manager's ability to forecast the sales in a given territory as a result of the allocation specified. If this were the result of model use, it would explain one reason why model users achieve higher profit performance (if they do). The hypothesis is that the more accurate the estimates, the greater is the understanding of the market response function in the environment. Another related measure is the confidence in these sales forecasts. Again, the hypothesis is that the greater the confidence in the knowledge of market responsiveness, the more likely it is that the recommendation of the model will be implemented.

3.4.1. L8: Impact on ability to forecast sales (FS)

In order to operationalize this measure, the manager may be asked, on several occasions and for several territories, to estimate the sales that will occur due to his/her specified allocation. The differences between this estimate and the real expected value provides a measure of forecast accuracy. This difference is standardized by the real expected value, to make it comparable across managers. So, the ability to forecast sales for regional manager r is represented as:

$$FS = \frac{1}{K} \sum_{k=1}^{K} \frac{|S_{kz} - \hat{S}_{kz}|}{S_{kz}},$$

where S_{kz} = the actual expected value of sales that would occur in the kth territory of regional manager r at allocation level z, and $\hat{S}_{kz}$ = the manager's estimate of S_{kz}.

A convenient way to elicit this measure is to utilize the parameterization responses to the model which are essentially sales forecasts of what would occur due to different allocation levels in an area. The measure must then be expressed as an average (i.e. it must be divided by the number of territories or control areas) when different managers have different numbers of territories to deal with. Note that if this elicitation procedure is used, then nonusers must be asked to respond to the model questions, at some point in time, in order to have measures across all users.

3.4.2. L9: Impact on confidence in sales forecasts (CF)

This measures the confidence in sales forecasts (in percentage terms) as the result of a budget allocation to a given territory. Specifically, it is the average percentage spread between a manager's maximum and minimum estimate for predicting the sales outcome he/she expects from the planned budget allocation. Confidence in sales forecasts for manager r is calculated as:

$$CF = \frac{1}{T'} \sum_{t'=1}^{T'} \sum_{k'=1}^{K'} \frac{(\max S_{kz} - \min S_{kz})}{\text{act } S_{kz}},$$

where

$\max S_{kz}$ = manager's maximum estimate of S_{kz},
$\min S_{kz}$ = manager's minimum estimate of S_{kz}, and
$\text{act } S_{kz}$ = the actual expected sales that would occur in territory k due to allocation z.

$T' < T$ and $K' < K$ when confidence estimates are elicited less frequently and across a smaller number of territories.

4. Other impacts from model use

4.1. Organizational impact

The benefits from a decision calculus system may extend beyond immediate performance measures. The decision aid may:
 (1) Allow the emergence of politically sensitive solutions.
 (2) Provide continuity as managers turn over in a given job.
 (3) Bring a new manager "up to speed" more quickly.
 (4) Act as a communications tool.
 (5) Lead to better documentation of past decisions.

(6) Suggest needs for future data and/or research.

(7) Broaden or enhance the perspective of the decision-maker.

(8) Increase attention to the logic of the analysis.

Such a perspective suggests that models of the decision calculus type might deserve evaluations that go beyond immediate decision impact.

4.2. Psychological validation

Another important issue in the evaluation of models, and decision support models in particular, is acceptance. It is sometimes argued that the ultimate criterion for model evaluation is a usefulness criterion and that if a model is not used then it must be given a poor evaluation [6, p. 10]. This leads to the concept of "psychological validation" [13, p. 11] or the reasons that might lead a manager to believe that a model will aid in decisions. Originally, it was suggested that a decision calculus model be evaluated on a set of six criteria [16]. These have been expanded to include methods for building and implementing models [35]. In addition, psychological validation of a model might be based on:

(1) The face validity of the model.

(2) The common sense or intuitive appeal of the model's results.

(3) The extent of use and acceptance of the model by respected individuals.

(4) Faith in the model supplier.

(5) The aesthetic appeal of the output.

(6) The fact that the answer comes from a computer.

(7) The fact that the manager has used the model and perceived it to be beneficial.

(8) The fact that the manager himself was involved in developing the model (or at least in requesting it and guiding its development).

Within such a perspective, the model could be evaluated on the basis of the user's perceptions of its benefits [9].

5. Contingency factors for model leverage

The impact (leverage) of a judgment-based marketing model may be contingent upon certain situational factors. These can be broadly classified according to fig. 1 as: (a) decision environment/situation factors (e.g. the number of control units or territories over which allocation are to be made); (b) decision-maker factors (e.g. a decision-maker's experience in trying to solve the problem without the aid of a model); and (c) decision calculus system factors (e.g. whether the response functions are modeled as stationary or nonstationary, whether the model uses a constrained budget allocation or an unconstrained optimization, etc.). A listed of such factors is provided in table 1.

Table 1
Factors that might affect leverage in a model usage situation

Decision situation factors	Decision model factors	Decision-maker factors
1. Number of control units (or territories) over which allocations are to be made. 2. Number of control variables which are (or can be) manipulated in arriving at a decision (e.g. just advertising, or advertising and personal selling as separate variables). 3. The level of interaction among the control variables (if there are more than one) and/or territories. 4. The degree of carryover from decision episode to decision episode of the influence from past levels of the decision variables. 5. The equality of the subunits (i.e. territories) in regard to their importance in the decision. Inequality effectively alters the "true" dimensionality of the problem. 6. The range of control variable settings in past decisions. If past operating ranges have been restricted, it is difficult to assess response functions over a broad range. 7. The amount of budget relative to the unconstrained budget across all territories. The severity of the constraint may influence the leverage achievable. 8. The degree of determinancy in the "reality generating" process relative to the control variables (i.e. noise in the environment). 9. The relationship between the length of the feedback period and the length of the control period. The lower the feedback to control ratio, the greater the likelihood of learning.	1. Formulation of the model: (a) Unit of analysis—individual consumer, market segment or total (aggregate) market. (b) Temporal perspective—static or dynamic response function. (c) Optimization — constrained or unconstrained. (d) Appropriateness of specification. 2. Consideration of elements in the decision-making environment. (a) Internal to the company—objectives for the product and comunality with organizational objectives, abilities, present and future marketing mix, etc. (b) External to the company—consumer, distribution channel and competitive response. 3. Model parameterization (a) Method—judgment, analysis of nonexperimental historical data, experimentation or hybred. (b) Type of data—cross-sectional, time series or pooled cross-sectional and time series. (c) Source of data—actual behavior. Behavior in an artificial environment or attitude data. 4. Uses of the model—description, understanding, conditional predictions.	1. The decision-maker's experience in trying to solve the problem with or without the aid of a decision support system. 2. The decision-maker's degree of understanding and training with the specific model. 3. The decision-maker's experience with models in general. 4. Cognitive style—personal ability or tendencies towards sensing and dealing with data and habits with respect to drawing conclusions. 5. Cognitive complexity—mental ability to handle many dimensions or concepts in mind at once. 6. Time spent to solve the problem on each decision episode. 7. Confidence in the model. 8. Degree of implementation of the model's suggestion. 9. Differences in cognitive biases—e.g. regression towards the mean, halo effects, etc. 10. Self-confidence, functional interest, attitude toward computers, models and quantiitative methods. 11. Quantitative ability and training. 12. Motivations. 13. Demographics—age/sex, etc.

Previous research has indicated that the relative cognitive difficulty of a particular task may have a strong effect on performance [28]. Cognitive difficulty is decomposed into the complexity of the decision situation and the cognitive abilities of a decision-maker which, in turn, are expected to affect leverage. Leverage may also be dependent on the particular judgment model (or DSM) being used. These models usually differ on (1) the formulation; (2) consideration of elements in the decision making environment; (3) method of parameterization; and (4) uses of the model.

Determining the usefulness of a model for a particular decision problem in a given environment for a designated decision-maker is then an empirical question. Past empirical evaluations have reported information sufficient to calculate a subset of the decision measures outlined in section 3 and to address a few of the contingency factors listed in table 1. In the remainder of this paper, we review these investigations.

6. Empirical evaluations using the multiple measure and contingency factor paradigm

Before reviewing the few studies that compare actual results from decisions made with and without a decision calculus system, it should be noted that there are a number of other approaches suggested in the literature that relate to how one might go about evaluating such models.

6.1. Internal or model-based evaluations

Frequently models are evaluated by taking them as "truth". Within the model framework, the performance of a management decision is compared to the performance of the model-based optimal decision which may be different from the optimum for the truth generating process (actual market). The difference is taken as a measure of the value of the model (e.g. [2,21–24,26,29,34]). While such results are certainly of interest, utilizing the model as the criterion biases the apparent improvement in favor of the model-based solution. Therefore, these evaluations are not dealt with here.

While the use of model-based evaluations is the only expedient approach in most field settings, sharper and more extensive measures are possible in the laboratory with the specification of a truth generating process. Knowledge of the truth generating process allows a determination of the optimum strategy and its corresponding profit. This permits the calculation of leverage measures L1 through L4, as well as L6 and L7. The measures L5, L8 and L9, however, do not require knowledge of the truth generating process and can hence be utilized in field settings. In certain field situations, such as competitive bidding, the true optimum strategy can be determined *post hoc* through an examination of the bids received. In such field situations all the leverage measures may potentially be calculated.

6.2. Model evaluation by tracking

With regard to the testing of models, tracking of historical outcomes has been suggested [16]. Tracking refers to the practice of using the model, as parameterized, to forecast historical data. This is one way to evaluate the adequacy of the model. Parameters can then be adjusted until the model tracks well. But it is acknowledged [16] that in most cases past operating ranges are so narrow that such tests are weak. In addition, the models sometimes have so many parameters that they will track past data reasonably well with various different sets of values all having different implications. For instance, in working with the ADBUDG model, Chakravarti, Mitchell and Staelin [4] demonstrated this point:

> We show that the different sets of parameters, which all give good fits to the data, yield optimum advertising decisions for the next period ranging from $0 to $2,860,000. This is strong evidence that different sets of parameters which reproduce past data equally well, can yield substantially different decision implications.

Thus it appears that tracking, while undoubtedly helpful, may not always signal the most appropriate parameters. This simply means that the manager's judgment is still the major influence in the model. Whether or not management decisions are improved by model use, then, remains as an important issue that tracking does not directly address.

6.3. Empirical tests

Therefore, we concern ourselves here only with objective evaluations of a decision calculus model based on external validation of results where one can compare model based performance to nonmodel based performance.

When the evaluation criteria are set this stringently, there are only four published empirical investigations (that we know of).

(1) Edelman [10] reported on the results of commercial bids prepared by managerial judgment without a model and bids generated by the same managers via a judgmentally parameterized decision calculus style model. The performance of each approach was then compared to the actual winning bids. In each of seven tests, the model bid was just below the lowest bid; the results being favorable for model use. Table 2 summarizes the comparative results of these seven consecutive bids.

Columns 2 and 3 contain the bids prepared without and with the use of the model. The lowest bid is shown in column 4. The measure of performance of

Table 2
Bidding model tests

Test	Manager's bid	Model bid	Lowest bid	Manager's bid: % under (over) lowest bid	Model bid: % under lowest bid
(1)	(2)	(3)	(4)	(5)	(6)
1	44.53	46.00	46.49	4.2	1.1
2	47.36	42.68	42.93	(10.3)	0.6
3	62.73	59.04	60.76	(3.2)	2.8
4	47.72	51.05	53.38	10.6	4.4
5	50.18	42.80	44.16	13.7	3.1
6	60.39	54.61	55.10	(9.6)	0.9
7	39.73	39.73	40.47	1.8	1.8

the model was chosen to be the comparison between columns 5 and 6 which are, respectively, the bids without and with the model relative to the lowest competitive bid.

Montgomery and Weinberg [27] suggest that the managers appeared to be over-reacting to the result of the previous bid. For example, in the first case, they undershot the next lowest bid by 4.2%, so in the second case they over-corrected and were 10.3% above the winning bid. The Edelman model seemed to provide a stabilizing effect on the bidding results.

(2) Chakravarti, Mitchell and Staelin [4,5] completed two replications of a study in which managers participated in a test of the ADBUDG model in a simulated setting. In the report on the first study it was concluded that the model *did not enhance* the ability of the participants to make market share estimates, *nor did it enhance* parameter estimation ability. The model *did*, however, provide a small (2.6%) but significant ($p < 0.10$) improvement in profit performance.. The second study confirmed the findings of the first, except that the profit improvement finding was not present. The authors attribute part of the reason for poor model performance to the fact that the model users demonstrated severe bias in their response to the parameterization questions. They found that the judgments were biased toward the current operating level of the user and that the more distant the true value of the parameter being estimated, the greater the bias that was exhibited. This phenomenon might be titled "anchoring of input judgments" in reference to an analogous tendency noted in the psychological literature [33]. The conclusions from these studies do not favor model use.

(3) Fudge and Lodish [11] used CALLPLAN in a controlled field experiment that pitted salesmen with the model against salesmen without it. Ten matched pairs of salesmen were included in the study. From each pair, one

salesman was randomly chosen to use the model, while the other received all the model input exercises, but not the model suggested call plan. The model group in this study achieved 8.1% higher sales during the 6-month test period ($p < 0.025$). Here again, results are favorable for model use.

(4) McIntyre [25] used a simplified model similar to CALLPLAN in a controlled laboratory experiment. Ninety-six MBA students played the part of a recently hired brand manager and made promotional allocations to a set of marketing territories in an attempt to maximize profit achievement. A $2 \times 2 \times 2$ full factorial design was used with "model availability", "dimensionality of the problem", and "noise level in the truth generating process" being the three factors involved. The dimensionality of the decision problem was manipulated at a low (three territories) and a high (six territories) level. The amount of "noise in the truth generating process" was also manipulated at a low and high level. Cognitive style (as measured by the Myers–Briggs instrument) and quantitative ability (as measured by GMAT scores) were determined and treated as covariates. Each subject made nine sequential decisions, the first four of which were just to gain some experience at the task. During the next five decisions half the subjects in each treatment condition were given the judgment-based model as a decision aid while the other subjects continued without the aid. The results from this experiment indicate that the model did help subjects to achieve greater profit under all conditions (high and low noise levels; three and six territories). Individual differences were found to have only a minor effect on performance (on average). These findings are again favorable for model use.

In order to further compare the findings of the four studies, we have attempted to calculate the leverage indexes in each case. The exact numerical results are difficult to compare because of the marked differences in the studies and the way in which the findings are reported. However, the direction of the findings is clear in a number of cases. Table 3 summarizes the leverage findings from the four studies.

7. Findings

In this section we speculate on what appear to be the generalizable findings from the four studies compared above.

(1) Model users show a marked tendency to anchor their judgments in the direction of past operating levels. Furthermore, the greater the difference between the current operating level and the parameter being estimated the greater will be the judgmental anchoring bias [5, p. 257; 11, p. 105]. This means that response functions tend to be estimated as too flat relative to the "truth". This finding is consistent with the phenomena reported in the psychological literature [32,33].

(2) The flattening of response functions is particularly detrimental in models
(e.g. ADBUDG) which attempt to arrive at overall budget levels as compared
to models (e.g. CALLPLAN) which attempt to arrive at across-activity allocations of a constrained budget. In an illustrative example, McIntyre [25, p. 140]
compared an unconstrained budget allocation to a constrained allocation for a
three-territory problem. A modified exponential was selected to represent the
promotional response function, the parameters of which were different for
each of the three territories.

Further, two cases were investigated: (1) wherein the user exhibits no bias in
the estimation of the parameters and (2) wherein the user underestimates the
saturation limit by 20% and overestimates the approach constant parameters
by 20%. The impact on profit differences from the unbiased and the biased
model was found to be 40 times greater in the *unconstrained* case as compared
to the *constrained* case [25, p. 140]. Beswick and Cravens [2] make a statement
which is relevant to the hypothesis that anchoring is not terribly critical in

Table 3
Leverage findings from four studies

	McIntyre [25]	Chakravarti, Mitchell and Staelin [5]	Fudge and Lodish [11]	Edelman [10]
L1: Higher average profits	yes [a]	no [j]	yes [n]	yes [p]
L2: Fewer very low profit periods	yes [b]	?	?	yes [q]
L3: Less profit volatility	yes [c]	?	?	yes [r]
L4: Faster profit improvement	yes [d]	no [k]	?	no [s]
L5: Less resource volatility (less movement of resources)	no [e]	?	?	?
L6: Less over-reaction (fewer shifts past optimum)	no [f]	?	?	yes [t]
L7: Greater confidence in allocation (perception that allocation is near optimum)	no [g]	?	?	?
L8: Better ability to forecast sales	no [h]	no [l]	?	?
L9: Greater confidence in sales forecasts	no [i]	?	?	?
Anchoring of input judgments	?	yes [m]	yes [o]	?

Notes

[a]   Subjects with the model achieved 21% more of their potential profit improvement when compared to nonusers ($p < 0.01$).

[b]   All users averaged 2.016 "low profit periods" during the four experimental decision episodes but model users experienced 0.633 fewer "low profit periods" relative to nonusers ($p < 0.05$).

[c]   All subjects had a profit volatility index of 0.27 but model users had a profit volatility 0.16 higher than nonusers. ($p < 0.01$).

[d]   Model advantage in the first period was 0.156 ($p < 0.10$). Two periods later, the model advantage had increased to 0.327 ($p < 0.01$).

[e]   All subjects had a resource volatility index that averaged 0.08 but model users had a resource volatility index 0.16 higher than nonusers ($p < 0.01$).

[f]   The model had the effect of increasing over-reactions by 0.0365 ($p < 0.01$).

[g]   Compared to nonusers, model users perceived that the optimum profit allocation would be higher than their current profit ($p < 0.10$). It is suggested that the reason for this outcome may have been that the model users were able to improve their profit performance more than nonusers and, therefore, may have reasoned that still more improvement might be possible. This occurred even though no subject was aware of anything about the experience of any other subject.

[h, i]   The model appeared to have no statistically detectable impact on the L8 and L9 leverage index measures.

[j]   While overall average performance was 0.813, those *not* exposed to the decision calculus model did 0.032 better than the grand mean performance ($p < 0.05$).

[k]   This follows from the L1 measure.

[l]   Subjects who were exposed to the model and also participated in a parameterization exercise experienced larger forecast errors than those who also used the model but did not so participate ($p < 0.05$).

[m]   The further the normalized distance from the true value of the parameter being estimated, the larger was the associated error. ($p < 0.01$). The net effect is an anchoring phenomenon wherein biases are made in the direction of the current operating level and these biases are greater the further from the current operating level is the true value of the parameter being estimated.

[n]   From the data and findings reported by Fudge and Lodish, it is not possible to calculate the actual leverage measures. However, it can be inferred from the fact that the users achieved 8.1% greater sales than the nonusers ($p < 0.025$) that the L1 measure, as a minimum, must be in effect.

[o]   Anchoring is apparent in the findings from the CALLPLAN experiment. The authors note: "It is evident that the salesmen and managers were conservative in their estimates of the sales response to changes in their call frequencies" [11, p. 105].

[p]   By making the assumption that costs were 80% of the average of the three bids (the manager's intuitive bid, the winning bid, and the model bid) it is possible to calculate the key leverage measures. Under these assumptions, L1 = 0.83 ($p < 0.01$).

[q]   The L2 measure also appears to be significant with the model making 0 "large errors" and the manager 3 "large errors" in the six trials. Thus, the large errors index would be 0 and 0.50, respectively.

[r]   The impact on consistency in the Edelman study is truly dramatic. The manager's intuitive approach appeared very erratic ranging from 10.6% under to 13.7% over the winning bid while the model based bids varied from 3.1% below the winning bid to 0.6% below the winning bid.

[s]   A plot of the L1 meAsure on a period by period basis reveals no apparent trend.

[t]   The L6 leverage impact of the Edelman study is also quite dramatic. The manager's intuitive approach generated three over-reactions as defined for the L6 index while the model based approach generated no such results (each out of five possible).

constrained allocation problems. In the authors' words:

> Because the model's responsiveness to selling effort was believed to be extremely conservative, the model was tested for sensitivity of this variable by rerunning the program with...the time elasticity...increased almost 40%....One encouraging result is that the effort allocations changed very slightly. The largest change in allocation was from 237% to 256% for territory B. Most important, the direction and relative magnitude of the changes from current effort levels where the same in every case. This result is especially encouraging because of the uncertainty in the estimate of the elasticity of the effort variable [2, p. 142].

This is an indication that altering all the response functions with similar anchoring may not much affect the optimal allocation of resources across the activities. The anchoring phenomenon may explain, in part, why the Chakravarti, Mitchell and Staelin experiments using ADBUDG (unconstrained optimization) did not yield increased profit performance for users as compared to nonusers of the model.

(3) The use of a decision calculus model does not appear to improve the decision-maker's ability to estimate response functions compared to a nonuser. This means that decision improvement (when there is one) comes about from better integration of judgments and not from some improvement in the basic judgments themselves [5, p. 261; 25, p. 257].

(4) When the response functions are nonstationary over a sequence of decision episodes, the user may include the shift in the response function as if it were part of the response function itself. In other words, if a decision-maker increases advertising in each of several periods and at the same time the response function is shifting upward, the decision-maker overestimates the slope of the response function since his increasing advertising is confounded with the upward shift (see fig. 2). Such use of historical information would be inappropriate, even though there is no error with regard to the model specification.

This factor can lead to serious distortions. Among the empirical tests described above, this problem was only present in the case of the ADBUDG test and may account, in part, for the failure of the model in that situation [5, p. 254].

(5) In some cases a decision calculus model can help to reduce inconsistency in decisions. Such a result is dramatic in the Edelman study [10, p. 56; 27].

(6) Decision calculus models do not provide marked improvement in the perception that better decisions are being made. This may explain why these models have not been implemented at a faster rate. In fact, the McIntyre study showed that even though the model clearly helped on the average, it certainly did not help every user to perform better than every nonuser in the same experimental conditions. Also, objective measures of decision confidence showed no enhancement with regard to model use [25, pp. 258–262].

(7) It appears that the cognitive style of the user (as measured by the

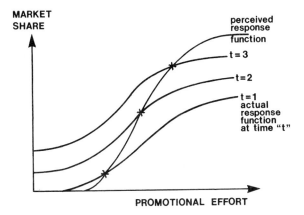

MARKET SHARE

perceived response function

t = 3

t = 2

t = 1 actual response function at time "t"

PROMOTIONAL EFFORT

Fig. 2. Shifting response function.

Myers–Briggs instrument) provides little explanatory power as to how an individual will perform with a decision calculus model [25, p. 242].

(8) Quantitative ability (as measured by GMAT scores) appears to have little explanatory power (though the power of McIntyre's test may have been quite low) as to performance with a decision calculus model [25, p. 242].

(9) Interestingly, manipulation of the degree of noise in the truth generating process appeared to have little impact on the relative advantage of using a decision calculus model. Apparently the detrimental effect of such environmental conditions works to the disadvantage of the model user and the nonmodel user in about equal amounts [25, p. 242].

(10) Also of interest is the fact that altering the decision complexity (as measured by the number of territories involved) appeared to have no marked effect on the relative advantage of model use (at least when the range of such manipulation is held to three territories versus six territories) [25, p. 242].

8. Summary

A synthesis of the above findings would suggest that decision calculus models can be expected to provide the best leverage potential in situations that do not involve nonstationary response functions over time. It also appears that such models do not need to take into account the cognitive style or quantitative ability of the user. Moreover, it appears that such models are likely to work about as well under high and lower noise levels and under higher and lower dimensionality. And finally, due to the existence of the anchoring phenomenon, it may be advisable to use models which attempt to arrive at across-activity allocations rather than models which attempt to arrive at overall budget levels.

References

[1] C.A. Beswick, Allocating selling effort via dynamic programming, Management Science 23 (March 1977) 667–678.

[2] C.A. Beswick and D.W. Cravens, A multi-stage decision model for salesforce management, Journal of Marketing Research 14 (May 1977) 135–144.

[3] R.D. Buzzell, Mathematical Models and Marketing Management (Harvard University, Graduate School of Business Administration, Division of Research, Boston, Mass., 1964) 136–156.

[4] D. Chakravarti, A. Mitchell and R. Staelin, A cognitive approach to model building and evaluation, in: B.A. Greenberg and D.N. Bellenger, eds., Contemporary Marketing Thought, Proceedings 1977 Educators' Conference (American Marketing Association, Chicago, Ill., 1977).

[5] D. Chakravarti, A. Mitchell and R. Staelin, Judgment based marketing decision models: An experimental investigation of the decision calculus approach, Management Science 25 (March 1979).

[6] C.W. Churchman, Reliability of models in the social sciences, Interfaces 4 (November 1973).

[7] G.S. Day, G.J. Eskin, D.B. Montgomery and C.B. Weinberg, Cases in Computer and Model Assisted Marketing: Planning (Hewlett-Packard, Cupertino, Calif., 1973).

[8] G.S. Day, D.B. Montgomery and C.B. Weinberg, New tools for teaching marketing: Computer and model assisted cases, Stanford Graduate School of Business, Research Paper 253 (April 1975).

[9] M.N. Dewaele, The design of decision aids for marketing managers based on Jungian personality types and other managerial styles, unpublished doctoral dissertation, University of California, Berkeley (1973).

[10] F. Edelman, Art and science of competitive bidding, Harvard Business Review 43 (July–August 1965) 53–66.

[11] W.K. Fudge and L.M. Lodish, Evaluation of the effectiveness of a salesman's planning system by field experimentation, Interfaces 8 (November 1977) 97–106.

[12] T.A. Glaze and C.B. Weinberg, A sales territory alignment program and account planning system (TAPS), in: R.P. Bagozzi, ed., Sales Management: New Developments from Behavioral and Decision Model Research (Management Science Institute, Cambridge, Mass., 1979).

[13] P.G.W. Keen, Interactive computer systems for top managers: A modest proposal, Sloan Management Review 18 (Fall 1976) 1–17.

[14] P.G.W. Keen, The evolving concept of optimality, in: M.K. Starr and M. Zeleny, eds., Multi-criteria Decision Making, Studies in the Management Sciences, vol. 6 (The Institute of Management Science, 1977) 31–57.

[15] P. Kotler, Marketing mix decisions for new products, Journal of Marketing Research 1 (1964) 43–49.

[16] J.D.C. Little, Models and managers: The concept of a decision calculus, Management Science: Applications 16 (1970) 466–485.

[17] J.D.C. Little, BRANDAID: An on-line marketing-mix model, Part 1: Structure, Operations Research 23 (1975) 629–655.

[18] J.D.C. Little, BRANDAID: A marketing mix model, Part 2: Implementation, calibration, and case study, Operations Research 23 (1975) 657–673.

[19] J.D.C. Little, Decision support systems for marketing managers, Journal of Marketing 43 (Summer 1979) 9–26.

[20] J.D.C. Little and L.M. Lodish, A media planning calculus, Operations Research 17 (1973) 1–35.

[21] L.M. Lodish, CALLPLAN: An interactive salesman's call planning system, Management Science 18 (1971) P25–P40.

[22] L.M. Lodish, A vaguely right approach to sales force allocation decisions, Harvard Business Review 52 (1974) 119–124.

[23] L.M. Lodish, Sales territory alignment to maximize profit, Journal of Marketing Research 12 (1975) 30–36.

[24] L.M. Lodish, Assigning salesmen to accounts to maximize profit, Journal of Marketing Research 13 (1976) 440–444.

[25] S.H. McIntyre, The leverage impact of judgment based marketing models, unpublished dissertation, Graduate School of Business, Stanford University (1979).

[26] D.B. Montgomery, A.J. Silk and C.E. Zaragoza, A multiple product sales force allocation model, Management Science 18 (1971) P3–P24.

[27] D.B. Montgomery and C.B. Weinberg, Modeling marketing phenomena: A managerial perspective, Journal of Contemporary Business (Autumn 1973) 17–43.

[28] A. Newell and H.A. Simon, Human Problem Solving (Prentice-Hall, Inc., Englewood Cliffs, N.J., 1972).

[29] A. Parasuraman and R.L. Day, A management oriented model for allocating sales effort, Journal of Marketing Research 14 (1977) 22–33.

[30] M.A. Sewall, A decision calculus model for contract bidding, Journal of Marketing 26 (1976) 92–98.

[31] R.J. Shanker, R.E. Turner and A.A. Zoltners, Sales territory design: An integrated approach, Management Science 24 (1975) 309–320.

[32] P. Slovic, From Shakespeare to Simon: Speculation and some evidence of man's ability to process information, Oregon Research Institute Bulletin 12 (1972) 1–29.

[33] A. Tversky and D. Kahneman, Anchoring and calibration in the assessment of uncertain quantities, Oregon Research Institute 12 (1972) 12–50.

[34] G.L. Urban, Allocating ad budgets geographically, Journal of Advertising Research 15 (1975) 7–16.

[35] G.L. Urban and R.I. Karash, Evolutionary model building, Journal of Marketing Research 8 (1971) 62–66.

[36] C.B. Weinberg, D.B. Montgomery and G.S. Day, Teaching notes for cases in computer and model assisted marketing, Technical Report 50, Graduate School of Business, Stanford University, Stanford, Ca. (1976).

[37] A.A. Zoltners, Prabhakant Sinha and Philip S.C. Cong, An optimal algorithm for sales representative time management, Management Science 25 (1979) 1197–1202.

[38] A.A. Zoltners and Prabhakant Sinha, Integer programming models for sales resource allocation, Management Science 26 (1980) 242–260.

TIMS Studies in the Management Sciences 18 (1982) 209–239
© North-Holland Publishing Company

A PROCESS MODEL FOR THE FAMILY PLANNING DECISION

John U. FARLEY and Donald E. SEXTON *

Columbia University

Patterns in sets of parameters estimated for a consumer behavior model describing the process by which couples adopt and continue to practice family planning suggest program design and target population segmentation strategies for family planning programs. For example, the results suggest that program planners should focus on providing product-specific (as opposed to general) information and on accessibility of contraceptive products. Efforts should also focus on younger couples nearing what they consider the "ideal" family size. The results are based on data from knowledge–attitude–practice (KAP) studies, familiar in family planning, from eight developing countries.

1. Introduction

Family planning programs which attempt to intervene directly in traditional reproduction patterns have received increasing attention as policies aimed at reducing rapid population growth were adopted by nearly 100 nations during the past two decades [16]. To be successful such programs must induce significant behavioral change by individual couples, particularly in situations in which average family size is large by tradition. Convincing couples to space children and ultimately to limit their number requires intervention at several points in the family's decision-making concerning fertility and family size. These interventions have generally been oriented toward one or more of the following:

(a) knowledge about family planning in general and about various specific methods;

(b) overall attitude toward "ideal" family size and toward family limitation; and

(c) use or willingness to use some modern method of family planning. Cross-sectional surveys, known in the field as KAP (knowledge–attitude–practice) studies, have traditionally focused on the values of these variables for consumers or potential consumers to provide benchmarks for program evaluation as well as guidance for program modification. While the primary program

*The authors are indebted to Dr. Robert Smith and Gary Damkoehler for providing the data from Westinghouse Population Center on which this model is based. Dr. Farley received support from the Mitsui Corporation during a portion of the study period; he is R.C. Kopf Professor of International Marketing.

goal is to create practice, various other measurements may provide guidance for specific activities. For example, unfavorable attitudes may indicate the need for heavy resource commitment to general communication, while favorable attitudes and high willingness to use contraceptives but low use may indicate problems in product-specific knowledge or product availability.

This paper develops and tests an integrating framework based on consumer choice models for use of KAP data. In addition to allowing more managerially relevant use of the information, such a model might be useful to program planners for pin-pointing key behavioral elements of changes in program configuration or policy modifications [3,10]. Since KAP studies have been done in many settings, such a model might also be helpful in making generalizations over cultures.

2. "KAP" and consumer choice models

KAP studies grew, like many applied research traditions, atheoretically from a combination of social science measurement technology and managerial needs. However, the data collected in most KAP studies contains the core variable structure of consumer choice models [17], which are built on presumed purposive behavior and learning, particularly in adoption of innovations such as family planning. Regression structures built on such models have been used to analyze adoption of new products or brands [11] and joint purchases of more than one related product [4]. A model of simple structure was used to track the introduction of a new contraceptive in Kenya [2]. Table 1 lists the six endogenous variables and 30 exogenous or predetermined variables used in the model development.

2.1. Endogenous variables

The key elements of the KAP measurements correspond to the key core endogenous variable structure common to consumer decision process models [7]:
● whether or not the couple communicates about family planning;
● whether or not the couple desires more children;
● general attitude towards family planning, measured on a five point scale;
● knowledge about family planning, measured as number of methods known on aided recall;
● whether or not the couple currently uses a modern family planning method;
● whether the couple is willing to use a modern family planning method.

2.2. Exogenous variables

In addition to relationships with each other, the endogenous elements are affected by various exogenous factors grouped under three general headings.

(1) The impact of prior behavior. In any cross section some couples will have experience with family planning (defined as the number of methods ever used) and feedback from this lagged endogenous variable could have a major impact on knowledge, attitude and behavior.

(2) Exogenous system variables. A second set of exogenous variables are factors determined more or less externally which are rather unique to the family planning decision and might not affect other family decisions as strongly.

(a) *Family decision descriptors* which provide the framework for decision making and include measures of sexual activity, the relationship between actual and desired number of children and the extent to which small children are present in the home.

(b) *Decision-making descriptors* which generally involve patterns of communication within the family, knowledge about fertility and feelings about whether births can be controlled.

(c) *Conditions of acquisition of data and materials* which indicate whether the respondent perceives family planning information and contraceptives as psychologically and physically accessible.

(3) Segmenting variables. The variable set also includes general characteristics of the family not specific to the family planning decision but which might still affect it. Primarily socio-economic descriptors, these variables are likely to be elements of a model describing any family choice activity—durables purchase, for example. Some are policy instruments (e.g. income and education) while others are more or less fixed, at least in the short run (e.g. occupation and place or residence). Besides helping describe users or potential adopters of family planning, some segmenting variables provide a basis for predicting the impact of longer-run programs (such as universal education) on family planning behavior.

3. Model specification

Table 1 shows the variable structure for the explicit specification of a system model. Since there are six endogenous variables, there are six equations. Variables included in a given equation are indicated in table 1 by an X in the column of the corresponding endogenous variable. This specification, which meets rank and order conditions for identification [18], has the following characteristics.

(1) The endogenous variables are specified as jointly determined—e.g. every endogenous variable affects every other one directly and is in turn affected by each other one by a feedback effect. This structure has been suggested as the most flexible approach to building models of this type [8] and is consistent with the feedback structure contained in most consumer behavior

Table 1
Variable configuration for behavioral model

	Word of mouth dis-cussed F.P.	Want to stop conceiving	Approve family planning	Number of methods known	Now using a product	Willing to use or using product
Endogenous variables						
Word of mouth discussed F.P.	a	X	X	X	X	X
Want to stop conceiving	X	a	X	X	X	X
Approve family planning	X	X	a	X		X
Number of methods known	X	X	X	a	X	X
Now using a product	X	X	X	X	a	X
Willing to use or using product	X	X	X	X	X	a
Prior behavior						
No methods ever used	X	X	X	X	X	X
Exogenous variables						
A. Exogenous systems variables						
1. Family situation descriptors:						
Age of youngest child	X	X				
Number of children at home	X	X				
Frequency of intercourse	X					
Actual – desired number of children		X				X
Actual – desired number of boys		X				
2. Decision-making descriptors:						
Talked with spouse about children wanted	X					

	1	2	3	4	5	6
Knows correctly when female is fertile	X	X		X		
Both generally make decisions	X	X				
Believes God decides number of children						X
Husband has final say in family size	X	X				X
Approve of F.P. for financial reasons			X			
Don't know where to get F.P. information				X		
Believes F.P. responsibility of both	X		X			
Believes contraceptive ads a bad idea						X
3. Conditions of purchase						
Cost may prevent contraceptive use					X	
Would go to store for contraceptives					X	X
Don't know where to go for F.P. information					X	X
Sources of contraception perceived convenient					X	X
B Segmenting variables						
Respondent is male	X	X	X	X	X	X
Years married	X	X	X	X	X	X
Woman now pregnant	X	X	X	X	X	X
Can read	X	X	X	X	X	X
Years of education	X	X	X	X	X	X
Owns radio	X	X	X	X	X	X
Monthly income	X	X	X	X	X	X
Rural resident	X	X	X	X	X	X
Age of wife	X	X	X	X	X	X
Husband has white-collar job	X	X	X	X	X	X
No. sources from which news is received	X	X	X	X	X	X

[a] Dependent variable.
X indicates the variable is included in the equation.

models. The endogenous variables are defined so that signs of coefficients linking them are by hypothesis positive.

(2) The segmenting variables are specified so that each affects each of the endogenous variables, allowing maximum flexibility for segment definition.

(3) A lagged behavior measure (number of methods ever used) is specified in each equation. This adjusts for extraneous patterns in the results traceable simply to experience with and prior exposure to family planning. As a result, a clearer picture of interrelationships among the contemporaneous endogenous variables should emerge [9].

(4) The exogenous family decision variables are specified to affect various components of the endogenous variable structure based on prior expectations and previous empirical results [1]. For example, variables describing conditions of purchase are specified to directly affect use and willingness to use contraceptives. Various decision-making descriptors are specified in different patterns of effects on attitudes, knowledge, communication and willingness to practice family planning and, through them, on practice.

The estimated model is multiplicative as described in the appendix. This specification has two useful characteristics: (1) it allows the variables to interact in generating the endogenous variable structure, and (2) the regression coefficients provide estimates of elasticities—i.e. a scaleless measure of *percentage change* in an endogenous dependent variable related to a 1% change in a particular explanatory variable. Direct comparisons of model parameters and hence model sensitivities across countries are thus possible even when the mean values of the variables differ over countries.

4. The data

Structured questionnaires were used in personal interviews with male and female members of fertile populations in eight countries (table 2) to obtain information relevant to the practice of contraception. Interviews were conducted with one member of a sample of couples in which the female was of childbearing age (between 13 and 44 years). Approximately equal numbers of males and females were interviewed. Multistage probability samples were used in the study, with a disproportionate allocation of samples to urban areas. All sampling frames involved random block cluster samples except Jamaica, where census enumeration districts were drawn. The resulting data sets generally overrepresented relatively high socio-economic groups. While this is a sample defect, these groups are also the most likely to be affected first by family planning programs. Specific details of the sampling procedures and detailed tabular analysis, particularly of the endogenous and exogenous system variables for various sample groupings, are reported in [24–31].

Table 2
Samples

Country	Number of individuals interviewed
Jamaica	895
Thailand	1,453
Iran	958
Philippines	1,996
Turkey	1,957
Panama	956
Venezuela	915
Korea	1,455

5. Patterns in average measurements

Average values of each variable for each country are shown in table 3. The means of the endogenous variables indicate a high degree of general approval of family planning. Half or more of respondents in all countries were willing to use contraceptive products in all eight countries. On average more than one method is known in every country and past usage of methods, while lower, indicates fairly wide multi-method experience. One half of each sample reported discussing family planning, indicating that some effort to encourage such discussion could be a useful element in program design. The percent now using some sort of product is surprisingly high, although it varies widely over countries. A substantial fraction of each population expresses a desire to stop conceiving, indicating a substantial segment of nonusers.

The segmenting variables indicate that the sample members are (relative to the corresponding populations) disproportionately urban, have relatively high incomes and educations and are disproportionately white-collar workers. Literacy rates are very high, as is radio ownership. The percent pregnant ranges from a tenth to a fifth, and years married also varies substantially.

In terms of exogenous descriptors closer to the family planning decision itself, six country samples have slightly fewer children and boys than they would consider ideal, while the other two samples have slightly more. Decision-making varies over countries, but the majority in all cases reported having discussed family size with their spouses. The majority of respondents in seven of the eight countries answered questions about fertility incorrectly, indicating the need for specific information. A significant fraction in all countries said the husband has the final say about family size, indicating a need for influencing the husband as well as the wife. About a fifth of each sample did not perceive sources of supply for contraceptives as convenient and about the same fraction said they would go to stores for contraceptives. Only a small fraction of each sample said they would not approve of contraceptive advertising, and a

Table 3
Mean values of variables

	Thailand	Iran	Jamaica
Endogenous variables			
Word of mouth-discussed F.P.	0.43	0.41	0.43
Want to stop conceiving	0.57	0.63	0.36
Approve family planning	0.80	0.84	0.80
Number of methods known	2.10	2.71	3.00
Now using a product	0.40	0.43	0.38
Willing to use or using product	0.73	0.75	0.73
Prior behavior			
No methods ever used	0.66	0.95	0.93
Exogenous variables			
A. Exogenous systems variables			
1. Family situation descriptors:			
Age of youngest child	3.46	4.22	4.25
Number of children at home	3.19	3.80	2.58
Frequency of intercourse (per week)	2.08	1.38	2.61
Actual–desired number of children	−0.25	0.53	−1.19
Actual–desired number of boys	−0.21	0.17	−0.69
2. Decision-making descriptors:			
Talked with spouse about children wanted	0.80	0.73	0.59
Knows correctly when female is fertile	0.17	0.20	0.21
Both generally make decisions	0.20	0.62	0.50
Believes God decides number of children	0.04	0.10	0.09
Husband has final say in family size	0.19	0.09	0.19
Approve of F.P. for financial reasons	0.59	0.80	0.55
Don't know where to get F.P. information	0.01	0.08	0.06
Believes F.P. responsibility of both	0.56	0.66	0.58
Believes contraceptive ads a bad idea	0.15	0.05	0.19
3. Conditions of purchase:			
Cost may prevent contraceptive use	0.09	0.005	0.07
Would go to store for contraceptives	0.23	0.29	0.21
Don't know where to go for F.P. information	0.45	0.55	0.47
Sources of contraception perceived convenient	0.80	0.77	0.76
B. Segmenting variables			
Respondent is male	0.49	0.51	0.49
Years married	9.38	14.48	15.41
Woman now pregnant	0.11	0.13	0.10
Can read	0.95	0.62	0.95
Years of education	5.89	7.61	7.88
Owns radio	0.91	0.94	0.92
Monthly income	1,368 baht	9,380 riak	$51
Rural resident	0.50	0.25	0.44
Age of wife	30.16	30.58	28.13
Husband has white-collar job	0.28	0.29	0.32
No. sources from which news is received	2.27	1.83	2.34

Philippines	Turkey	Panama	Venzuela	Korea	Median	Range
0.52	0.60	0.61	0.47	0.52	0.49	0.41 to 0.61
0.50	0.62	0.57	0.46	0.67	0.57	0.36 to 0.67
0.90	0.85	0.90	0.83	0.91	0.85	0.80 to 0.91
1.22	1.64	1.48	1.78	1.54	1.66	1.22 to 3.00
0.14	0.32	0.44	0.37	0.35	0.37	0.14 to 0.44
0.46	0.72	0.64	0.69	0.68	0.71	0.46 to 0.75
0.56	0.95	0.82	0.71	0.86	0.84	0.56 to 0.95
1.35	1.86	1.72	1.54	1.74	1.79	1.35 to 4.25
1.91	1.54	1.64	1.73	1.81	1.86	1.54 to 3.80
1.24	1.72	1.68	1.72	1.13	1.70	−1.19 to 0.62
0.63	0.66	0.66	0.60	0.56	0.60	−0.69 to 0.66
0.89	0.83	0.92	0.87	0.88	0.85	0.59 to 0.92
0.23	0.33	0.23	0.15	0.65	0.22	0.15 to 0.65
0.37	0.39	0.32	0.68	0.45	0.42	0.20 to 0.68
0.11	0.03	0.02	0.08	0.08	0.08	0.03 to 0.11
0.30	0.40	0.16	0.07	0.30	0.19	0.09 to 0.40
0.74	0.63	0.88	0.75	0.77	0.76	0.55 to 0.88
0.06	0.03	0.01	0.03	0.01	0.03	0.01 to 0.06
0.50	0.26	0.55	0.83	0.52	0.58	0.26 to 0.83
0.10	0.17	0.14	0.22	0.14	0.14	0.05 to 0.22
0.35	0.10	0.09	0.07	0.11	0.08	0.05 to 0.35
0.27	0.66	0.29	0.35	0.21	0.28	0.21 to 0.35
0.06	0.14	0.07	0.05	0.01	0.10	0.01 to 0.55
0.87	0.73	0.85	0.76	0.74	0.77	0.74 to 0.87
0.50	0.50	0.50	0.50	0.48	0.50	0.49 to 0.51
2.49	2.48	2.33	2.37	2.75	2.62	2.33 to 15.43
0.21	0.14	0.13	0.16	0.12	0.13	0.10 to 0.16
0.97	0.88	0.99	0.98	0.95	0.95	0.62 to 0.99
2.65	2.59	2.70	2.56	2.70	2.60	2.56 to 7.88
0.93	0.92	0.89	0.96	0.93	0.93	0.89 to 0.96
3.50	7.89	22.1	20.90	61.1		
0.50	0.46	0.22	0.19	0.49	0.47	0.19 to 0.49
20.5	20.92	23.31	20.87	24.04	23.71	20.50 to 30.54
0.20	0.51	0.51	0.50	0.23	0.29	0.18 to 0.51
1.51	1.58	1.58	1.65	1.37	1.62	1.37 to 2.34

Table 4
Significance and signs of coefficients in structural equations

	Endogenous variables						
	Word of mouth discussion	Want to stop conceiving	Approve family planning	No. of methods known	Using a product	Willing to use a product	Total
Endogenous variables:							
Specified	40	40	40	40	40	40	240
Positive and significant	21	13	21	14	15	27	111
Positive and not significant	12	13	12	11	10	9	67
Other	7	14	7	15	15	4	62
Prior behavior							
Specified	8	8	8	8	8	8	48
Positive and significant	8	7	7	8	8	4	42
Positive	0	1	1	0	0	3	5
Negative and not significant	0	0	0	0	0	1	1
Exogenous variables							
A. Exogenous systems variables [a]							
1. Family situation descriptors							
Specified	24	32	0	0	0	8	64
Positive and significant	5	16	—	—	—	4	25
Positive and not significant	6	6	—	—	—	2	14

Negative and not significant	6	4	—	—	—	0	10
Negative and significant	7	6	—	—	—	2	15
2. Decision-making descriptors							
Specified	32	16	16	16	0	24	104
Positive and significant	11	0	10	11	—	1	33
Positive and not significant	9	3	4	4	—	8	28
Negative and not significant	9	3	0	1	—	9	22
Negative and significant	3	10	2	0	—	6	21
3. Conditions of purchase							
Specified	0	0	0	0	32	24	56
Positive and significant	—	—	—	—	7	9	16
Positive and not significant	—	—	—	—	1	7	8
Negative and not significant	—	—	—	—	2	7	9
Negative and significant	—	—	—	—	22	1	23
B. Segmenting variables							
Specified	88	88	88	88	88	88	528
Positive and significant	26	23	9	27	11	10	106
Positive and not significant	24	20	26	34	34	26	164
Negative and not significant	23	28	37	17	26	32	163
Negative and significant	15	17	16	10	17	20	95
Median R^2	0.154	0.554	0.320	0.351	0.550	0.365	
Range of R^2	0.116 to 0.286	0.339 to 0.633	0.310 to 0.753	0.249 to 0.430	0.327 to 0.642	0.248 to 0.494	

[a] Number of coefficients varies over equations because of specification differences shown in table 1.

substantial fraction (in all but one case the majority) believed that family planning is the responsibility of both the parents, again reinforcing the importance of activities involving the male.

6. General patterns in estimated parameters of the model

The first task is to establish that the results of fitting the models to the eight samples described earlier are not simply random. The basic framework is provided by significance testing of the coefficients, under which about 5% of the coefficients would be statistically significant by chance. Table 4 shows that, overall, patterns in the regression coefficients reflect the existence of a structure of relationships like the one suggested in table 1.

For all equations, nearly three-quarters of the coefficients linking endogenous variables are positive as expected, and 46% are significant. Over 85% of coefficients involving prior behavior measurements are positive and significant. More coefficients of exogenous variables are significant than the 5% that would be expected by chance. Over half of the coefficients involving exogenous system variables (133 of 224) are significant, while two-fifths of the coefficients (201 of 528) involving the segmenting variables are significant. However, patterns of signs vary over countries, probably indicating cultural differences.

Overall, the models provide more explanatory power about the endogenous variables than would be expected by chance. All coefficients of determination (R^2's) are significant in ANOVA tests, and are in most cases larger than would be expected in disaggregated cross sections of this type [6].

These general patterns carry over to the individual explanatory variables (last two columns of table 5) where at least a quarter of the signs are significant in all cases and at least half are significant for 22 of 36 variables.

Among specific explanatory endogenous variables, willingness to use or using products, the desire to stop conceiving, and general approval of family planning have the strongest explanatory power. It is not possible to create an unambiguous hierarchical sequence of the endogenous variables [20], but it is possible to make a rough ordering to check on the relative impact of forward versus feedback relationships among the endogenous variables. The following order was used as a tentative "hierarchy of effects":

(a) knowledge of methods involving a contraceptive product,
(b) word of mouth discussion,
(c) want to stop conceiving,
(d) approve family planning,
(e) willingness to use a product,
(f) using a product.

Using this hierarchy, 57 coefficients are significant involving various relationships downward, while 54 upward (involving feedback) are significant. Experimenting with alternative hierarchies produced similar results. This indicates that the model structure should involve both forward and feedback effects, a feature of the original specification.

Among the exogenous system variables, the most consistent explanatory power is provided by the relationship between the desired and actual family size, the belief that God decides the number of children, approval of family planning for financial reasons, knowledge of where to get family planning information, willingness to get contraceptives at stores and perceptions that sources of supply are convenient. Segmenting variables best describing groups with special characteristics are sex of respondent, age of wife, length of marriage, years of education, and whether the woman was pregnant at the time of interview.

7. Coefficient patterns in individual equations

Patterns of coefficients governing each dependent endogenous variable are compared over countries in terms of goodness of fit, patterns in signs and significance of coefficients using tables 4 and 5.

7.1. Word of mouth discussion of family planning

The coefficients of determination (R^2), while all significant, are the lowest of any of the six equations showing that the model is least successful in explaining this endogenous variable. Twenty-one of 40 endogenous variable coefficients are significant, with each variable significant in two or more cases. Knowledge of methods and willingness to use a product show the most consistent explanatory patterns over the eight countries. The number of methods known and approval of family planning are strongly linked to discussion, indicating that communication programs working on knowledge and attitude will affect conversation as well. Lagged behavior is a significant causal factor in all eight countries. Among exogenous systems variables, more conversations about family planning occurred for those with younger children, those who had discussed the family size with their spouses, and those who share decision-making. Among the segmenting variables, male respondents reported less conversations than female respondents. Conversation is associated with literacy, the number of years of the marriage, education, urban residence and receipt of news from several sources.

7.2. Wishing to stop conceiving

The coefficients of determination ranging from 0.34 to 0.63 (median 0.55) indicate that the general fit was best among the six equations. Among the

Table 5

Number of significant regression coefficients for eight countries in fitted six-relationship structural model

	Word of mouth-discussed F.P.		Want to stop conceiving		Approve family planning	
Endogenous variables						
Word of mouth-discussed F.P.	a		1		4	
Want to stop conceiving	3		a		8	
Approve family planning	3		7		a	
Number of methods known	7		0		3	
Now using a product	2		2		0	
Willing to use or using product.	6		3		6	
Prior behavior						
No methods ever used	8		7		7	
Exogenous variables						
A. Exogenous systems variables (effect)	+	−	+	−	+	−
1. Family situation descriptors:						
Age of youngest child	2	2	0	4		
Number of children at home	1	3	3	2		
Frequency of intercourse	2	2				
Actual − desired number of children			8	0		
Actual − desired number of boys			5	0		
2. Decision-making descriptors						
Talked with spouse about children wanted	5	0				
Knows correctly when female is fertile			0	2		
Both generally make decisions	3	1				
Believes God decides number of children			0	8		
Husband has final say in family size	2	0				
Approve of F.P. for financial reasons					8	0
Don't know where to get F.P. information						
Believes F.P. responsibility of both	1	2			2	2
Believes contraceptive ads a bad idea						
3. Conditions of purchase						
Cost may prevent contraceptive use						
Would go to store for contraceptives						
Don't know where to go for F.P. information						
Sources of contraception perceived inconvenient						
B. Segmenting variables (effect)	+	−	+	−	+	−
Respondent is male	0	5	1	2	0	0
Years married	4	1	8	0	1	1
Woman now pregnant	0	3	0	5	2	0
Can read	5	0	2	0	1	2
Years of education	5	0	0	3	0	1
Owns radio	3	0	0	1	0	2
Monthly income	1	1	0	1	2	1
Rural resident	1	0	1	2	2	2
Age of wife	0	4	7	0	1	2

Number of methods known		Now using a product		Willing to use or using product		Total for variable:	
						Specified	Significant
6		1		5		40	17
1		4		4		40	20
3		2		6		40	21
a		0		4		40	14
0		a		8		40	12
4		8		a		40	27
8		8			4	48	42
+	−	+	−	+	−		
						16	8
						16	9
				4	2	16	10
						8	8
						8	5
						8	5
						16	6
4	0					8	4
				0	4	16	12
				1	0	16	3
						8	8
						8	7
7	0					16	7
				0	2	8	2
		0	7	1	0	16	8
		7	1	2	1	16	11
		0	6			8	6
		0	8	6	0	16	14
+	−	+	−	+	−		
1	5	1	2	1	2	48	23
0	2	2	0	0	5	48	24
0	1	0	8	4	1	48	24
5	0	1	0	0	1	48	17
7	0	3	0	0	2	48	21
2	0	1	1	1	0	48	11
2	1	1	1	1	2	48	14
1	0	1	0	1	0	48	11
1	0	0	1	0	6	48	22

Table 5 (continued)

	Word of mouth-discussed F.P.		Want to stop conceiving		Approve family planning	
Husband has white-collar job	3	1	2	1	0	1
No. sources from which news is received	4	0	2	2	0	1
Coefficient of determination (R^2)	8		8		8	

Blank cell means that variable is not specified in that particular relationship.
Number indicates the number of countries for which that coefficient is significant on the basis of one-tailed tests for the endogenous and two-tail tests for the exogenous variables
[a] Dependent variable

endogenous variables, approval of family planning is significant in seven cases, and lagged behavior is also significant in seven cases.

Among the exogenous system variables, families which are large relative to the desired family size are more likely to wish to stop conceiving, and those that believe that God decides family size are less likely to wish to stop. Families with young children are less likely to want to stop completely, which suggests a strategy based on spacing of children in approaching them.

Among the segmenting variables, years married is positively related in all cases to wishing to limit fertility. Older women are more likely to want to stop, while women currently pregnant are less likely to.

7.3. General approval of family planning

This is the "attitude" element of the conventional KAP research package. The coefficients of determination range more broadly than for any other equation, indicating more differences over countries in the explanatory power of the model.

Among the endogenous variables, Want to Stop Conceiving and a feedback effect from Willingness to Use or Using Products are quite consistent over countries, and prior behavior is significant in all cases.

Among the exogenous system variables, the significant positive effect of approval of family planning for financial and economic reasons suggests a powerful cross-cultural appeal. No clear pattern exists over countries of the segmenting variables, indicating that segmenting occurs more sharply in other elements of the system.

7.4. Number of methods known

Knowledge, the K in KAP, is defined as the number of methods cited in aided recall. Coefficients of determination of regressions explaining Knowl-

Number of methods known		Now using a product		Willing to use or using product		Total for variable:	
						Specified	Significant
2	1	0	2	1	0	48	14
6	0	1	2	1	1	48	20
	8		8		8	48	48

edge range from 0.25 to 0.43, with a median of 0.35.

Among the endogenous variables, Use or Willingness to Use Products is significantly related in six cases to Knowledge, as is Discussion, indicating that word of mouth is an important source of information. Lagged behavior is significant in all countries, indicating that experience is an important source of information.

The exogenous system variables indicate that respondents who do not perceive that they have easy access to family planning data know fewer methods, and poor knowledge about reproduction is also related to low levels of knowledge. Among the segmenting variables, the number of sources from which news is received, the ability to read and education are related to knowledge. It is important to note that males tend to know fewer methods than females.

7.5. Willingness to use a product

Prediction of willingness to use a contraceptive product varies over countries, with the coefficients of determination centered about 0.35 and ranging from 0.25 to 0.5.

The endogenous explanatory behavioral variables are strongest in this equation, as indicated by the fact that 27 of the 40 coefficients are positive and significant. Approval of Family Planning and (not surprisingly) Current Use show the most consistent patterns over countries. Prior behavior again is a significant effect in all cases.

Patterns among the segmenting variables and the exogenous system measures differ over countries, although those who perceive contraceptives as available are more likely to be willing to use a product. Older women and those with longer marriages are less willing to use a product, indicating that conversion of general approval into action will be more difficult for these segments.

7.6. Current use of contraceptive products

For Current Use (the "Practice" element of KAP), coefficients of determination ranged from 0.32 to 0.64 and center at over 0.5. Willingness to Use Products and Desire to Stop Conceiving are the most consistent predictors over countries. Prior Behavior (as is often the case in decision process models of this type) is a strong and consistent correlate of behavior in all countries.

The exogenous system variables are more strongly related to Current Usage than to any other endogenous variable. Measures related to access (Willingness to Use a Store as Outlet, and Perception that Supply is Convenient) are positively related to use, reflecting the importance of supply source on current practice of family planning. Relationships between use and lack of knowledge of sources of information and sensitivity to cost reflect the fact that access to information and cheap supplies are important.

Among the segmenting variables, the fact that those families with the wife currently pregnant are in all countries less likely to be current users provides a useful check of internal consistency for the data set and for the model.

8. "Strong patterns" in the exogenous variables

Some relationships with particular exogenous variables have similar patterns over countries. With "similar" defined as all eight regression coefficients having the same sign and at least six of eight significant (a severe definition given the results in table 5), some interesting implications emerge (table 6). For example, it appears that contraceptive trial encourages discussion. Older women with families nearing or exceeding the desired size are more likely to want to stop conceiving, while those believing that "God decides" the number of children are less likely to wish to stop. The fact that the most likely reasons to approve family planning are related to family finances suggests a promotional theme. Knowledge about methods is likely to be affected by knowledge of where to get information and also by education. Older women express less willingness to buy contraceptives. Current use is affected (not surprisingly) by prior use, by whether the woman is currently pregnant and by perceptions of cost and convenience of supply.

9. Numerical values of the coefficients

Each estimated coefficient in the system is an elasticity measuring the percentage by which the dependent endogenous variable will change as a result

Table 6

Exogenous variables with highly similar [a] effects for all countries

Word-of-mouth discussion	Wish to stop conceiving	Approve family planning	No. of methods known	Using a product	Willing to use a product
Prior behavior (+)	Prior behavior (+)	Prior behavior (+)	Prior behavior (+)	Prior behavior (+)	Age of wife (−)
	Actual-desired Number of children (+)	Approval for financial reasons (+)	Don't know where to get information (−)	Cost may prevent use (−)	
	God decides number of children (−)		Years of education (+)	Sources of contraceptives inconvenient (−)	
	Years married (+) Age of wife (+)			Woman pregnant (−)	

[a] Defined as (1) all coefficients have the same sign and (2) at least six are significant.

of a 1% change of the explanatory endogenous or exogenous variable. Some useful patterns emerge from the numerical values of these coefficients.

(1) In no case is any single estimated elasticity greater than one for any country, equation or variable. By implication, there is no single variable among those discussed in the previous section that would provide a more than proportionate impact on any endogenous variable in the system. Furthermore, the relatively small values indicate that impact of any changes in the system will be small and more or less immediate. Second-order effects of a change rippling back through the system should be relatively minimal.

(2) Not surprisingly, the greatest numerical impact involves the prior behavior measure (table 7), although all significant elasticities lie between 0 and 1. Median elasticities reinforce the importance of past behavior on both knowledge and current use, and suggest serious attention to strategies related to retention of practicers of family planning and to motivating past adopters to start again.

(3) The endogenous variables affect each other, but again on the basis of median elasticities, the impacts are fairly subtle (table 8).

It appears that the most impact on the system is provided by product-specific information aimed at increasing knowledge about and willingness to use specific products.

(4) In the same way as the endogenous variables, certain of the exogenous systems variables appear to have more leverage than others. These general patterns in significant elasticities involving exogenous systems variables (table 9) again suggest strategies oriented about providing specific knowledge and reasons to practice family planning, concurrent with providing perceived easy access (both physical and economic) to contraceptive supplies and to information. Encouraging discussion of how big a family the household really wants should also have some impact.

(5) Patterns of elasticities of the segmenting variables differ much more over countries. In addition, most are not subject to direct manipulation, although they provide some insight for program configuration. However, some

Table 7
Median significant elasticities for lagged behavior

Endogenous variables	Median significant elasticities
Word of mouth discussion	0.093
Wishing to stop conceiving	0.051
Approval of family planning	0.033
Willingness to use a product	0.035
Number of methods known	0.431
Current use	0.240

Table 8
Median significant elasticities among endogenous variables

Endogenous dependent variable

Explanatory endogenous variable	Word of mouth discussion	Wish to stop conceiving	Approve family planning	Willing to use a product	Number of methods known	Current use
Word of mouth discussion	[a]	0.013	0.036	0.077	0.160	0.028
Wish to stop conceiving	0.042	[a]	0.055	0.063	0.046	0.043
Approve family planning	0.092	0.105	[a]	0.178	0.136	0.037
Willing to use a product	0.074	0.039	0.070	[a]	0.079	0.314
Number of methods known	0.102	n.s.	0.020	0.392	[a]	n.s.
Current use	0.032	0.039	n.s.	0.036	n.s.	[a]

[a] Dependent variable.
n.s. = none significant.

Table 9
Median significant elasticities for exogenous systems variables

Endogenous variable	Explanatory variable	Median significant elasticity
Word of mouth discussion of family planning	Discussion of family size	0.160
	Participation by both in family decision-making	0.054
Wishing to stop conceiving	Number of children at home	0.059
	Difference between ideal and current family size	0.380
Approval of family planning	Existence of a specific reason for approval	0.360
Number of methods known	Correct knowledge of period of fertility	0.105
	Knowledge of where to get family planning information	0.267
Willingness to use a product	Frequency of intercourse	0.039
	Perception that supply is convenient	0.103
	General approval of advertising	0.078
	Willingness to secure contraceptives at stores	0.160
Current use	Perception of acceptable cost	0.073
	Knowledge of where to get family planning information	0.230
	Perception that supply is convenient	0.197

useful and consistent patterns (table 10) emerge. Over the long run, education programs affect both discussion of family planning and knowledge of methods, and in the short run a multiple media strategy is suggested by the impact of multiple sources of news used on both discussion and specific knowledge of methods.

Older families offer some differential opportunities related to high motivation to stop conceiving, but they are generally disapproving and unwilling to use contraceptives. Approval and use of products is also low for rural residents. It appears that older rural segments will be the most difficult to reach directly, although willingness to use products will be affected exogenously by growth of nonagricultural segments of the economy.

10. Prediction and the "reduced form" equation

Some additional insight is provided by one of the reduced form equations associated with the structural system in table 1. In the reduced form, each of

Table 10
Median significant elasticities of key segmenting variables

Segmenting variable	Endogenous variable					
	Word of mouth family planning	Wish to stop conceiving	Approve family planning	Number of methods known	Willing to use products	Using product
Years married	0.030	0.140	−0.017	–	−0.051	−0.003
Age of wife	–	0.185	–	–	−0.191	–
Literacy	0.110	–	–	0.151	–	–
Education						
Number of sources from which news is received	0.061	–	–	0.182	–	–
Husband has white-collar job	–	–	–	–	–	–
Rural resident	–	–	−0.034	–	–	−0.012

– No strong segmenting effect.

the endogenous variables in the system is predicted on the basis of all of the exogenous variables, regardless of whether that particular exogenous variable is specified in the corresponding structural equation. The coefficients of the reduced form can be used for policy purposes to predict impact of shifts in exogenous variables which may be either induced externally or expected to occur naturally due to external factors. Key for our purposes is encouraging the use of products, so only the reduced form for Current Use is examined (table 11). Four exogenous variables have coefficients which are significant and have the same sign for all countries.

(1) Prior use is associated with current use. This suggests strategies aimed at continuation, particularly as the fraction of couples who ever used a method becomes sizable.

(2) Perceived low costs encourages contraceptive use, so programs which provide low cost contraceptives should be effective.

(3) People would go to stores for contraceptives if supplies were available there were perceived as not too costly, so subsidized schemes using retail stores as outlets may be useful program components [1–3].

(4) Those who do not know where to go for contraceptive information and who perceive sources of supply as inconvenient are less likely to be users, indicating that priority be given to making both supplies and materials physically as well as psychologically accessible.

Variables for which signs of coefficients are all the same (although not all are significant) include those in which:

(a) the woman is pregnant, again indicating face validity of the measurements;

(b) the family has is fact discussed family size;

(c) the actual number of children in the family is larger than the number perceived as desired, with some similar indication for the desired versus actual number of boys;

(d) the family approves of family planning for reasons of family finances; and

(e) the wife is older, and hence presumbaly the family is nearer to completed size.

These results suggest appeals which might be made to specific target groups.

Less generalizable but directional indications are higher contraceptive use for those who have intercourse frequently, those who think advertising of family planning was not a bad idea, and families in which the husband has a white-collar job. These results suggest segments that might be particularly responsive and that advertising may be effective in reaching these segments.

The fact that socio-demographic measures do not generalize well suggests that programs will probably have to develop idiosyncratically for specific countries at this level.

Table 11

Statistical tests on reduced form equations with product use as dependent variable

	Reduced form regression coefficients			
	Positive		Negative	
	Sig-nifi-cant	Not signifi-cant	Sig-nifi-cant	Not signifi-cant
Prior behavior				
No. methods ever used	8	0	0	0
Exogenous variables				
A.Exogenous systems variables				
1. Family situation descriptors:				
Age of youngest child	2	0	2	4
No. children at home	2	3	1	2
Frequency of intercourse	5	2	0	1
Actual − desired no. of children	2	6	0	0
Actual − desired no. boys	1	3	0	4
2. Decision-making descriptors:				
Talked with spouse about children wanted	4	4	0	0
Knows correctly when female is fertile	1	2	0	5
Both generally make decisions	1	2	0	5
Believes God decides no. of children	1	4	1	2
Husband has final say in family size	3	1	3	1
Approve of F.P. for financial reasons	6	2	0	0
Don't know where to get F.P. information	2	3	1	1
Believes F.P. responsibility of both	2	2	2	2
Believes contraceptive ads a bad idea	0	1	2	5
3. Conditions of purchase				
Cost may prevent contraceptive use	0	0	8	0
Would go to store for contraceptives	8	0	0	0
Don't know where to go for F.P. information	0	0	8	0
Sources of contraception perceived inconvenient	0	0		0
B. Segmenting variables				
Respondent is male	2	2	1	3
Years married	2	3	1	2
Woman now pregnant	0	0	6	2
Can read	3	8	0	0
Years of education	3	3	0	2
Owns radio	1	4	1	2
Monthly income	1	4	2	1
Rural resident	1	2	3	1
Age of wife	0	0	4	4
Husband has white-collar job	1	3	1	3
No. sources from which news is received	0 5	2	3	3
Coefficient of determination (R^2)	8	0	0	0
Intercept (constant)	8	0	0	0

11. Cross-cultural comparisons

An important question in any cross-cultural research is the extent to which results stand up over different cultural settings. The question is not whether the results are exactly the same for the eight countries (which would be unexpected) but rather which elements of the analysis seem to generalize and which do not. While there is some variation (table 12), the qualitative patterns in the model coefficients just described are similar over countries. Based on the fraction of coefficients in each category for each country, the conclusion that the endogenous variables are interrelated stands up over countries, as does the impact of prior behavior on the system. Similar patterns were found in parameters of a smaller model used for program evaluation in Kenya [2]. The variables describing conditions of purchase generally have a strong effect, implying that programs (contingent upon local conditions) should consider strengthening activities that involve availability of contraceptives and of information about them.

There are also some patterns which indicate intercultural differences. The impact of family situation descriptors is sharpest in Panama, Thailand and Iran, while descriptors of family decision-making have the greatest effect in Turkey and Thailand. The segmenting patterns are also different over countries. For example, they are sharpest in Thailand, even though the model fit for Thai data is no better than for other countries.

In terms of fit, the model has varying ability to explain endogenous variables over countries, but the range of the coefficients of determination for the various equations are similar over countries.

12. Discussion

Planners of family planning programs must allocate scarce resources among several potentially effective activities—improving attitudes toward family planning, encouraging the development of a "small family ideal", providing general information about family planning, expanding distribution systems, etc. The planner often has available survey data on knowledge, attitudes and behavior of a relevant target population. This paper has suggested a behavioral model of the way families decide to practice family planning that may help the planner sort out the complex elements that govern these intra-family decisions in order to try to induce nonusers to adopt the modern practice of family planning: while the results on eight countries are not perfectly consistent with prior expectations based on theories of consumer behavior, several important patterns emerge from the results.

(1) *Relationships among the endogenous variables are consistent with expectations under a consumer behavior model.* Overall it is clear that behavioral

Table 12
Significant structural coefficients by country

	Number of coefficients of each type in each country model	Jamaica	Thailand	Iran	Panama	Turkey	Philippines	Korea	Venezuela
Endogenous variables	30	17	21	15	9	11	14	14	10
Prior behavior	6	6	6	6	5	5	5	4	5
Exogenous variables									
A. Exogenous system descriptors:									
1. Family situation descriptors	8	4	7	7	7	2	6	3	4
2. Decision-making descriptors	13	7	8	6	7	9	5	7	7
3. Conditions of purchase	7	5	5	3	6	5	6	4	5
B. Segmenting variables	66	27	34	20	21	29	25	23	22
Coefficients of determination:									
Median		0.422	0.345	0.391	0.456	0.423	0.279	0.325	0.333
Range over six equations		0.116 to 0.750	0.116 to 0.643	0.221 to 0.753	0.123 to 0.591	0.286 to 0.502	0.241 to 0.634	0.154 to 0.556	0.240 to 0.686

elements of the decision process structure are related in more than a random pattern. Program design should thus concentrate on several behavioral elements rather than single aspects—e.g. attitude or behavior.

(2) *Prior behavior is important.* Similarly, lagged behavior plays a very important role, and it may be productive to concentrate on prior users as one aspect of program design. The implication of this fact is that programs, especially as the level of initial trial builds up, should not yield to the temptation of focusing on only new adopters, but should devote substantial attention to retaining current practicers [1].

(3) *The various segmenting variables impact the system at different points and, to a somewhat lesser extent, in different patterns over countries.* General socio-demographic segmenting variables are important for understanding the structure of the choice situation, but they do not contribute to discrimination among groups of respondents as well as the behavioral state variables or the exogenous descriptors closer to the specific choice situation [23].

(4) *The variable set,* particularly the exogenous system descriptors and the segmenting variables, *enters the system in a rather complex pattern.* The impact of most of these on actual use is indirect—education and news sources impacting knowledge and knowledge in turn impacting behavior, for example. Under these circumstances, it is not likely that relatively simple experimental designs or tabular displays of survey data will yield sharp answers in terms of either program evaluation or policy implication.

(5) *Specific program elements should stress product-specific information and easy access to supply.* The battle for general approval of family planning and for a reasonable level of desire to stop conceiving has proceeded successfully enough that what is required now is measures which facilitate contraceptive use by those who approve and wish to stop or delay conception. Specific information about products and about reproduction are needed, as is easy physical, psychological and economic access to low priced supplies.

(6) *Even large shifts in a given variable will have modest immediate impact on the system.* All of the estimated elasticities are less than unity, implying that a 1% induced shift in the value of one of the variables will induce a shift in others of only a fraction of 1%. Similar patterns of relatively low elasticities have been found in other studies using consumer choice models as general frameworks [13]. Managers should thus expect relatively modest impacts of program changes of the types suggested here rather than being disappointed by them. Of course, even a modest shift in the fraction of a large population practicing family planning can have a sizeable effect in the short run in the number of children born.

(7) *The approach may generalize to other settings and other cultures.* Patterns among the endogenous variables show similarity over cultures and to other applications of this approach, including an analysis of a contraceptive test market. Since the variable set used here is also qualitatively similar to that used

in surveys in several fields (political polling and market research about consumer products, for example), the type of model used here might be applied to other types of situations in which a planner wishes to use cross-sectional survey data as a basis for target market identification and resource allocation.

Appendix: The regression model

A.1. Model configuration

The model is configured multiplicatively: $i = 1,\ldots,6$ indicating the endogenous variable

$$Y_{ikl} = \prod_{j=1}^{m} X_{ijkl}\beta_{ijk}, \tag{A1}$$

where

$j = 1,\ldots, m$ indicating the explanatory variables in that particular equation (table 3),
$k = 1,\ldots,8$ the country,
$l = 1,\ldots, r$ members of the sample.

The choice of a nonlinear form of the model is motivated by evidence that consumer behavior models with nonlinear specifications and variable interactions are superior in terms of explanatory power to linear approximations [21].

A.2. Variable definitions

Most variables in the data set are discrete and all but one endogenous variable is binary. In order for estimated values of the two-valued variables to be interpreted as probabilities (e.g. probability of favorable attitude), the variables must be transformed in such a way that after linearization (e.g. the taking of logarithms as described above), these two values are 0 and 1. For example, the couple either does ($Y(l) = 1$) or does not ($Y(l) = 0$) discuss contraception. This is accomplished by setting each variable to l ($\ln l = 0$) in the absence of the activity and to e ($\ln e = 1$) presence. The regression coefficients (the β's) are then measures of relative sensitivity of the endogenous dependent variable to each explanatory variable. In this multiplicative form with the coefficients specified as exponents, the estimated coefficients are elasticities (percentage change of the endogenous variable which would result from a 1% change in the observed value of the explanatory variable, averaged over all respondents and over all values in the range of the endogenous and exogenous variables.)

The basic model in (A1) is converted into linear form by taking logarithms of all transformed variables:

$$\ln Y_{ikl} = \sum_{j=1}^{m} \beta_{ijk} \ln X_{jkl},$$

with the subscripts defined as above. The coefficients can then be estimated with linear regression methods by the addition of appropriate statistical disturbance terms to the basic multiplicative model specifications.

A.3. Estimation

Model parameters are estimated equation by equation using ordinary least squares methods. While more sophisticated methods exist, it was not feasible to use them because no computer program could be found to accommodate such a large variable set and such large data sets. Ordinary least squares (OLS) have been shown to have certain desirable practical properties in situations like the one described here [5,18].

The OLS estimates may also be somewhat conservative, as tentative results are available to show that two-stage least squares estimates of elasticities in systems such as these are on average larger than OLS estimates [13]. For statistical tests of relationships among endogenous variables, one-tailed tests tests for positive values are used, because the theory upon which the model is based predicts positive relationships: two-tail tests are used with the exogenous variables because the theory is less strong about predictions of their signs.

References

[1] Lhabdi R. Bhandari, John U. Farley, James Hulbert, and Donald E. Sexton, Some Applications of Social Research to Family Planning, Working Paper, Columbia University (1976).

[2] Timothy R.L. Black and John U. Farley, Response to advertising contraceptives, Journal of Advertising Research 17 (October 1977) 49–56.

[3] Timothy R.L. Black and John U. Farley, Retailers in social program strategy: The case of family planning, Columbia Journal of World Business 12 (Winter 1977) 33–43.

[4] John U. Farley, A "soft" approach to modeling relationships among elements of nutrition, breast feeding and family planning decisions in Sri Lanka, Working Paper, Columbia University (1979).

[5] John U. Farley, Estimating parameters in marketing systems, Proceedings of the American Marketing Association (1967) 316–321.

[6] John U. Farley and John A. Howard, Control of "Noise" in Market Research Data (D.C. Heath, Lexington, Mass., 1975).

[7] John U. Farley, John A. Howard and Donald R. Lehmann, A "working version" car buyer behavior model, Management Science (November 1976) 179–187.

[8] John U. Farley and Jarrold Katz, Patterns in survey results on consumer decision making, Working Paper, Columbia University (1977).

[9] John U. Farley, Jarrold Katz, Donald R. Lehmann and Russell Winer, Two approaches to enriching specifications of consumer decision process models, Working Paper, Columbia University (1979).

[10] John U. Farley and Harold J. Leavitt, Private sector logistics in population control—A case in Jamaica, Demography 5 (1965) 167–176.

[11] John U. Farley and Donald R. Lehmann, An overview of empirical applications of buyer behavior system models, in: W.D. Perrault, Ed., Advances in consumer research (Association for Consumer Research, 1977) 36–41.

[12] John U. Farley and L. Winston Ring, Empirical specification of a buyer behavior model, Journal of Marketing Research 11 (February 1974) 89–96.

[13] John U. Farley, Donald R. Lehmann, and Michael J. Ryan, Generalizing from imperfect replication, Working Paper, Columbia University (1980).

[14] John U. Farley, Donald R. Sexton, Robert B. Smith and Steven S. Tokarski, A behavioral segmentation scheme for family planning program management, Proceedings, American Marketing Association, Portland, Oregon (August 1974) 31–34.

[15] John U. Farley and Steven S. Tokarski, Law and population policy: Some suggestions for determining priorities and estimating impacts, Columbia Human Rights Law Review 6 (1974) 415–446.

[16] John U. Farley and Steven J. Samuel, Predicting the impact on birth rate of changes in laws governing contraceptive marketing, Working Paper, Columbia University (1980).

[17] John A. Howard and Jaydish N. Sheth, The Theory of Buyer Behavior (John Wiley and Sons, 1969).

[18] Jack Johnston, Econometric Methods (McGraw-Hill, New York, 1963).

[19] Jerrold Katz, An examination of sample survey research in marketing in the context of a buyer behavior model, Ph.D. Dissertation, Columbia University (1974).

[20] Robert K. Lavidge and Gary A. Steiner, A model for predictive measurement of advertising effectiveness, Journal of Marketing (October 1961) 61–67.

[21] Michael LaRoche, A new approach to non-linear consumer behavior models and market segmentation by the use of orthogonal polynomials, Unpublished Ph.D. Dissertation, Columbia University (1974).

[22] Boone A. Turci, The Demand for Children (Ballinger Publishing Co., Ballinger, Mass., 1975).

[23] David Weinstein and John U. Farley, Market segmentation and parameter inequalities in buyer behavior models, Journal of Business 48 (October 1975) 526–540.

[24] Westinghouse Population Center, Distribution of Contraceptives in the Commercial Sector of Iran (Columbia, Maryland, 1973).

[25] Westinghouse Population Center, Distribution of Contraceptives in the Commercial Sector of Jamaica (Columbia, Maryland, 1973).

[26] Westinghouse Population Center, Distribution of Contraceptives in the Commercial Sector of Thailand (Columbia, Maryland, 1973).

[27] Westinghouse Population Center, Distribution of Contraceptives in the Commercial Sector of Philippines (Columbia, Maryland, 1973).

[28] Westinghouse Population Center, Distribution of Contraceptives in the Commercial Sector of Turkey (Columbia, Maryland, 1973).

[29] Westinghouse Population Center, Distribution of Contraceptives in the Commercial Sector of Panama (Columbia, Maryland, 1973).

[30] Westinghouse Population Center, Distribution of Contraceptives in the Commercial Sector of Venezuela (Columbia, Maryland, 1973).

[31] Westinghouse Population Center, Distribution of Contraceptives in the Commercial Sector of Koreo (Columbia, Maryland, 1973).

TIMS/Studies in the Management Sciences 18 (1982) 241–269
North-Holland Publishing Company

ANALYZING NATURAL EXPERIMENTS IN INDUSTRIAL MARKETS

Gary L. LILIEN
Pennsylvania State University

and

A. Api RUZDIC
Northwestern University

In most industrial markets, buyers and sellers have long-standing relationships, and sales, marketing and market share data are not collected with the same frequency and degree of precision found in consumer markets. For these reasons it is difficult to make quantitative inferences about the effectiveness of marketing instruments. This paper presents an approach for studying industrial markets where the effect of marketing spending can be measured and analyzed. We call these market situations natural experiments. The analysis best applies in those situations where marketing experimentation cannot be justified because of time or cost constraints or for competitive reasons.

First, we develop a procedure to identify markets where sufficient historical variability has occurred to enable statistical analysis. Then a model of industrial market response follows from a set of theoretical conditions. Finally, the model is applied to six case studies with encouraging results. The models fit well and the signs of all estimated coefficients are consistent with *a priori* expectations.

The approach allows quantitative analysis of market response and provides answers to market budget questions such as whether an increase in marketing spending will increase or decrease profitability.

1. Introduction

Industrial marketing is the marketing of goods and services to organizations for use in their business operations. Industrial markets themselves differ dramatically. Products may be high or low ticket items, frequently or infrequently purchased, with many or few customers. Such diversity suggests that a single approach to market analysis is unlikely to fit all situations.

Consider a range of product–market settings. At one extreme, products such as copiers have as potential customers almost all organizations. Potential volume is large, and much variation occurs in the marketing mix (use of broadcast media, frequent price discount programs, targeted direct mail campaigns, etc.). This situation, with a large customer base and high number of purchases per year, has many properties of consumer markets. We refer to this as a "general" purchase situation, to indicate that a large subset of all possible industrial customers comprise the potential market. Other examples include office supplies, business forms, word processing equipment, and telecommunication products and services.

At the other extreme are "products" like off-shore oil rigs whose potential customers are few and well-defined, where no two products are identical—each meets a specific set of demand dimensions—and where the purchase takes months and often years of negotiation. We refer to this as a "custom" purchase situation, where "custom" means that a specially designed marketing effort may be developed for each sale. The sale of products and services to governments and other institutions, and joint development projects between a supplier and a potential customer fall into this category.

Suppose we wish to determine quantitatively the sales response to marketing spending for these two extreme types of situations. For general situations, where there are a large number of purchase occasions, market experimentation, suitably modified for industrial settings, is a feasible and suitable approach for quantitative analysis of sales response. On the other hand, custom situations do not usually provide data bases sufficient for statistical inference, which requires grouping at one stage or another; instead customer-by-customer, situation-specific analyses are required there.

But what of the situations in between? These are characterized by a moderate number of customers and moderate sales rate. With relatively small markets, if the expenditure for marketing experiments is analyzed on the basis of the value of added information, the cost cannot justify the expense. (For a discussion of evaluating marketing spending in this way, see Blattberg [2] and Peters and Summers [37].) Furthermore, buyer–seller relationships are often long-term so that the historical variability needed to read response to marketing strategy variation is usually missing. Finally, it should be noted that analogies to Nielsen and SAMI data, i.e. regularly and frequently collected product–class sales data, do not exist in industrial markets. This lack of data makes sales response modeling difficult and/or extremely expensive.

Some of these products do hold promise for analysis, however. They have markets that have gone through a significant disruption—a major competitive entry, a product modification or some similar event. This disruption gives us knowledge both of causality and of the magnitude of the effect. Following Stouffer [50] and Campbell [6], we refer to the event as a *natural experiment* and the resulting overall change in the market-equilibrium situation as a *market in transition.* Table 1 summarizes our proposed classification.

The objective of this paper is to develop an approach for analyzing natural experiments in industrial markets. We proceed by discussing what characterizes a market-in-transition. A model of market response follows along with an estimation procedure for the model. The procedure is then applied to

Table 1
A classification of industrial marketing situations and analyses

Type of purchase situation	Typical products	Type of market	Preferred mode of analysis
Custom (few customers/purchases)	Oil rigs	Customized	Customer by customer examination
Intermediate	Machine tools	Mixed	Analysis of natural experiments
General (many customers/purchases)	Copiers/supplies	Mass/general	Experimentation

six cases and the results are evaluated. Few examples of time-series analysis of response to marketing spending for industrial products exist in the marketing literature; Weinberg [57] is a well-known exception. The procedure, and the six cases analyzed, represent a contribution in this area.

2. Industrial markets in transition

Most intermediate industrial products will not show enough historical variation in marketing spending levels and competitive activities to allow a statistically significant estimation of marketing effects. A standard approach to overcome this difficulty and to get a clear causal direction of the effects would be to perform a controlled field experiment. As previously mentioned, this is frequently impossible because of timing, costs and institutional constraints. Results are typically wanted yesterday; a field experiment, especially if the product is a durable, may take years to complete and evaluate. The results may be readily available to competitive scrutiny. Costs of performing the experiment may exceed the potential value of the added information. Furthermore, it may be impossible to vary, say, sales call frequency without disrupting long-term marketing programs. Thus, a *natural experiment* in a market-in-transition may be the only viable mechanism to permit response modeling.

Two examples of markets in transition are illustrated in fig. 1. Fig. 1(a) is drawn from the data in case A (see the Appendix). Here, as can be seen, the company introduced marketing spending in a market where nothing had been spent historically. The result was a dramatic increase in market share. Fig. 1(b) illustrates a very different effect (case C, appendix). Here, a number of competitors entered a company's market over a period of years, cutting into market share in a significant way.

Intuitively, a natural experiment can be said to have occurred when some

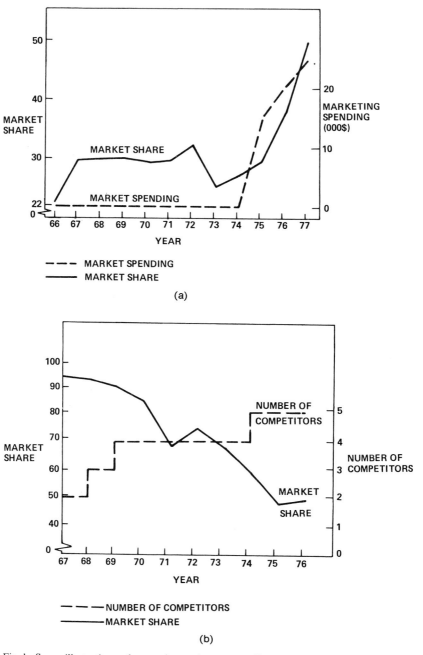

Fig. 1. Some illustrations of natural experiments. (a) Case A—company A's introduction of marketing dramatically increased its market share. (b) Case C—company C's share went down as its number of competitors grew.

dramatic change in the company's historical behavior or in the competitive environment has occurred that could be expected to affect the company's market position. The event or events should be identifiable and the cause-and-effect relationship clear, both intuitively and statistically, for a situation to be acceptable for analysis. This view is articulated by Cook and Campbell [10, p. 296]: "The event being evaluated has to be abrupt and precisely dated, and not a reaction to prior change in the level of the indicator."

Several procedures exist in statistics to operationalize this concept, typically by detecting changes in time series (e.g. see Box and Tiao [4]; Bagshaw and Johnson [1]; Quandt [38]; Chow [9]; Farley and Hinich [15]). All these procedures are founded on the notion of a departure from stationarity of a stochastic time series. Similarly, the theory of statistical quality control (Shewhart [47]) draws upon the same notion, i.e. to establish bounds beyond which an "assignable cause" of variation is expected to have occurred.

None of the above approaches can be used here because of our limited data bases. However, we can use the underlying concept of nonstationarity and design a test suitable for our limited data base. We shall say that a natural experiment has occurred in a market if either the time series of observations on the dependent variable (market share, in general) or any of the independent variables (marketing spending, competitive spending, etc.) is found to be generated by a nonstationary process. The departure from stationarity is observed at the time of a change in the market or the environment and it is identified by the company participating in the analysis. The associated market will be called a market-in-transition.

Following this convention we shall characterize a natural experiment by its deviation from an autoregressive model. In an autoregressive process of order r, the current observation of the variable (market share, m_t, for example), is generated as a weighted average of past observations going back r periods together with a random disturbance, e_t, in the current period. The process can be represented with the following equation:

$$m_t = d_0 + d_1 m_{t-1} + d_2 m_{t-2} + \ldots + d_r m_{t-r} + e_t. \tag{1}$$

The necessary and sufficient condition for stationarity of this process is given by Box and Jenkins [3]:

$$|d_1|, |d_2|, \ldots, |d_r| < 1.$$

Or, the process is nonstationary if

$$|d_1|, |d_2|, \ldots, |d_r| \geqslant 1. \tag{2}$$

To identify conditions for a natural experiment we look for situations where expression (2) holds. Condition (2) is a very strong one from the standpoint of looking for stationarity, much stronger in fact than those proposed by Box and Tiao [4] or by Farley and Hinich [15]. However, the data series that we will be working with are quite short, requiring clear, strong conditions of non-stationarity to permit parameter estimation.

Just as large differences are required to see statistically significant differences between two populations when their sample sizes are small, so we must require strong conditions on nonstationarity here, with our short data series.

Ideally, one would like to make a statement about the statistical properties of the estimates in (2). In practice this leads to difficulties, due to (a) the short time series we have available (except for stationary time series which we are not interested in here, when Hibbs' [21] approximation could be used) and (b) the fact that any statistical statement of the characteristics of the auto-regressive coefficient in a nonstationary series depends on the process one assumes is generating the nonstationarity (see Box and Jenkins [3, ch. 6]).

For our purposes, we consider (2) a condition to be satisfied and apply it to the variables (dependent or independent or both) that we hypothesize have undergone a change. The reason for considering both independent and dependent variables, and requiring only one for a disruption, is that marketing activities may vary widely and not affect share (an interesting, and analyzable event); also, share may change without noticeable influence from marketing spending (perhaps from a new sales strategy), suggesting a need to analyze the situation and discover reasons for the change.

3. Analytic approach for industrial markets

Our objective is to assess market response in industrial markets-in-transition. In the previous section, we proposed a small sample procedure to identify such markets. Many candidate products were discarded from the data base of products collected for the ADVISOR project (Lilien [26]) because of insufficient data for complete analysis even if a natural experiment had occurred. This was because, in the industrial markets we were able to observe, data collected more frequently than on an annual basis were misleading and/or impossible to obtain. We found difficulty in separating purchase commitment from signed sales orders and orders from shipments; these quantities were frequently moved forward or backward in time to balance sales quotas. Finer reading of effects simply registered additional noise. Due to personnel turnover and other causes, time histories in many products were difficult to trace, so data streams were often very short. We were forced to discard products whose sales history did not generate quite a few more points than the number of model parameters we wish to estimate.

Fig. 2 presents a flow chart of our analysis. We started with 131 potential

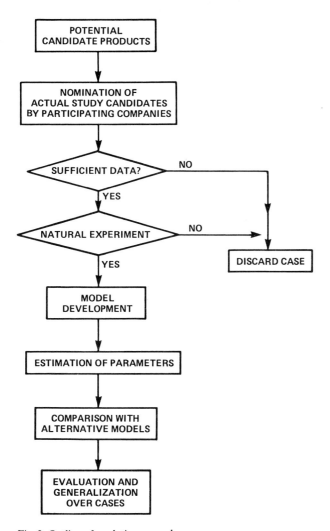

Fig. 2. Outline of analytic approach.

candidate products. Of these, 10 were nominated by participating companies as study candidates, following identification of a potential natural experiment. Of these 10, 3 data base were insufficiently large to enable even small sample estimation and 1 additional case was discarded as not passing the test for nonstationarity. For the products that passed both screens, coefficients of a model, presented in the next section, were estimated. This was done for each situation. Finally, the models of different situations were compared across the cases in search of generalization.

In the next three sections we develop a modeling and estimation approach and then apply it to a number of product-specific situations.

4. A model of industrial market effectiveness

We are interested in a model of industrial marketing effectiveness that is both conceptually sound and managerially useful. Little [31,32], Urban [53] and Lilien [26] discuss strategies related to building marketing models which we follow here. As we were particularly interested in model relevance and use, we interacted heavily with company representatives in the study design, data collection, case study development, modeling and interpretation of results. Recalling that we are dealing with intermediate products, if we draw from Corey [11], Webster [56] and Choffray and Lilien [8], we assert that an effective model of industrial market response should exhibit the following properties:

● The model should relate sales and/or profit to major company control variable(s).
● Market share should vary only between 0 and 1.
● Competitive activity should be explicitly included.
● Zero marketing effort should not necessarily imply zero sales.
● The effectiveness of a marketing program should be greater when the company spends more.
● Long-term relationships between the buyer and seller should be explicitly included in the structure. Reciprocity and long-term buyer–seller relationships are often the rule in industrial markets, so interruptions of marketing should not immediately stop sales.
● The model should have a symmetric structure. By this we mean that if a market has two identical producers with two identical product–market relationships and the same marketing effectiveness, then the model should show these situations as identical.
● The total market for the product is exogeneously given and is not affected in a major way by selling and advertising activities.

The conditions we wish to model incorporate a situation where a few competitors, using product and market "weapons" are "battling" for sales. Lanchester's [24] models of warfare, first introduced into the management science literature by Kimball [23] (and applied by Little [32] in a marketing context), address these issues. Those models also include the special kind of competitive framework one finds in industrial markets where there are few competitors who all know each other well, i.e. a market that could be described in a game-theoretic framework (Von Neumann and Morgenstern [55]). In these analyses companies divide a relatively fixed market and a reasonable model should incorporate the competitive nature of those markets.

For expository simplicity, first assume a market with two competitors, companies 1 and 2. These companies can compete only by changes in the effectiveness of their marketing programs. (Marketing effectiveness will be operationalized later; one can think of it as the dollar amount of marketing spending for now.)

Let

s_i = sales of company i (function of time),
ε_i = marketing effectiveness of company i, either constant or a function of time,
M = market sales = $s_1 + s_2$ (function of time),
m_i = market share of company i (function of time).

For two competitors, a model consistent with the above conditions is:

$$\frac{ds_1}{dt} = \varepsilon_1 s_2 - \varepsilon_2 s_1 \quad \text{and} \quad \frac{ds_2}{dt} = \varepsilon_2 s_1 - \varepsilon_1 s_2. \tag{3}$$

The complete solution for (3) follows from:

$$M = s_1 + s_2 \quad \text{or} \quad s_2 = M - s_1. \tag{4}$$

Thus,

$$\frac{ds_1}{dt} + (\varepsilon_1 + \varepsilon_2)s_1 = \varepsilon_1 M \tag{5}$$

or

$$s_1(t) = \frac{1}{\mu(t)}\left[M \int \mu(t)\varepsilon_1 \, dt + c \right], \tag{6}$$

where

$$\mu(t) = \exp\left[\int (\varepsilon_1 + \varepsilon_2) \, dt \right]. \tag{7}$$

In particular, if

$$s_1(0) = C_1, \quad s_2(0) = C_2 \tag{8}$$

and ε_1 and ε_2 are constant, we get

$$s_1(t) = \left[\frac{\varepsilon_2 C_1 - \varepsilon_1 C_2}{\varepsilon_1 + \varepsilon_2} \right] \exp\left[-(\varepsilon_1 + \varepsilon_2)t \right] + \frac{M\varepsilon_1}{\varepsilon_1 + \varepsilon_2}. \tag{9}$$

The steady-state solution to this equation is the second item in (9):

$$s_1 = \frac{\varepsilon_1}{\varepsilon_1 + \varepsilon_2} M \quad \text{or} \quad \frac{s_1}{M} = \frac{\varepsilon_1}{\varepsilon_1 + \varepsilon_2}. \tag{10}$$

If a large number of observations are available at frequent intervals, parameters of the transient portion of the model can be estimated. However, the steady-state solution can be used in the analysis provided that changes in the market occur within a time period shorter than our period of observation. Little [32] gives evidence of the short duration of advertising influences primarily in consumer markets, which is supported by unpublished research findings from one of our participating companies in an industrial setting.

Eq. (10) generalizes in the case of n competitors to

$$\frac{s_1}{M} = \frac{\varepsilon_1}{\sum\limits_{i=1}^{n} \varepsilon_i}. \tag{11}$$

Assuming that market shares reach equilibrium annually (our unit of measurement), we can use eq. (11) as our response model.

An important issue here is the specification of the functional form of the sales response to marketing. Empirical evidence is not clear on this relationship. In a variety of settings from retail outlet management (Hartung and Fisher [20]; Lilien and Rao [28]) to the measurement of sales call effectiveness (Hyman [22]) there is evidence for a region of increasing returns to marketing effort. The PIMS study (Schoeffler et al. [45]) supports this contention indirectly in a cross-sectional analysis, indicating that decreasing levels of marketing (as a percent of sales) are needed to maintain a given level of sales across a wide range of industry situations. Also, Rao [39] presents evidence in a variety of consumer goods categories for regions of increasing returns, and Wittink [58] finds larger coefficients of advertising spending variables at larger advertising rates, indicating increasing returns to scale.

However, there is also empirical evidence on decreasing returns: Simon [48] reviews a number of studies and concludes that there is diminishing returns to individual brand advertising, and Weinberg [57], in a study of sales response to industrial advertising, concludes that in the region observed there is decreasing returns to spending.

Much of the evidence is inconclusive (Ferguson [16]) but both increasing and diminishing return hypotheses can be accommodated with an S-shaped sales to marketing response hypothesis, the position we take here. This view is supported in the consumer marketing literature by Cardwell [7], Longman [34], Rao and Miller [40], Rao [39], and Little [32] on an aggregate basis and by McDonald [35] at the individual consumer level.

There are several aggregate S-shaped functions that can be used in model (11). Domencich and McFadden [13] indicate that these several closed form S-shaped functions are difficult to discriminate between, and suggest adopting a logistic form for computational reasons. In this case, eq. (11) can be rewritten in the form:

$$\frac{s_1}{M} = \frac{e^{a_0 + a_1 X_1}}{e^{a_0 + a_1 X_1} + e^{a_2 X_2}}, \tag{12}$$

where

X_i = marketing effort for product i
a_i = coefficient of marketing effectiveness, $i = 1, 2$,
a_0 = constant (Srinivasan [49]).

(Note that a little algebra will show that only one intercept term can be specified in eq. (12).) Here marketing spending is the only influence on brand share.

Let us now define marketing effectiveness as the impact of all the components of a brand's activities on its sales. The current marketing effort component of effectiveness can be divided into:

X_i^1 = advertising spending for product i,
X_i^2 = personal selling spending for product i,
X_i^3 = technical service spending for product i.

That is, $\varepsilon_i = f(X_i^1, X_i^2, X_i^3)$.

Variable effectiveness of communications programs (copy/media effectiveness for example) can be included as factors multiplying spending levels.

Dorfman and Steiner [14] suggest that the model should also include variables such as price and product quality. In general, we denote

X_{ki} = market factors, such as communications spending, introduction of new products, etc. for product i ($k = 1,...,K$).

Then, the general model becomes, for two competitors:

$$\frac{s_1}{M} = \frac{\exp\left(a_0 + \sum_k b_k X_{k1}\right)}{\exp\left(a_0 + \sum_k b_k X_{k1}\right) + \exp\left(\sum_k c_k X_{k2}\right)}. \tag{13}$$

In the cases investigated, the nonmarketing factors included technological change (e.g. a clear quality change) and competitive market entries. In the 131 cases examined, no situation was observed where product managers indicated competitive pricing variation was important. This result is perhaps not surprising since oligopolists are considered to substitute nonprice for price competition (see Scherer [47, pp. 334–337]).

Two key simplifying assumptions should be pointed out here. First, we assume the model coefficients are stable during the period in question and that we can ignore higher order interactions in the exponents. Our data will not generally permit these kinds of complications. If sufficient data exist, the model can be extended to examine such complexities as when $\varepsilon = \varepsilon(t)$. A classical treatment of this issue can be found in Forsyth [17, p. 158] with numerical solution tables available in Richards [42, p. 351]. Also, interaction terms can be estimated (see Lerman and Manski [25]).

Secondly, although the generating equation for the model incorporates competitive effort, no mechanism for specifying competitive reaction to a specific company's spending level has been included within the model itself, and competitors have been lumped together as a single competitor for purposes of analysis here.

5. Estimation procedure

The parameters of eq. (13) can be estimated either using regression analysis or a maximum likelihood method (MLE). We decided against a weighted least squares approach (WLS) such as suggested by Cox [12]; Domencich and McFadden [13] have shown that in small samples WLS estimates have a larger systematic bias and mean square error than the MLE, the approach we follow here.

The logistic response function represented by eq. (13) can be written in the following form:

$$\frac{S_1}{M} = \frac{\exp\left(a_0 + \sum_k b_k X_{k1}\right)}{\exp\left(a_0 + \sum_k b_k X_{k1}\right) + \exp\left(\sum_k c_k X_{k2}\right)} + \eta_t, \tag{14}$$

where η_t = a stochastic term with zero mean and variance σ^2.

In constructing a likelihood function here, we assume (and test) whether the successive values of η_t are independent. The results of the test for autocorrelated disturbances is described in section 6.

Oliver [36] has derived solutions for the maximum likelihood estimators of the parameters in (14) and discussed their properties. He has shown, using Monte Carlo simulation, that except under very special data conditions, the maximum of the likelihood function obtained from eq. (14) is unique, even for small samples. His estimator is unbiased and consistent and is the one used here.

6. Application

We have applied the approach to products from the ADVISOR study (Lilien [27]). The results of the stationarity analysis for the relevant variable in the seven products retained for study (see fig. 2) are displayed in table 2. Although first, second and third order autoregressive schemes were estimated, for expository clarity only the first order scheme results are presented here. The stationarity test led to the elimination of one of the cases, case F. (Note that, as described earlier, the paucity of data limits our ability to make statistical inferences about the d's.)

Coefficients of the model defined by eq. (14) were estimated for the six cases studied. Sketches of the case situations are given below, with more detail available in the appendix. Graphs of the critical changes are displayed in fig. 3(a–d), as well as in fig. 1(a and b).

Briefly, the situations are as follows:

Case A: The company discovered marketing, having produced this material since 1966 but only having started a formal marketing effort in 1975.

Case B: This case deals with a significant quality improvement in a widely used material, halting a long-term market share decline.

Case C: In this case, during the period from 1968 to 1974, four new competitors entered the market for a specialty chemical, cutting company market share in half.

Case D: Here, competitors introduced a technological innovation as well as a new end-use form (in 1970 and 1972, respectively). The results affected the OEM and replacement markets differently, and they are studied separately here.

Case E: This case deals with vertical integration, the company adding equipment to what had been previously a supply business only. The

Table 2

Test for stationarity: Coefficients of the autoregressive model indicate that A through E are nonstationary, F is stationary

Case	$|d_1|$	Series tested
A	1.24	Marketing
B	1.23	Share
C	1.07	Share
D (new)	1.22	Marketing
D (replacement)	1.11	Marketing
E	1.21	Marketing
F	0.81	Marketing

resulting marketing activity around an integrated system led to a share increase.

It is important to emphasize that the companies were able to provide detailed data for all important variables except competitive marketing spending. These expenditures were generated using the ADVISOR norm model for marketing spending (Lilien [27]). These estimates of competitive spending were then reviewed by the marketing management and reconciled with their esti-

MARKET SHARE

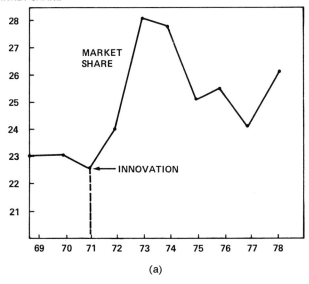

(a)

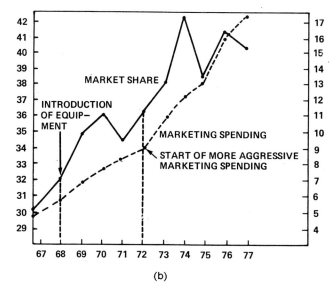

(b)

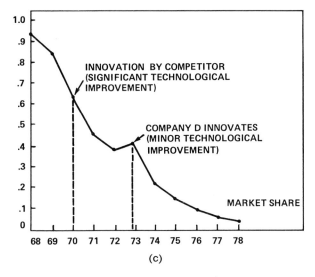

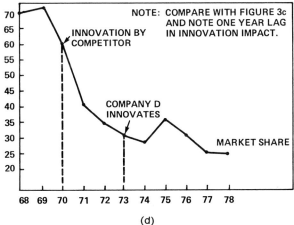

Fig. 3. (a) Case B—company B's introduction of a product improvement boosted its market share temporarily. (b) Case E—company E's introduction of equipment and more aggressive spending program in marketing yielded share growth. (c) Case D (OEM). Market share for product is eroded by market entry of competitive materials in 1970. (d) Case D (replacement). Market share for replacement sales of product is also eroded by market entry of competitive materials, but fall is more gentle, less severe than with OEMs.

mates of competitive spending; in most cases there was no difficulty in resolving differences.

Each of the models was of the general form specified in eq. (14); the key independent variables are defined as:

● Our marketing: Total $ level of marketing effort in year t associated with the product.

● Our sales inertia: Past year's sales in $, an instrumental variable for sales inertia.
● Competitive marketing: Total $ level of competitive marketing spending.
● Competitive sales inertia: Past year's sales of competition.
● Environmental factor: a 0–1 or multi-valued variable depending on the case (e.g. in case B it is a dummy variable equalling 1 when the new material was introduced and 0 before).

For none of the models did sufficient data exist to separate out the differential effects of the elements of the marketing mix—personal selling, technical service and advertising; they are aggregated here.

The results of the estimation together with some qualitative descriptors of each particular situation are presented in table 3. The results show that all coefficients have the a priori expected sign; for example, an increase in our marketing effort results in an increase in market share while an increase in competitive marketing effort has the opposite effect in all cases. The majority of adjusted t-statistics indicate that the coefficients are significant above the 90% level. As an index of goodness of fit (roughly analogous to R^2) we use one minus the ratio of the log of the likelihood functions (Theil [51], Richards and Ben-Akiva [41]):

$$\ell^2 = 1 - \frac{L^*(a)/(i-k)}{L^*(0)/(i-1)}, \tag{16}$$

where $L^*(a)$ is the value of the log likelihood function for the vector of estimated coefficients and $L^*(0)$ is the value of L^* for the coefficient vector $= 0$, i is the number of observations, and k is the number of variables. Note that ℓ^2 lies between 0 and 1.

A test for the presence of autocorrelated disturbances developed for use in a regression analysis framework was performed using (1) Theil's BLUS estimator and (2) the Durbin and Watson test (or a modified Durbin test for the inconclusive cases). In all six cases the hypothesis that the disturbances were not autocorrelated could not be rejected at the 5% level.

The very small sample sizes for the six models limits our confidence in the estimation results: small errors in measurements of the variables could result in large errors in the estimated coefficients, the corrected t-statistics, and ℓ^2. Thus, all results must be treated with caution; they are more suggestive of the general magnitude of the effect than its exact level.

Other ways of evaluating the sensitivity of parameters besides the corrected t-statistics—such as jack-knifing—(Tukey [52], Sharot [46]) might have been used. However, these methods assume all points to be equally important while our analysis is based on the premise that points around the natural experiment are the most important and thus cannot be excluded from the analysis. For this reason jack-knifing would simply demonstrate that the points around the time

Table 3
Estimation results/case summaries

Product case Independent variable	A	B	C	D (New)	D (Repl)	E
Our marketing	0.659(−5) [a] (2.56) [b]	0.195(−6) (1.03)	0.318(−5) (2.05)	0.473(−5) 2.70)	0.640(−5) (2.76)	0.402(−7) (2.01)
Our sales inertia	0.361(−6) (1.76)	0.189(−8) (3.75)	0.194(−7) (1.81)	0.505(−7) (1.41)	0.540(−6) (1.02)	0.319(−8) (3.82)
Environmental factor	[c]	+0.212 (2.21)	−0.967(−1) (1.96)	−1.01 (1.72)	−0.81 (1.59)	0.921(−2) (1.62)
Competitive marketing	0.217(−5) (1.73)	0.547(−7) (1.82)	0.871(−6) (2.01)	0.195(−5) (1.26)	0.133(−5) (1.43)	0.781(−7) (1.51)
Inertia of competition	0.123(−6) (1.26)	0.972(−9) (1.65)	0.128(−7) (1.42)	0.873(−7) (1.91)	0.226(−7) (1.82)	0.112(−8) (1.07)
Kind of change	add marketing	innovation	new com- petition	comp. innov.	comp. innov.	add equipment
Number of observations	12	11	11	12	12	11
Overall ℓ^2 fit	0.92	0.94	0.90	0.80	0.80	0.86

[a] (−5) means $\times 10^{-5}$.
[b] (2.56) is corrected t-statistic.
[c] not relevant in this case.

Table 4
Relative effects of marketing spending, sales inertia and other factors on market share show that
the relative marketing effects differ considerably

Case	Marketing	Sales inertia	Other
A	0.29	0.71	–
B	0.67	0.10	0.23
C	0.49	0.08	0.43
D (new)	0.50	0.03	0.47
DR	0.17	0.41	0.42
(replacement)			
E	0.11	0.88	0.01

Note: These effects are computed as of the end of the last year of the respective analysis period.

of the natural experiment are very influential in parameter estimation.

Let us then consider what would be a minimal number of observations to obtain statistically valid estimates of coefficients given (a) that the variables of the model are drawn from normal distributions (over intervals before and after change), (b) that coefficients have a 10% confidence level, and (c) that effects have the same magnitude as our estimates. We performed a simulation study to investigate this issue and found the number of points to be about 15; 7 before the change in the market, 7 after, and 1 during the change. Since none of our models has this quantity of data, we must be careful not to overemphasize the accuracy of the parameter estimates.

Assuming for the moment that the parameter estimates are reasonable, what do the models say about the influence of marketing spending on market share? To answer this important managerial question, consider a simple way of relating the relative size of the effects—by multiplying each coefficient by the value of the associated variable and then normalizing. This allows us to compare the relative magnitude of effects across models. Table 4 performs these calculations, showing great variability. For example, note that the new and replacement markets in case D show similar responses to the change in market conditions; however, the new market is much more responsive to marketing effort than the replacement market. Case E shows that the new addition of equipment is not effective in influencing sales (effect $= 0.01$) while case B shows a much more effective innovation (effect $= 0.23$). In sum, then, the relative effects of marketing spending compared to other market factors varies widely over the cases studied here.

7. Evaluation and further research issues

The models and the procedure should now be evaluated in terms of statistical fit, conceptual soundness, managerial use and parsimony. As the previous section noted, the models fit adequately. With respect to conceptual soundness, the models were built to satisfy a set of predetermined criteria and used structural forms motivated by other work in marketing and allied fields. The models are intuitively appealing and their soundness is supported by the fact that all the estimated coefficients have the right logical sign.

Since the models are market share response models, they can be incorporated in a profit function to evaluate anticipated marketing program changes. In this sense the models meet the use criterion as well. At the same time, the models cannot be used in a precise, prescriptive manner because coefficient estimates, clearly based on a small number of data points, are sensitive to variations in the data. However, the models suggest policy inferences of the following sort: (a) spend much more, (b) spend more, (c) stay about the same, (d) spend less, or (e) spend much less, than what you are spending now. This type of inference can be made with reasonable assurance and, from a decision-maker's standpoint, is a valuable result. It is an important way of summarizing what is in the data that is available to the manager.

These results were reviewed with the participating companies (Galper [19]) with generally supportive results: the managers interviewed concurred with the recommendations of the model and some plan to modify future spending plans following the analysis.

Finally, the model was compared with time-series extrapolation models. If the model explains real market factors, it should perform better in terms of statistical fit whenever a change occurs. As reported elsewhere (Lilien and Ruzdic [30]) the model performs significantly better than three time-series extrapolation models: the model was compared with a linear trend, an exponential growth model and an autoregressive trend. Several measures of comparative fit were calculated; an indication of the quality of the results is that the *largest* percentage root mean square error (RMSE) for any of the cases was 15% for our model while the smallest RMSE was 44% for any of the extrapolation models.

This discussion suggests that the model and the associated estimation procedure seem to perform adequately in the situations tested. Hence, the procedure developed here appears reasonable for studying markets-in-transition.

An issue we are currently studying is whether the results about market response and the relationship between marketing spending and profitability can be generalized from markets-in-transition to a larger universe of industrial products. This is an important issue as the universe of natural experiments is small.

Investigations of the determinants of industrial product profitability have been correlated by economists and marketers for many years. Economists (e.g. Scherer [43], Vernen [54]) have, by and large, focused on variables that managers cannot control such as the number of competitors and concentration ratios. Marketers (Schoeffler, Buzzell and Heany [45] and Buzzell, Gale and Sultan [5]) have used cross-sectional data, generally without strong guiding theory, to study this problem.

All these results have been cross-sectional in nature. A limitation of cross-sectional analysis is that directions of causality—i.e. what causes high profitability—are often unclear. Firms with large market shares may make more profit, but the high share and the profit may result from high product quality or value. High market share does not "cause" high profit. The company with a poor product and consequent low market share can do nothing worse than try to "buy" market share (Fruhan [18]).

The importance of this research is that our analysis rests on knowledge of the direction of causality. As such, at least in the region close to the current spending level, it can be expected that changes in marketing spending will result in predictable sales and profit changes. As a first step in this direction, consider Π_m, where

$$\Pi_m = \frac{\partial \text{ profit}}{\partial \text{ marketing}} \tag{17}$$

and

profit = revenue $\times$ contribution

= industry sales $\times$ contribution $\times$ market share. $\tag{18}$

Our preliminary results analyzing Π_m using our earlier models as input have been encouraging. If we consider the markets-in-transition as representative samples from the universe of industrial products, then it would be desirable to see if we can relate variations in Π_m to observable product and market characteristics. The development of such a model is beyond the scope of our study here. The work needs development in terms of data generation, theory and estimation. The PIMS and ADVISOR results, however, encourage further work in this direction of cross-section analysis of industry operating relationships.

8. Conclusion

This paper develops a procedure for identifying and assessing market response in markets undergoing natural experiments. A response model and associated estimation procedure has been developed and applied to six case situations.

The situations studied varied greatly, as did model parameters. The results are consistent with *a priori* expectations and provided useful, managerial guidance. There are, however, several limitations. The models assume stable coefficients in changing markets. Competitive reaction is not specifically included: competitive firms are viewed similarly and aggregated into a single "competitor". From the standpoint of estimation, the results are based on small data sets, the situation found in such markets.

There are several directions research in this area can lead. First, we have isolated a set of situations in an industrial marketing setting where causally sound modeling leads to useful managerial results. The concepts and the procedure can, thus, be applied elsewhere. Further research in this area should be aimed at a more integrated procedure, allowing for more elaborate models in those cases where more data are available. That data may be available through longer time series or, more likely, through geographic breakdowns of shorter time series. Given better data a scientific and philosophical basis for analyzing markets-in-transition is required, extendable to different length series; in particular, a theory dealing with the tradeoff between variability and the length of the series should be developed.

Our most promising direction for research is the development of a causal relationship between profitability and marketing spending as applied to the wider universe of industrial products. This would use natural experiments to generate the data base on which to test hypotheses about the determinants of responsiveness and profitability in industrial markets.

Acknowledgements

The work described in this paper was performed as part of the ADVISOR project. Many individuals from the participating companies gave generously of their time and support. Our colleagues at MIT, John D.C. Little, Glen L. Urban, Alvin J. Silk, and Manohar Kalwani, provided many valuable comments on earlier drafts. We would also like to acknowledge the efforts of Mort Galper of Babson College who collected the information and wrote it up in case study form.

Appendix: Case details

Case A

The company selling the product here was founded in 1937 as an equally owned joint venture subsidiary of two companies. The company's initial product is still an important part of the company's line. The major part of the product line consists of construction products for a variety of applications. Constructed from a proprietary material, this material is produced in a rigid cellular form in blocks by a baking process. It is lightweight, waterproof, vaporproof, and noncombustible. These characteristics, coupled with its dimensional stability and high compression strength, make it well suited to construction applications.

The special situation involves a product application that is totally removed from the company's main business direction. The product is basically the application of the company's cellular material to a specialized need of restaurants and fast food outlets.

The company manufactures material that is sold to distributors who cut and wrap the material, and sell to restaurant supply wholesalers who in turn sell to restaurants. The customer for this market is the restaurant. The material normally is supplied to the restaurant by the restaurant supply wholesalers. There are over 400 restaurant-supply wholesalers in the United States and over 500,000 food service outlets.

These materials are a very small cost of the food service operation and produces low volume for the restaurant-supply wholesaler. Thus, restaurant management is not aware of the cost and usage of the supplies used; rather, their concern centers around attributes such as ease of use, residue remaining, and safety of the process. Restaurant supply wholesalers are in the position of being the buying influence, i.e. their influence is the key to what material is used or not used.

The company had been aware since 1966 that its material has been used for this purpose and began to monitor its sales in this market since then. A research report suggested giving this particular market-opportunity specific company attention and support. This involved a full marketing program, including product design and packaging, branding, authorized distributorships, and a comprehensive communications program directed at restaurant management and restaurant supply houses. As part of this study a restaurant survey was conducted which revealed that in 1973 approximately 50% of the food outlets responding used some form of specialized product; an equivalent survey in 1977 indicated that 60% used such iems. Over this period national market share for the product increased from 25 to 50%, according to the company. (It should be noted that none of the competitors offers exactly the same product.)

Formal marketing effort for the product by the company did not commence until 1975 and due to the length of the distribution channel (three stages) there is lag between the initiation of marketing communication expenditures and the occurrence of a change in sales. Through 1977 the marketing effort expended has been exclusively in the form of personal selling to the company's distributors (converters). In 1978 the company started a low level media campaign directed at restaurant managers, as a form of "pull" strategy to increase awareness, stocking, and promotion by restaurant supply houses. A coupon offer in the ad for a free sample is a key part of the promotional concept.

Fig. 1(a) graphically depicts the market effects.

Case B

The company is one of the world's leading manufacturers in its field, currently holding a 25% share of the world-wide market for this basic industrial product. In 1976 the company's major business accounted for over 50% of its approximately $600 million in sales.

The main product can be broadly divided into two areas. One portion is generally considered to be the more technically sophisticated of the two and is classified by size, shape and material used. The other is also varied by size, shape and material based on the application. Product B is part of this business.

The market for product B has grown since 1967, increasing from nearly $100M in sales to approximately $250M in 1977. Since the product line is a production supply, it is closely related to the level of economic activity. As a result, industry sales have shown some volatility within the overall growth trend. The market is highly diverse by industry segments as well as by annual use. The company estimates that there are in excess of 15,000 user locations that purchase these products. The company, as well as its two major competitors, service the market through networks of selected distributors. Each of these participants has a distribution organization of approximately 600 outlets. Approximately 95% of the company's sales volume is handled by these distributors.

Since World War II, the company had seen its market share in its major business steadily decline as new competitors emerged to offer specialized products and services in limited geographic market areas. This decline was particularly noticeable in the area under study. The company has identified more than 40 competitors in this product area; it considers two to be major competitors and one other to be an important minor one. The top three participants, which include the company, have controlled more than 85% of business over the past several years.

The decline in market share continued unchecked until 1972, when the company introduced a revolutionary new patented material which significantly outperformed existing materials in most applications. Its major advantages were longer life, fast production rates, less operator fatigue and improved operator efficiency (at user organizations).

Initial shipments of this new material in the line took place in the fourth quarter of 1972. The introduced was supported by a major increase in marketing effort which incorporated personal selling, advertising, and dealer promotions. An important objective of the introductory program was the specific effort to "go after" competitive business. This new product program not only stemmed the market share decline, but also reversed the trend, resulting in an increase in market position. This continued until 1975, when a number of internal and external factors combined to intervene and halt the gain. Most significant among these factors were the entry in 1974 and 1975 of the two major competitors with comparable products. This came about as a result of the company's decision to license these two competitors rather than battle them in a lengthy and expensive patent suit.

Fig. 3(b) details the market share history of the product.

Case C

Company C manufacturers a diverse line of specialty chemicals produced primarily from renewable natural fats and oils—the oils of soybeans, coconuts, pine trees, cotton seeds and animal fats. The company's products are used by a wide range of industries in highly diverse applications. In fiscal year 1977 a sales peak of $183.8 million was achieved.

Product C's line are viscous liquids produced by the polymerization of fatty acids. Two important characteristics that these products impart to other materials are thermal stability and flexibility. These products have been used in a variety of applications. Among the most important are surface coatings (paints), synthetic lubricants, inks, and adhesives. The company introduced these products in 1950 and was the sole merchant (noncaptive) supplier for almost 10 years.

The market for the product line expanded rapidly in the early seventies after being stable for several previous years. This growth reflects a shift away from petroleum-based chemicals in favor of those with a more consistent and renewable supply. Since 1973, when approximately 26 million pounds were shipped, the market dropped more than 25%, reflecting the 1974–75 recession. Current shipment levels reflect an improved market situation, though company executives indicated the industry has excess capacity. Prices have become less stable over the past five years as a result of volatile raw material costs and dramatically expanded competition. An important element in the market structure for this product is the limited number of prospective customers, which has been estimated by company executives to be approximately 300. Company C currently supplies products to about 65% of these.

One of the most significant aspects of this market is the rapid change that took place in the competitive environment during the period from 1968 to 1974. Until that time the company and one other firm shared the market with most of the competitors' capacity being used internally. By 1974 there were four additional firms supplying the product for the merchant market and two companies with substantial capacity dedicated to internal requirements. In 1976 the company was still the dominant supplier in this market, but it had an expanded number of competitors.

Since 1968, when the third participant entered the field, the company has seen a steady drop in its market position in the merchant market. From 93.5% in 1968 its share has dropped to just under 50% in 1976. This loss of market share very closely parallels the increase in competition witnessed over this same period. In addition, the decline in participation was undoubtedly accelerated by a reduction in marketing communications expenditures during these years as well. Most notable was a nearly 55% reduction in technical service support over the 10-year period.

Fig. 1(b) gives details of the rise in number of competitors along with the associated drop in market share.

Case D

Company D is the world's leading manufacturer of its class of products, which are manufactured in two basic forms: (1) one type used in construction products, and (2) the other used for weaving fabrics and for reinforcing plastic, rubber and paper products. In 1976 the company reached the billion dollar sales level; it has grown dramatically since 1973, nearly doubling its sales between then and 1976.

Product D is made from filament, which is produced through an extrusion process. The filament is then impregnated (coated) with rubber and combined through twisting with other impregnated filaments into a yarn. This is the form in which the product is sold to its customers. These customers then weave the yarn into a fabric that is cut into specific sizes and shapes required for their use.

The particular application of this material is a fairly recent development. Experimental work began in 1964 with significant commercialization first appearing in 1967. The development work on this product was supported by the company in cooperation with major customers. This close working relationship between company D and its customers led to a rapid acceptance of this material once the product's superior performance characteristics were demonstrated. Those advantages led to a doubling of the average operating life of the users' products when compared with existing materials.

After initial market introduction, market development and acceptance occurred very rapidly with the announcement of a major customer end product on national television in 1969. An extensive and aggressive promotion effort led to strong consumer acceptance of the end product over the next few years.

According to trade sources there were 219.6 million end products sold in 1976. The market is segmented further into products sold as original equipment (OE) and those sold for replacement. In defining the market served by company D, we have segmented the end use market, since the company's marketing and product development efforts have been directed at specific areas.

With the introduction of product D in 1967, the company became an important factor in this business. It enjoyed dominant market shares in both the OE and replacement markets through 1970, when the aggressive introduction of competitive materials reduced its market position. In 1972–73 a new end use product form was introduced as a premium long-life product. This form also received considerable recognition for the improvements in operating efficiency it provided. The oil embargo and the subsequent concern over energy conservation provided a timely boost to the interest in this product. This culminated in the OE market going heavily into this form in 1974. The company saw its market position in the OE segment deteriorate rapidly over the period. It was, however, making both a technical and a market research effort to determine if a medium priced niche could be developed for its material. These efforts proved successful, and the company introduced its design in 1975, which ultimately led to two OE manufacturers accepting the product for use in 1977.

The company's marketing effort accelerated sharply during the period from 1965 to 1970 and has remained relatively constant since that time in spite of significant loss of market position. Technical service and sales efforts were directed at the customers' customers as well as direct customers. Extensive advertising and sales promotion resources (trade shows, POP displays, and advertising support) as well as sales effort were directed at both independent distributors as well as large retailers. The company considered and rejected a direct consumer campaign as too costly.

Figs. 3(c and d) depict the dynamics of company share movements in this market.

Case E

Company E is a widely known diversified manufacturer. Its 1977 sales volume of over $2 billion reflects steady growth in sales since 1968, increasing by over 240%. Product E represents the supply portion of the product line being studied. The company presently markets a complete system of products and services, including equipment, supplies and support services under a single brand name. The major properties of the product E line are derived from the use of a tough moisture-resistant plastic as the base material. This material was applied to product E in the early 1960s and provided the company with important product advantages in quality and consistency that were well received by users. As a result, the company has been able to receive a 10–15% price premium for its supplies over most competitive brands.

The market for the product has grown nearly three-fold in unit volume since 1969. The market for these products consists of institutions and individual users, totalling approximately 14,000 customers. Most of these products are marketed through specialty distributors (estimated at 300 organizations nationally) who provide inventory services for both individual and institutional users.

The company markets its line of products through a 180-person dedicated sales force. This organization is responsible for servicing 250 distributors as well as approximately 8,000 users. This channel handles over 90% of the company's business in this product line.

The company has approximately eight significant domestic and foreign competitors in this product area. Until recently one competitor held the dominant market share, received a premium price for its product, and matched company E in technological advances in the field. Of late, the leadership position has been yielded to company E due to inattention, according to some company executives.

Since 1960, company E has gained an increasing share of this expanding market. A closer investigation reveals that the gains in unit-based market share have come about at three discrete intervals since 1960. The first of these occurred between 1963 and 1965, when the company's market share increased from 20.8 to 29.2%. The principal factor behind this movement was the introduction of a major technological improvement. The second significant jump in share took place between 1967 and 1969 (29.8 to 34.8%), and this has been ascribed to the company's entry into the equipment business, which permitted it to market an integrated system. This development enhanced the company's reputation as the technological leader in the field. The third sizeable gain took place between 1972 and 1974. Company managers attribute this improvement to their aggressive marketing posture, which is revealed in significant increases in their communication expenditures. In addition they recently implemented programs designed to assist the user in managing his business, training his staff, and enhancing the quality of service. There is also some feeling, as noted previously, that the major competitor's attention may have been diverted to other businesses at this time, which permitted the company to assert industry leadership.

Fig. 3(b) details the market share and market spending history for the product through 1977.

References

[1] M. Bagshaw and R.A. Johnson, Sequential procedures for detecting parameter changes in a time-series model, Journal of the American Statistical Association 72 (1977) 593–597.

[2] R.C. Blattberg, The design of advertising experiments using statistical decision theory, Journal of Marketing Research 16 (1979) 191–202.

[3] G.E.P. Box and G.M. Jenkins, Time Series Analysis, Forecasting and Control (Holden-Day, San Francisco, 1970).

[4] G.E.P. Box and G.C. Tiao, Intervention analysis with applications to economic and environmental problems, Journal of the American Statistical Association 70 (1975) 70–79.

[5] R.F. Buzzell, B. Gale and R. Sultan, Market share: A key to profitability, Harvard Business Review 53 (January–February 1975) 97–107.

[6] D.T. Campbell, Factors relevant to the validity of experiments in social settings, Psychological Bulletin 54 (1957) 297–314.

[7] J.J. Cardwell, Marketing and management science—a marriage on the rocks? California Management Review (Summer 1968) 3–12.

[8] J.M. Choffray and G.L. Lilien, Market Planning for New Industrial Products (John Wiley and Sons, New York, 1980).

[9] G. Chow, Tests of equality between two sets of coefficients in two linear regressions, Econometrica 28 (1960) 561–605.

[10] T.D. Cook and D.T. Campbell, Quasi-Experimentation (Rand McNally, Chicago, 1979).

[11] E.R. Corey, Industrial Marketing, Cases and Concepts, 2nd edn. (Prentice-Hall, Englewood Cliffs, 1976).

[12] D.R. Cox, Some procedures connected with the logistic qualitative response curve, in: M.F. David, ed., Research Papers in Statistics (John Wiley and Sons, New York, 1966).

[13] T.A. Domencich and D. McFadden, Urban Travel Demand (North-Holland, Amsterdam, 1975).

[14] R. Dorfman and P.O. Steiner, Optimal advertising and optimal quality, The American Economic Review 44 (1954) 826–836.

[15] J.U. Farley and M.L. Hinich, A test for a shifting slope coefficient in a linear model, Journal of the American Statistical Association 65 (1970) 1320–1329.

[16] J.M. Ferguson, Advertising and Competition: Theory, Measurement and Fact (Ballinger, Cambridge, Mass., 1974).

[17] A. Forsyth, Theory of Differential Equations (Cambridge University Press, 1903).

[18] W.E. Fruhan, Pyrrhic victories in fights for market share, Harvard Business Review 50 (September–October 1972) 100–108.

[19] M. Galper, Improving communications spending decisions for industrial products, Unpublished D.B.A. Thesis, Harvard University, Devision of Research (1979).

[20] P.H. Hartung and J.L. Fisher, Brand switching and mathematical programming in market expansion, Management Science 11 (1965) 231–243.

[21] D.A. Hibbs, Jr., Problems of statistical estimation and causal inference in time series regression models, in: H.L. Costner, ed., Sociological Methodology—1973–1974 (Jossey-Bass, San Francisco, 1974).

[22] M. Hyman, Unpublished AT&T Long Lines Study of Sales Call Effectiveness (1979).

[23] G.E. Kimball, Some industrial applications of military operations research methods, Operations Research 5 (1957) 201–204.

[24] F.W. Lanchester, Aircraft in warfare: The dawn of the fourth arm, Engineering 78 (1914) 422–423.

[25] S. Lerman and C. Manski, The estimation of choice probabilities from choice-based samples, Econometrica 45 (1977) 1977–1988.

[26] G.L. Lilien, Model relativism: A situational approach to model building, Interfaces 5, no. 3 (1975) 11–18.

[27] G.L. Lilien, ADVISOR 2: Modeling the marketing mix decisions for industrial products, Management Science 23 (1979) 191–204.

[28] G.L. Lilien and A.G. Rao, A model for allocating retail outlet building resources across market areas, Operations Research 24 (1976) 1–15.

[29] G.L. Lilien, M. Galper and A.A. Ruzdic, ADIVSOR 2: Multiple situation analysis—Final report (Marketing Center, MIT, 1979).

[30] G.L. Lilien and A.A. Ruzdic, Market response in industrial markets: Models, estimation and applications, Working Paper 1968–79 (Sloan School of Management, MIT, 1979).

[31] J.D.C. Little, Models and managers: The concept of a decision calculus, Management Science 16 (1970) B466–B485.

[32] J.D.C. Little, Aggregate advertising response models: The state of the art, Operations Research 27 (1979) 629–667.

[33] L.M. Lodish, CALL PLAN: An interactive salesman's call planning system, Management Science 18 (1971) 25–40.

[34] K. Longman, Advertising (Harcourt, Brace, Jovanovich, New York, 1971).

[35] C. McDonald, What is the short-term effect of advertising?, in: The Practical Applications of Marketing Research (Esomar Congress, Barcelona, 1970).

[36] F.R. Oliver, Aspects of maximum likelihood estimation of the logistic growth function, American Statistical Association Journal 61 (1966) 697–705.

[37] W.S. Peters and G.W. Summers, Statistical Analysis for Business Decisions (Prentice-Hall, Englewood Cliffs, 1968).

[38] R.E. Quandt, Tests of the hypothesis that a linear regression system obeys two separate regimes, American Statistical Association Journal 55 (1960) 324–330.

[39] A.G. Rao, Advertising response functions: A survey, paper presented at the XXIV International TIMS Meeting, Honolulu, Hawaii (June 1979).

[40] A.G. Rao and P. Miller, Advertising/sales response functions, Journal of Advertising Research 15 (1979) 7–15.

[41] M.G. Richards and M. Ben-Akiva, A Disaggregate Travel Demand Model (Lexington Books, Lexington, Mass., 1975).

[42] R. Richards, Manual of Mathematical Physics (Pergamon Press, New York, 1953).

[43] F.M. Scherer, Industrial Market Structure and Economic Performance (Rand McNally, Chicago 1970).

[44] D. Schendel and G.R. Pattern, A simultaneous equation model of corporate strategy, Management Science 24 (1978) 1611–1621.

[45] S.R. Schoeffler, D. Buzzell and D.F. Heany, The impact of strategic planning on profit performance, Harvard Business Review 52 (March–April 1974) 137–145.

[46] T. Sharot, The generalized jackknife: Finite sample and subsample sizes, Journal of the American Statistical Association 71 (1976) 451–454.

[47] W.A. Shewhart, Statistical Method From the Viewpoint of Quality Control (The Department of Agriculture, Washington, D.C.; 1939).

[48] J.L. Simon, New evidence for no effect of scale in advertising, Journal of Advertising Research 9, no. 1 (1969) 38–41.

[49] V. Srinivasan, Network models for estimating brand-specific effects in multi-attribute marketing models, Management Science 25 (1979) 11–21.

[50] S.A. Stouffer, Some observations on study design, American Journal of Sociology 55 (1970) 355–361.

[51] H. Theil, Principles of Econometrics (John Wiley and Sons, New York, 1971).

[52] J.W. Tukey, Bias and confidence in not quite large samples, Annals of Mathematical Statistics 29 (1958) 614.

[53] G.L. Urban, Building models for decision makers, Interfaces 4, no. 3 (1974) 1–11.

[54] J.M. Vernon, Market Structure and Industrial Performance: A Review of Statistical Findings (Allyn and Bacon, Boston, 1972).

[55] J. von Neumann and O. Morgenstern, Theory of Games and Economic Behavior (Princeton University Press, Princeton, 1947).

[56] F.E. Webster, Industrial Marketing Strategy (John Wiley and Sons, New York, 1979).

[57] R.S. Weinberg, An Analytical Approach to Advertising Expenditure Strategy (Association of National Advertisers, New York, 1960).

[58] D. Wittink, Exploring territorial differences in the relationship between marketing variables, Journal of Marketing Research 14 (1977) 145–155.

TIMS/Studies in the Management Sciences 18 (1982) 271–274
North-Holland Publishing Company

NOTES ABOUT AUTHORS

Joseph Blackburn ("Litmus: A New Product Planning Model") is Associate Professor of Management in the Owen Graduate School of Management at Vanderbilt University, Nashville, TN 37203. He received his B.S. Ch.E. from Vanderbilt University, M.S. Ch.E. from University of Wisconsin and Ph.D. in operations research from Stanford University. He has previously taught at the University of Chicago, Stanford University and Boston University. He has published articles in *Management Science, Decision Sciences, Journal of Operations Management* and *Production and Inventory Management*. His current research interests are new product introduction models and material requirements planning systems. He is a member of TIMS, ORSA, AIDS and APICS.

John Bradford ("Stochastic Dominance Rules for Product Portfolio Analysis") is a doctoral candidate in marketing at the Graduate School of Business, Columbia University. He received a B.A. in economics and M.B.A. in management science from The Ohio State University. His research has appeared in several proceedings and marketing journals.

Marcel Corstjens ("Optimal Strategic Business Unit Portfolio Analysis") is an Assistant Professor of Marketing at INSEAD. He holds a licence in applied economics from the University of Antwerp (UFSIA) and a Ph.D. in marketing from the University of California, Berkeley. His major research interests include the areas of multiattribute decision-making, marketing strategy, and modeling in retail management. He has published in *Management Science* and the *Journal of Marketing*.

Kevin John Clancy ("Litmus: A New Product Planning Model") is Director of the Doctoral Program and Associate Professor of Marketing in the School of Management, Boston University where he teaches graduate level courses in marketing research, advertising management and marketing consulting. Prior to joining B.U., Dr. Clancy held joint appointments in marketing and sociology at the Wharton School and, before that, served six years as Vice President for Research Services of BBDO Inc., Advertising. Dr. Clancy holds B.A. and M.A. degrees in sociology and economics from the City University of New York and a Ph.D. in sociology and statistics from New York University. He has published extensively on the issue of reliability and validity of social science and marketing research methods and measures in the sociological and marketing literature.

Imran S. Currim ("Evaluating Judgment-Based Marketing Models: Multiple Measures, Comparisons and Findings") is an Assistant Professor of Marketing at the Graduate School of Management, University of California, Los Angeles, California 90024. He received a B.E. (electrical engineering) degree from the University of Bombay, India, a M.B.A. degree from the University of Wisconsin-Milwaukee, and M.S. (statistics) and Ph.D. (marketing) degrees from Stanford University. His previous publications have appeared in *Journal of Marketing Research* and *Journal of Consumer Research*. He is a member of ORSA, TIMS and AMA. His current interests include probabilistic models of consumer behavior, and consumer preference assessment.

Robert J. Dolan ("An Aspect of New Product Planning: Dynamic Pricing") is Associate Professor of Business Administration in the marketing area at the Graduate School of Business Administration, Harvard University. Previously, he was on the faculty of the Graduate School of

Business, University of Chicago. He holds a Ph.D. in operations research from the Graduate School of Management, University of Rochester. His major research interest is various aspects of pricing policy: pricing over the product life cycle, quantity discounts, and pricing adjustments in inflation. His publications on pricing have appeared in the *Bell Journal of Economics, Journal of Marketing,* and *Industrial Marketing Management.* He is a member of TIMS and the American Marketing Association.

John U. Farley ("A Process Model for the Family Planning Decision"), R.C. Kopf. Professor of International Marketing at Columbia University, has also taught at the London School of Business Studies and Handelshogskolan in Gothenburg, Sweden. He is section editor of *the Journal of Marketing* for International Marketing. He has published widely in marketing and in the management and social sciences. He has worked on "social marketing" programs in family planning for over a decade.

Abel P. Jeuland ("An Aspect of New Product Planning: Dynamic Pricing") is Associate Professor of Marketing at the Graduate School of Business, University of Chicago. He holds a Ph.D. in management science from the Krannert School of Business Administration, Purdue University. His interests include modeling of purchasing behavior, quantitative relationships between advertising and sales, new product modeling, modeling channels of distribution. His articles have appeared in *Management Science, Operations Research,* the *Journal of Marketing* and publications of the American Marketing Association. He is a member of the review board of the *Journal of Marketing* and is an Associate Editor of *Management Science.* He is a member of TIMS and the American Marketing Association.

Gary L. Lilien ("Analyzing Natural Experiments in Industrial Markets") is Research Professor of Management Science in the College of Business Administration at The Pennsylvania State University, University Park, PA 16802. Prior to coming to Penn State, he taught at MIT. He holds B.S., M.S., and D.E.S. degrees, all from Columbia University. He has numerous publications in the fields of marketing and management science and is co-author of a book, *Market Planning for New Industrial Products.* He belongs to the American Marketing Association, TIMS, ORSA, Tau Beta Pi and Alpha Pi Mu. He is Departmental Editor for Marketing for *Management Science,* is on the editorial board of the *Journal of Marketing,* and will be editing the journal, *Interfaces,* in 1982.

Vijay Mahajan ("Stochastic Dominance Rules for Product Portfolio Analysis") is an Associate Professor of Marketing at the Wharton School, University of Pennsylvania. He received a B.S. in chemical engineering from the Indian Institute of Technology, Kanpur and a M.S. in chemical engineering and a Ph.D. in management from the University of Texas at Austin. He has published extensively in several major marketing journals.

Shelby H. McIntyre ("Evaluating Judgment-Based Marketing Models: Multiple Measures, Comparisons and Findings") is an Assistant Professor at the University of Santa Clara, Santa Clara, California 95053. He received a B.Sc. in industrial engineering, an M.B.A. and a Ph.D., all from Stanford University. His current research interests focus on the improvement of business decisions by the use of judgment-based models. His research has appeared in the *Journal of Applied Psychology,* the *Journal of Marketing Research,* and the *Academy of Management Journal,* among others. He is an active business consultant.

Andrew A. Mitchell ("A Discrete Maximum Principle Approach to a General Dynamic Market Response Model") is Associate Professor of Marketing in the Graduate School of Industrial Administration, Carnegie-Mellon University, Pittsburgh, PA 15213. He received his Ph.D. from the University of California, Berkeley, and has recently published articles in *Management Science,*

Journal of Marketing Research, Journal of Consumer Research and *Journal of Marketing*. He is a member of TIMS, AMA, ACR, APA and CSS.

Thomas E. Morton ("A Discrete Maximum Principle Approach to a General Dynamic Market Response Model") is a Professor of Industrial Administration at Carnegie-Mellon University, Pittsburgh, Pennsylvania 15213. He received a B.S. in mathematics from California Institute of Technology, an M.S. in mathematics, an M.B.A. in business (economics) and a Ph.D. in business (operations research), all from the University of Chicago. His published work in operations research and operations management has appeared in numerous professional journals. His principal research areas include inventory theory, planning horizon theory, scheduling and production heuristics, forward simplex methods, robotico.

Edgar A. Pessemier ("Strategy Development for New Product Introductions: Predicting Market and Financial Success") is Professor of Management at the Krannert Graduate School of Management, Purdue University. He earned his doctorate in business administration at the Harvard Graduate School of Business Administration. His publications include four books, two research monographs, and more than one hundred articles and papers. These works deal principally with product research and development, product and merchandise management, experimental methods in marketing, and decision support systems. He is a member of TIMS, ORSA, ASA, ACR and AMA.

A. Api Ruzdic ("Analyzing Natural Experiments in Industrial Markets") is an Instructor of Marketing at the J.L. Kellogg Graduate School of Management at Northwestern University, Evanston, Illinois 60201. He received his B.S. in electrical engineering from the University of Zagreb, Yugoslavia. He was a Fulbright scholar at MIT where he received his M.S. in management and is about to receive his Ph.D. in marketing. His research has focused on discrete choice models and new product management. He is a member of the Sigma Xi Society, TIMS, and the American Marketing Association.

Donald E. Sexton ("A Process Model for the Family Planning Decision"), Professor of Business at Columbia University, has also taught at INSEAD. He has broad research experience and consulting in marketing and in international business. He has worked in various applications of marketing in not-for-profit settings, including the arts and family planning. Publications include numerous journal articles, as well as *Marketing and Management Science* (with W.A. Clark) and *A Growth Perspective on Teheran*.

Hermann Simon ("PRICESTRAT—An Applied Strategic Pricing Model for Nondurables") is Professor of Management Science and Marketing at the University of Bielefeld, West Germany. Formerly he was at the University of Bonn from where he holds a Dr. in management science and a diploma in economics. In 1978–79 he was a Visiting Fellow at the Sloan School of Management, MIT. His research interests focus on product life cycle- and long term-oriented pricing and advertising issues. He has published articles in *Management Science, Journal of Marketing Research, Journal of Advertising Research* and several European Marketing Academy, AMA and German professional associations.

Prabhakant Sinha ("Integer Programming Model and Algorithmic Evolution: A Case from Sales Resource Allocation") is an Associate Professor of Quantitative Studies at the Graduate School of Management, Rutgers University, Newark, N.J. 07102. He has contributed to *Management Science, Operations Research,* and *Mathematical Programming.* His research interests are in resource allocation in menu planning and marketing.

David Weinstein ("Optimal Strategic Business Unit Portfolio Analysis") is an Associate Professor of Marketing at INSEAD. He holds a B.A. in economics and statistics from Tel-Aviv University and a Ph.D. in marketing from Columbia University. His major research interests include the areas of industrial marketing, marketing strategy and sales force management. He has published in the *Journal of Business, Journal of Marketing* and *Multivariate Behavioral Research*.

Yoram Wind ("Stochastic Dominance Rules for Product Portfolio Analysis") is a Professor of Marketing and Director of the Wharton Center for International Management Studies at the Wharton School, University of Pennsylania. He is an editor of the new *Journal of Marketing Science* and was the previous editor of the *Journal of Marketing*. He received his doctoral degree from Stanford University in 1966 and is the author of several books and over 150 articles and monographs.

Eitan Zemel ("A Discrete Maximum Principle Approach to a General Dynamic Market Response Model") is an Associate Professor of Decision Sciences at the J.L. Kellogg Graduate School of Management, Northwestern University. He is currently visiting the L. Recanati Graduate School of Business Administration Tel-Aviv University. Professor Zemel's research interests are mainly integer and combinatorial programming and complexity analysis of algorithms. His papers appeared in *Mathematics Programming, Mathematics of Operations Research, Operations Research, Networks, Operations Research Letter, SIAM Journal on Applied Mathematics,* and *SIAM Journal on Computing*.

Andris A. Zoltners ("Integer Programming Models and Algorithmic Evolution: A Case from Sales Resource Allocation") is an Associate Professor of Marketing in the Graduate School of Management at Northwestern University, Evanston, Illinois 60201. He received an M.S. in mathematics from Purdue University and an M.S. and Ph.D. in industrial administration from Carnegie-Mellon University. His major research interest is in the application of management science concepts and computer-oriented decision systems in marketing. His research articles have appeared in several journals including *Management Science, Journal of Marketing Research, Journal of Marketing, Operations Research, Mathematical Programming,* and *ACM*.

Fred S. Zufryden ("A General Model for Assessing New Product Marketing Decisions and Market Performance") is currently Associate Professor of Marketing at the University of Southern California. He rceived a B.A. in mathematics, M.B.A. and a Ph.D in business administration from the University of California at Los Angeles. His numerous publications have appeared in the *Journal of Advertising Research, Management Science,* the *Operational Research Quarterly,* the *Journal of Business,* the *Journal of the Market Research Society,* and other publications. His industrial experience includes previous positions with Planning Research Corporation and Litton Industries. He has also been consultant to a number of companies and research firms.

TIMS Studies in the Management Sciences 18 (1982) 275–276
© North-Holland Publishing Company

AUTHORS' ADDRESSES

Joseph D. Blackburn
Vanderbilt University, Owen Graduate School of Management, Nashville, TN 37203

John W. Bradford
Columbia University, New York, NY 10027

Marcel Corstjens
INSEAD, Marketing Department, Boulevard de Constance, F-77305, Fontainbleau Cedex, France

Kevin J. Clancy
Boston University, Boston, MA 02215

Imran S. Currim
Graduate School of Management, UCLA, Los Angeles, CA 90024

Robert J. Dolan
Harvard University, Cambridge, MA 02138

John U. Farley
Columbia University, Marketing Department, 523 Uris Hall, New York, NY 10027

Abel P. Jeuland
University of Chicago, Graduate School of Business, 1101 East 58th Street, Chicago, IL 60637

Gary L. Lilien
Pennsylvania State University, 310 Business Administration Building, University Park, PA 16802

Vijay Mahajan
University of Pennsylvania, The Wharton School, Philadelphia, PA 19104

Shelby H. McIntyre
University of Santa Clara, Graduate School of Business and Administration, Santa Clara, CA 95053

Andrew A. Mitchell
Carnegie-Mellon University, Graduate School of Industrial Administration, Schenley Park, Pittsburgh, PA 15213

Thomas E. Morton
Carnegie-Mellon University, Graduate School of Industrial Administration, Schenley Park, Pittsburgh, PA 15213

Edgar A. Pessemier
Purdue University, Krannert Graduate School of Industrial Management, West Lafayette, IN 47907

A. Api Ruzdic
Northwestern University, Evanston, IL 60201

Donald E. Sexton
Columbia University, Marketing Department, 523 Uris Hall, New York, NY 10027

Hermann Simon
University of Bielefeld, Postfach 8640, D-4800 Bielefeld 1, Federal Republic of Germany

Prabhakant Sinha
720 Fairacres Avenue, Westfield, NJ 07090

David Weinstein
INSEAD, Marketing Department, Boulevard de Constance, F-77305, Fontainbleau Cedex, France

Yoram Wind
University of Pennsylvania, The Wharton School, Philadelphia, PA 19104

Eitan Zemel
Northwestern University, Evanston, IL 60201

Andris A. Zoltners
J.L. Kellogg Graduate School of Management, Nathaniel Leverone Hall, 2001 Sheridan Road, Northwestern University, Evanston, IL 60201

Fred S. Zufryden
University of Southern California, School of Business Administration, Department of Marketing, University Park, Los Angeles, CA 90007